BUSINESS COMMUNICATION

BUSINESS COMMUNICATION

[For B Com, BCA, BBA, MBA Students]

Dr. V. K. JAIN

M. Com., M.Phil, LL.M., Ph.D. (Tax), ACS,

Higher Diploma in English

Ex-Reader, G.S. College of Commerce & Economics, Nagpur

Recipient of Best Teacher Award, RTM Nagpur University

Dr. OMPRAKASH BIYANI

M.A. in English (Gold-medallist), Ph.D.

Former lecturer in Business Communication and English at
SIES College, Mithibai College (Mumbai), &
YCCE, Kamala Nehru Mahavidyalaya, Dhanwate National College (Nagpur)
Visiting professor at Tata Institute of Social Sciences & Department of English,
RTM Nagpur University

S. CHAND
PUBLISHING

S. Chand And Company Limited

(ISO 9001 Certified Company)

S. Chand And Company Limited
(ISO 9001 Certified Company)
Head Office: D-92, Sector–2, Noida – 201301, U.P. (India), Ph. 91-120-4682700
Registered Office: A-27, 2nd Floor, Mohan Co-operative Industrial Estate, New Delhi – 110 044, Phone: 011-49731800
www.**schandpublishing.com**; e-mail: **info@schandpublishing.com**

Marketing Offices:

Chennai : Ph: 23632120; chennai@schandpublishing.com
Guwahati : Ph: 2738811, 2735640; guwahati@schandpublishing.com
Hyderabad : Ph: 40186018; hyderabad@schandpublishing.com
Jalandhar : Ph: 4645630; jalandhar@schandpublishing.com
Kolkata : Ph: 23357458, 23353914; kolkata@schandpublishing.com
Lucknow : Ph: 4003633; lucknow@schandpublishing.com
Mumbai : Ph: 25000297; mumbai@schandpublishing.com
Patna : Ph: 2260011; patna@schandpublishing.com

First Edition 2007
Reprints 2008, 2009, 2010
Second Revised Edition 2011, 2013, 2014, 2015
Reprints 2017 (Twice), 2019, 2020, 2021, 2022 (Twice), 2023

Reprint 2024

ISBN: 978-81-219-2870-0 **Product Code:** H8BCO48BMGT10ENAB11O

PRINTED IN INDIA
By Vikas Publishing House Private Limited, Plot 20/4, Site-IV, Industrial Area Sahibabad, Ghaziabad – 201 010 and Published by S. Chand And Company Limited, A-27, 2nd Floor, Mohan Co-operative Industrial Estate, New Delhi – 110 044.

This book is dedicated to

You the user - student, teacher, businessperson, manager…

"May great ideas come to us from all Creation." – **Rigved**

"If you don't give them more listening power, pray give me more speaking power." **–Mirza Ghalib**

"Give everyone your ear but to only a few your tongue." – **Shakespeare**

"Life is short, art is long." – **Ancient Roman saying**

"Best speech comes from the heart and reaches the heart, touches the heart." – **Persian saying**

"Talking to the daughter, telling the daughter-in-law." -- **Marathi saying**

"Commune with Nature." **Ralph Waldo Emerson (USA)**

"Find beauty, life, bliss in the silence of the soul." – **Anonymous**

PREFACE

Dear Business Communicator:

Easy and in-depth writing on your subject is the aim of this book. The authors have put in here the fruits of their wide-ranging and first-hand knowledge of BizCom - business writing and speaking. It is enriched with extensive references. All is presented in units that are readable, graspable by the beginner – lighting his/her path a long way.

Reader-friendly Style

With a little thought, you will see that Asian business has to develop a new style so as to come out of the age-old British patterns.

Traditional	New option
1. Sign at petrol pumps (2006): ENSURE REGISTER SET TO ZERO BEFORE DELIVERY.	WHEN BUYING PETROL SEE THAT METER IS ON 0.0.
2. Sign on private property: NO THOROUGHFARE	CARE! THIS IS NO PUBLIC ROAD.

Indian English novelist Raja Rao (winner of the Neustadt Prize and guiding star to thousands of writers worldwide) tells us, "We cannot write like the British. We should not."

On every page of your book you will see how a simpler style of English is balanced with your need. You as a business communication expert have the job of understanding the difficult and making it easy. That is what the book is about. Deep secrets of business speaking and writing, listening and managing are given in a you-friendly way.

Wide Coverage

Your book covers the current UGC (University Grants Commission) syllabus, hence it puts you in a position to pursue your studies in any part of India. You may be a student of graduation, a manager or a businessman of any place from Ahmedabad to Arunachal, Bangalore to Bangladesh, Kochi to Kashmir, or, infact, the subcontinent and you will find this book addressed to you. The book is useful in other Asian countries as well.

You have discussions on a timeless form of communication like a smile as also the talk-of-the-time - videoconferencing. Specimens are in plenty.

Answer the questions at the end of each chapter, get an evaluation, rewrite - and you can transform your score, your business, even your outlook on life.

Global Glamour and You

This century has brought in an Age of International Travel. People are flying for studies, business, medicare and pleasure on a never-before scale. The world is calling. Are you ready to cash in? Management guru Sanjay Arora (of Shells Advertising) inspires you with this music: "Opportunity dances with you if you have got onto the dance floor." Your polish and grace in communication can well be YOUR dance floor.

Today there are more speakers of English in countries where it is NOT the first language, than in English-speaking countries. As such, the power-centre of the language is with anyone who uses it better than others or an economic superpower. Interestingly, 20th century's greatest writers of English were born in countries where it is not the first language: Sri Aurobindo (India), Mother Mirra (France), Franz Kafka's translator Max Brod (Germany), Vladimir Nabokov (Russia)… . European radio stations use English that is better understood worldwide than Voice of America.

Traditional British and American usages are being replaced by simpler, international usages:

Traditional	International option
(a) "Beg your pardon." (British for"Pray/Please repeat.")	"I didn't get you." (Used on European airlines)
(b) Cellphone instruction no. 1: "The standby mode is home base and indicates your phone is in standby mode." (*User's Guide*, *2006*, in American English)	"As you switch on your phone, the first screen view you get is called the standby mode or position." (Suggested English for the wide world)

We (the authors) offer our heartfelt thanks to the CEO of S.Chand & Co. Ltd Shri Amit Gupta, Shri Navin Joshi, EVP (S.Chand Group) and Shri Bhagirath Kaushik , General Manager (Sales) for associating us with this prize project.

We present this book in a humble spirit, knowing we have much to be humble about. Your suggestions to improve the book in any way will be very welcome.

Happy communication! Happy communion!

Dr. V. K. Jain

1st March, 2011 **Dr. Omprakash Biyani**

Power your way as a business communicator.

1. Learn to listen deeply. Read the speaker's face, too, and listen to his/her silences.
2. Speak into your listeners' hearts – whether to one at a time or a million at a time. Touch that point in humans which makes them move.
3. Read the best writers – and read them till their writing echoes in you. Discuss what you read.
4. Practise writing – and rewriting – till you get the final polish. Imitate – creatively – the masters of writing.
5. Think over what you hear, view, sense, read or imagine. Reflect over great sayings, great audio-visuals... analyse them... internalise them.
6. New technology is connecting six billion heads and hearts. Stay in tune with it, day after day.
7. Beyond words, enter the magic world of the mind. Meditate.

STRENGTHEN THE POWER-CENTRE OF COMMUNICATION IN YOU.

CONTENTS

Chapter 3
LISTENING AS A TOOL OF COMMUNICATION 44–48

Chapter 4
GROUP COMMUNICATION 49–69

Chapter 5
BUSINESS LETTER WRITING 70–85

Chapter 6
ENQUIRIES, QUOTATIONS AND TENDER NOTICES 85–97

Chapter 7
PLACING ORDERS AND THEIR FULFILMENT 98–104

Chapter 8
COMPLAINTS (CLAIMS) AND ADJUSTMENTS 105–112

Chapter 9
CIRCULAR AND SALES LETTERS 113–125

Chapter 10
COLLECTION LETTERS 126–130

Chapter 11
STATUS ENQUIRIES AND CREDIT LETTERS 131–141

Chapter 12
EXPORT-IMPORT CORRESPONDENCE 142–150

Chapter 13
CORRESPONDENCE WITH BANKS 151–156

Chapter 14
CORRESPONDENCE WITH INSURANCE COMPANIES 157–163

Chapter 15
JOB-RELATED LETTERS, GROUP DISCUSSION, AND INTERVIEWS 164–180

Chapter 16
CORRESPONDENCE WITH PUBLIC AUTHORITIES 181–194

Chapter 17
INTERNAL COMMUNICATION 195–206

Chapter 18
PRÉCIS AND SUMMARISING

Chapter 19
REPORT AND PROPOSAL WRITING

Chapter 20
CORPORATE COMMUNICATION

Chapter 21
PRESENTATION SKILLS AND PUBLIC SPEAKING 269–277

CHAPTER

1

Basic Ideas in the Study of Communication

What should you know?

1.1 Nature of Communication
1.2 Importance of Communication
1.3 Process of Communication
1.4 Barriers to Communication
1.5 Principles of Effective Communication
1.6 Communication Theories and Models
1.7 Audience Analysis
1.8 Self-development and Communication
1.9 SWOT Analysis

1.1 NATURE OF COMMUNICATION

Communication occurs wherever life exists.

The transmission of any meaningful message is communication. It is as natural a phenomenon as existence itself. Whether we recognise it or not, we have no option but to communicate.

The *we* here stands for all things living. A baby cries to convey its hunger. A dog barks to warn his master of an intruder. Corporate organisations which, after all, consist of the human element, use information-based systems like Management Information System (MIS), Decision Support System (DSS) and Strategic Information System (SIS) to run businesses successfully.

This is what communication is all about. Communication is an integral part of human existence. Communication contributes enormously to the success or failure of every human activity. Communication is essentially the ability of one person to make contact with another and to make himself understood. Since man is a social animal, it is vital that he express his feelings and emotions, receive and exchange information. It is here that communication comes into play.

In case of organisations, it becomes even more important as people working in different departments have to achieve common objectives. The working of inter-personal relationships is possible only through communication. Apart from binding its various components internally, communication is what links an organisation with the external world. Thus, communication is regarded as the foundation of a successful organisation. No group can exist without communication.

Communication has a significant impact on the ultimate potency of an organisation. *It is only through communication that ideas, information, attitudes or emotions get conveyed from one person to another.* At the individual level also, effective communication skills are responsible for success. According to a survey of America's most successful managers by a leading American magazine, *Fortune*, excellent communication skill was one of the prime determinants of success.

1.1.1 Defining Communication

The word communication has been derived from the Latin word *communis,* which means to share or to participate. Thus, communication stands for sharing or transmission of information, an idea, an opinion, an emotion, a fact or an attitude. *It includes both, the act of communicating as well as the message to be communicated.*

Attempts have been made by different authors to define communication. A few are enumerated below:

"Communication means to share in, to give to another, or the interchange of - thoughts, opinions or information." **Webster**

"Communication is an exchange of facts, ideas, opinions, or emotions by two or more persons." **W. H. Newman and C. F. Summer Jr.**

"Communication in its simplest form is conveying of information from one person to another." **Hudson**

"Communication is the process of passing information and understanding from one person to another." **Keith Davis**

"Communication is a continuing and thinking process dealing with the transmission and interchange with understanding of ideas, facts and courses of action." **George R. Terry**

"Communication is the transmission of information, ideas, emotions, skills, etc. by the use of symbols, words, pictures, figures, graphs, etc. It is the act or process of transformation that is usually called communication. " **Berelso and Steiner**

Thus communication is the process of passing information and understanding from one person to another with three sides to it:

– Transmission of *subject-matter or message*

– Involvement of *two parties* to complete the process of communication

– The person to whom the message is transmitted *understands it in the same sense* in which the sender of message wants him to understand it

According to Harold D. Lasswell, a convenient way to describe an act of communication is to answer the following questions:

Who
Says What
In Which Channel
To Whom
With What Effect?

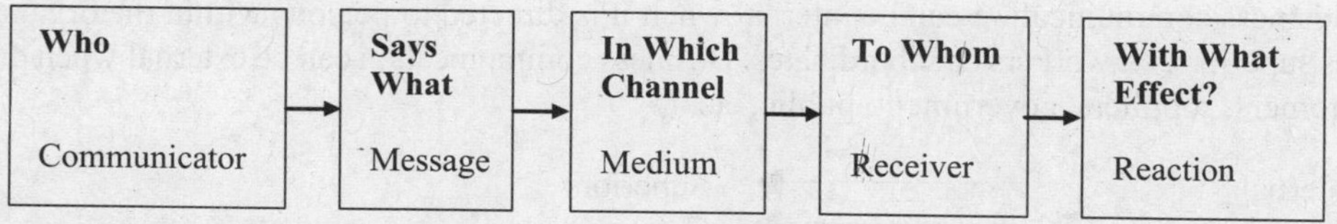

Characteristics of communication

"Communication maintains and animates life. It creates a common pool of ideas, strengthens the feeling of togetherness through exchange of messages and translates thought into action." UNESCO – Many Voices One World

(i) **Interchange of information:** The basic characteristic of human communication is that it aims at exchanging information. It is a two-way process. The exchange can be between two or more persons. It may be at the individual or the organisational level.

(ii) **Continuous process:** Communication is a continuous process. It is not static. It is constantly subject to change and is dynamic. The people with whom communication is held, its content and nature, and the situation in which communication is held – all keep changing.

(iii) **Mutual understanding:** The main purpose of communication is to bring about mutual understanding. The receiver should receive and understand the message in the manner that the sender intended him to.

(iv) **Response or reaction:** Communication always leads to some response or reaction. A message becomes communication only when the receiving party understands and acknowledges it, and also reacts and responds to it.

(v) **Universal function:** Communication is a universal function, which covers all levels of authority.

(vi) **Social activity:** Communication is a social activity, too. The components of a society are into a relationship of sharing, be it information, feelings or emotions. The same holds true for business communication. It involves the effort of people to get in touch with one another and to make themselves understood. The process by which people attempt to share meaning and relate to one another is, thus, a social activity.

1.1.2 Purposes of Communication

Communication is meant

- To inform
- To reassure
- To teach
- To deliver news, whether good or bad
- To understand
- To explain
- To persuade
- To transact
- To organise
- To control
- To co-ordinate
- To direct…

among other things.

1.2 IMPORTANCE OF COMMUNICATION

The importance of communication to an organisation cannot be overemphasised. It is critical to the success of any organisation and has a very significant impact on the ultimate effectiveness of the whole organisation. Communication is a means by which behaviour is modified, change is effected, information is made productive and goals are achieved.

Business communication can be internal when it is directed to persons within the organisation such as superiors, co-workers or subordinates. Business communication can be external when directed to customers, suppliers, government, public, etc.

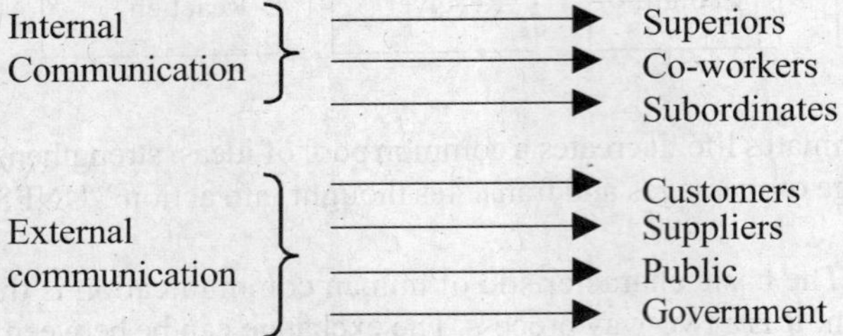

Effective internal communication works towards establishing and disseminating of the goals of an enterprise, evolving plans for their achievement, organising human and other resources in an efficient way. It helps in selecting, developing and appraising members of the organisation, in motivating and encouraging people to put in their best, and in controlling their performance.

Growth in the size and multiple locations of organisations require keeping in touch with employees spread over different states of a country or over different countries. Sending directions and getting feedback from them would be possible only through effective communication. Rapid technological advancements deeply affect not only the methods of work but also the composition of groups. In such a situation, proper communication between superiors and subordinates becomes very necessary.

External communication relates an organisation to the environment outside. No enterprise can thrive in a vacuum. It has to be aware of the needs of the customers, the availability of suppliers, regulations of the government and the concerns of a community. Only through effective communication can an organisation become an open system interacting with its environment.

Thus communication:

- Binds people together.
- Improves the morale in an organisation.
- Helps in proper planning and co-ordination.
- Forms the basis for decision-making.
- Helps in the efficient running of an organisation.
- Helps in achieving increased productivity at lower costs.
- Builds up mutual trust and confidence.

1.2.1 Factors Contributing to the Importance of Communication

The importance of communication cannot be denied nor should it be underestimated in this era of globalisation dominated by modern management education. With the passage of time, society has also become increasingly complex and businesses more global. All these factors have added to the importance of communication. Let us have an overview of the factors that have contributed to this growing importance of communication.

(i) **Big size of organisations**: Modern organisations are gigantic as compared to those of yesteryears. Moreover, they are in a continuous process of expansion. Communication is the only link among the large number of people in the set-up.

(ii) **Growing importance of human relations:** Modern management has brought in the concept of human resource management. Its importance cannot be ignored. The style of working has changed considerably over the years. It is no longer a management-decides-and-workers-follow kind of working pattern. Participative management has become the watchword. Men will not cooperate unless they are treated humanely. This has only increased the importance of communication in business organisations.

(iii) **Public relations:** Just like human beings, organisations cannot function in isolation. Every organisation has certain social responsibilities. It also has to interact with different segments of society. The responsibilities are towards customers, shareholders, suppliers, traders, trade unions, media, government and the people in general.

(iv) **Advances in behavioural sciences:** Modern management lays great stress on the theories of behavioural sciences like sociology, psychology, philosophy, spiritualism and transactional analysis. Their growing importance can be judged by the tremendous surge in the sale of books on these subjects. The essence of all the writings is that we change the way of looking at human nature. Improvement in communication skills can do this effectively.

(v) **Technological advances:** Today's computer age affects not only the methods of working, but also the composition of groups. Communication is the only way to meet the challenge and to strengthen the relationship between superiors and subordinates. Teleconferencing has become a key link for immediate decision-making and feedback in large business organisations.

(vi) **Growth of trade unions**: The last century has seen a tremendous increase in the size of the unions of workers. These unions occupy a very important place in an organisational set-up. Hence, mutual understanding between the management and the unions is very important. Communication, therefore, has a vital role to play.

(vii) **Consumerism (increase in the demand for consumer goods)**: Communication has become an inevitable cycle since the growth of consumerism. In this era of the global marketplace, the competition is real ly tough, and companies are under constant pressure to attract clientele and to perform. The effort to persuade customers to buy a product is virtually never-ending. This has led to a tremendous growth in communication. From pamphlets, brochures and advertisements in the print and the electronic media, to workshops, demonstrations, contests and attractive schemes, consumerism has spawned a whole new way of communication.

(viii) **Distance education**: The advent of the open university system has led to an increase in communication. In many countries, a large segment of population is receiving distance education. In India, IGNOU (Indira Gandhi National Open University) is an example.

1.3 PROCESS OF COMMUNICATION

The process of communication involves seven major elements –sender, message, encoding, channel, receiver, decoding and feedback.

Sender: The sender is the person who transmits a message. He is the communicator. He is the one who gets the entire process of communication started. He wants to get his opinions, ideas, facts, thoughts or information across to the receiver. He is, therefore, also said to be the transmitter of a message.

Message: A message is the actual information that has to be conveyed. Communication is unthinkable without a message. A message triggers a response from the receiver. Messages can broadly be divided into **verbal** and **non-verbal**. The message must be clear, complete, unambiguous and courteous.

Encoding: The seeds of communication are sown the moment the sender thinks of transmitting a certain message. These thoughts have to be converted into suitable words, pictures, charts or symbols so that they can be delivered to the receiver. This process of converting thoughts into suitable words, charts, symbols or any other form in which they can be understood by the receiver is called encoding. The choice of the method of communication is made here – will the message be verbal or non-verbal?

Channel: How does one communicate? This is what a channel deals with. Communication is achieved through a channel. The channel can be a letter, an email, a fax, a telephone or memos, reports, bulletins, posters and manuals. The choice depends on the relationship between the sender and the receiver as well as on the message that has to be communicated. Other factors that tend to influence the choice of a channel include the gravity of the message, the number of receivers, the costs involved and the amount of information.

Receiver: The person who receives the message, decodes it and understands it or attaches some meaning to it is the receiver. The receiver has to perform three functions:

(i) Reception of the message: This is the stage when a message sent by the sender is sensorily taken in by the receiver.

(ii) Decoding the message: After receiving the message, the receiver has to attach some meaning to it.

(iii) Understanding the message: He then has to interpret it in the same way and in the same sense as the sender meant it.

Feedback: The return of communication from the receiver to the sender is known as feedback. It is the response, reaction or reply to the communication. It is always directed towards the sender. This completes the cycle of communication. Thus, in feedback, the receiver sends his reply or response to the sender, indicating that he has understood the message received. In face-to-face communication, the feedback is quicker than in written communication.

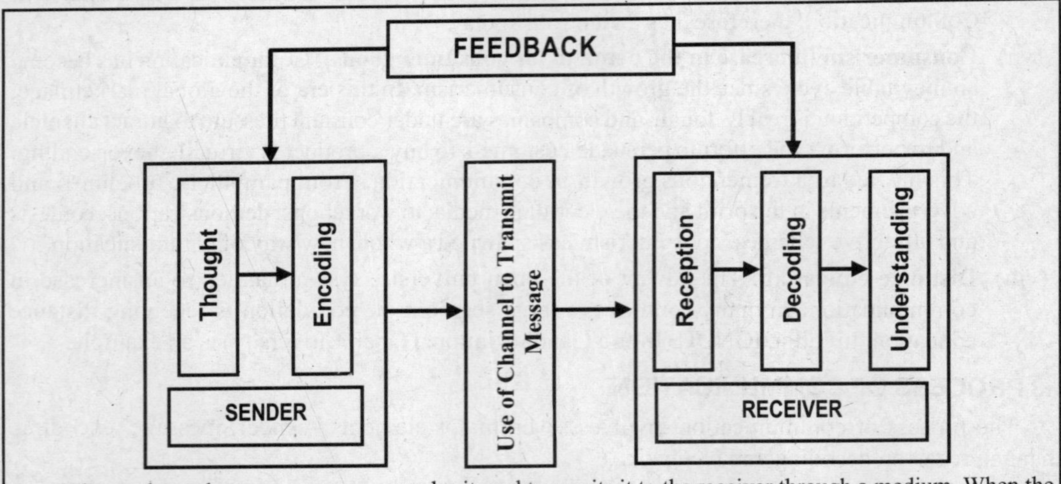

[The sender makes up a message, encodes it, and transmits it to the receiver through a medium. When the message reaches the receiver, he decodes it and gives an internal response to the perceived message. Only when there is feedback does effective communication take place.]

1.4 BARRIERS TO COMMUNICATION

If the sender's message does not reach the receiver as it is meant to, then there must be some barrier or hindrance. What can it be? And how to avoid such barriers?

Good organisers of communication need to anticipate the barriers and remove them. The barriers range from a poor microphone to an emotional attitude that rejects the message before it is received (e.g. a child unwilling to heed to reason unless its demand is fulfilled first).

For convenience of analysis, we may classify the barriers into five types:

I. Mechanical barriers

II. Physical barriers

III. Psychological barriers
IV. Semantic and language barriers
V. Status barriers

I. Mechanical barriers : Faulty mechanism

A communication may not reach properly if the mechanism that carries it breaks down. To take an extreme case, if the computer typing has been done in devnagari ,and while taking the printout the computer is in the Roman mode, not a single letter would be understood. Similarly, if the mirror image of a letter is sent by some mechanical fault, it will be hard to decipher.

Some possible mechanical failures are:

(a) A weak microphone or poor sound spread (acoustics) of the meeting place
(b) Defective telephone lines
(c) Electricity/computer breakdown
(d) Poor printing quality or paper, spread of ink, overlap of colours
(e) Atmospherics on radio or TV, especially in a cloudy weather

II. Physical barriers : noise, space, time

Sometimes background noise, whether in a face-to-face meeting or at either end of the telephone, reduces the audibility of the spoken word. Also, if the listener is too far from the speaker, he may not be able to hear him, in which case distance is the barrier. Similarly, the time taken for the message to reach its destination can become a barrier, e.g. a telegram delivered too late.

III. Psychological barriers

These are numerous and require greater effort to overcome.

(a) **A person of weak hearing or eyesight** cannot always receive the communication in full.

(b) **The age of the listener** puts its own limitations on his ability to receive messages. One may be too young or too old to understand certain things.

(c) **A person's educational level** governs his understanding. Some background knowledge is required to understand certain messages.

(d) **There are gender barriers** too. Boys and girls in general have their own areas of specialisation where they understand faster. Boys are more outdoors oriented while girls tend to take a major interest in housework. A boy who is told to do a "girl's" job may put up a psychological barrier.

(e) **A wandering mind** cannot fully gather the inputs given to it. While roving is a natural tendency of the mind and the attention span of a listener is limited, there may be other causes of inattention too. These may be visual or audio distractions – gaudy pictures or songs in the neighbourhood.

(f) **Ideological loyalties** may form a barrier to communication. One may have a political party membership, a philosophical principle (like hedonism, i.e. devotion to sensory enjoyment), a religious affiliation that has already bound the way one thinks. Such a person may not be receptive to the ideas counter to his ideology.

(g) **Loyalty to a brand or an organisation** is also a barrier. One who is loyal to a certain brand may not be receptive to a rival product's ad. One may not be receptive to the praises of an organisation other than one's own, a team other than one's country's, and so on.

(h) **Emotional states of a person** can act as barriers. If someone is in a fit of anger, he /she may not listen to reason. They may also find it difficult to communicate soberly with a person who has not contributed to his anger. There is a spillover effect – the emotion generated by one transaction spilling over into an unrelated transaction.

(i) **One's prejudices** act as a hindrance to reason. A prejudice is a judgment formed without proper information. One may have a racial prejudice, a caste prejudice and so on. This is the opposite of an open mind. A liberal education is meant to remove irrational notions which stay on as prejudices.

(j) **Personality limitations**, too, put a barrier. These are similar to ideological barriers, as some personalities are naturally attracted to certain ideologies. However, personality variations are far too numerous. One's aspirations, viewpoints, analyses make one open or closed to certain messages. One bent on getting into a job for livelihood may not listen to the advantages of entrepreneurship.

(k) **Fixed images about other people** stand as barriers to see them in a new role. A comedian coming in as a hero of a film may not be acceptable to an audience which sees him typed in comedy roles.

(l) **Poor retention power is a barrier.** If one fails to take timely notes when instructions are given, hoping to remember them all, one has perhaps given away a part of the communication.

IV. Semantic and language barriers

Semantics is the study of how words convey meanings. What happens if the speaker/writer means one thing and the listener/reader takes it in another meaning? An advertiser offered to sell a "big, bad dog". While the word "bad" is meant to convey its attacking power to guard a house, some readers may take it otherwise. The context changes the meaning of the word. One has to ask, is the word conveyed in its proper context? Words are indeed so tricky to use that one can hardly ever convey the same thing to all receivers in given words. The words generate different meanings in different minds, according to their previous associations and language levels. Literary texts, created by master writers and read by expert critics, are continually open to reinterpretations. Some of these conflict with one another.

Yet in business life, dealing with matter-of-fact situations, semantic barriers arise from the inability to read the receiver's mind. If the sender knows the receiver's level of understanding, fine. If not, there is a barrier. A good communicator takes the trouble of removing all ambiguity and wrong colouring of words. As a receiver, he tries to read the words and between the lines.

Semantic barriers arise when:

(a) The sender's experience with words differs from the receiver's.

(b) Words from one environment are taken out and put into an environment where they don't fit.

(c) Opinions are given as facts. "XYZ bike is the most reliable."

(d) An abstract word is used (in order to be more general and more safe) when a concrete word is required. One may want to say that students of a particular college are rowdy, but in order to avoid naming names, one may abstract and generalise, and put the blame on college students as a whole. Similarly, some young men may be impatient, but one might say "Youth is impatient."

(e) Complex phrases and long constructions are used. Also, when idioms are meant to be understood in the idiomatic sense but are taken in the literal sense. E.g., *dot you i's and cross your t's*. This may even generate unintended humour.

As for language barriers (other than semantic barriers), we all experience how different regional groups, sometimes due to their previous language habits, distort English vowels. Thus, "He is good at batting" may be changed to "He is good at betting". Lack of proper language skills may lead to wrong choice of words, or of words with wrong associative values. One hears people saying,"My boss's behaviour is good," whereas the proper thing to say way would be, "My boss's treatment of his juniors is good." But the rudeness may be unintended. Homonymns (words with the same sound) cause difficulty in understanding: *there* and *their, one's* and *once*.

Speakers with different accents find it hard to understand each other. The American accent is insufficiently understood in India while Americans may have a hard time making sense of Indianised English.

Inadequate vocabulary in a new language is a handicap to communication. Hence the praises of wordpower. Short of words, one may straightaway use a native language word in a foreign language: "Today I met an *aamdaar*". What the speaker means is an MLA, but the listener may try to associate the word with a *mango* and get nowhere.

Symbols (non-verbal) create the same problems as languages. The swastik is revered by Hindus but the reverse swastik was a Nazi symbol.

Poor organisation of one's speech and a harsh voice may also act as barriers. In writing, long paragraphs are out of fashion. They are hard to read. Clusters of big words put a barricade to speed reading.

V. Status barriers

This again is a kind of psychological barrier, where the higher or lower social status of the other party disables one from expressing one's meaning fully. A modest farmer, asked to express his problems to a high-ranking official or politician, may feel nervous or ill at ease.

Status symbols (e.g. luxury of the surroundings) may halt communication. A candidate from a modest background may be awestruck to see the glitz and glamour of a multinational company where he has to appear for an interview.

Cultural barriers are a special case of collective psychological barriers. A culture brings its own habits, modes of dressing, greeting, eating, food preferences etc. Most people have an element of xenophobia (fear or aversion of foreigners). *Time* magazine once commented sharply on American businessmen's need to allow for differences between American culture and Oriental culture. Only then would they be able to do business with eastern countries. This advice can, in fact, be universalised. Media power which the English speaking countries enjoy tends to give them a false sense of universal acceptability of their culture. In Indian business, it is a grassroot reality that Indian words and Indianisms are freely used. Exposed to native speakers of English, Indian businessmen are often at a loss.

Resistance to the written word exists as a barrier. The written word demands a commitment. People prefer to listen (if possible in their regional language) and act. Letters remain unreplied while personal visits or telephone calls serve the purpose.

How to remove communication barriers

A proper understanding of the nature of barriers helps us to arrive at a solution. All the same, good communicators have to form a new set of general habits and recognise the potential barriers in order to put their meaning across.

(i) **Good listening**: This topic is dealt with at length in the chapter "Listening as a Tool of Communication." In brief, deep and comprehensive listening helps to overcome barriers. One has to listen to the words as well as the tone. An overworked employee may say, "I'll do it" with just a little touch of despair. The boss needs to show understanding. One may develop a better listening capacity by systematically testing oneself on listening comprehension. TOEFL (Test of English as a Foreign Language) is meant to find out, among other things, how well one listens.

(ii) **Practice in simplifying and clarifying one's message**: Writers are known to rewrite their text several times to achieve clarity, precision and beauty. Hence regular writing is advisable. The art of writing, says an expert, is the art of rewriting.

(iii) **Obtain feedback, analyse it and respond**: Advertisements are often tested for their pulling power. A slight rearrangement of words or font or layout can make an ad more appealing.

(iv) **Repetition**: Repetition of a message through multiple channels helps to remove barriers which may exist at the first appearance of an idea. Thus one removes the resistance to the new.

(v) **Ambience**: Find the receiver in a receptive mood and ambience. If the audience is, for instance, given more comfortable chairs, it may digest a speech better.

(vi) **Actions speak louder than words**: If the communicator's sincerity is shown through his actions, people go out to listen to him.

(vii) **Cross-cultural get-togethers**: A systematic effort to bring together people of different cultures goes to increase receptivity. Also, respect for their cultural icons makes the message welcome.

(viii) **Informality is useful**: If the rank and file in an organisation are in awe of the superior (due to his position, education, dress, quality of visitors, excellence in speech, etc.) such a manager may step out of his cabin and go out to the juniors. Politicians are always doing it during election campaigns – coming out into the street and going door to door. Multinationals also send out door to door salespersons to reduce the distance created by celebrity endorsement (backing by a famous person) of their products.

1.5 PRINCIPLES OF EFFECTIVE COMMUNICATION

What you say may be important, but how you say it is even more important.

This is a major theme of this book. We particularly refer the reader to Chapter 4 "Business Letter Writing" where the eight C's of effective letter writing are discussed: correctness, completeness, clarity, conciseness, courtesy, consideration, concreteness, and convincing power.

However, talking of communication in general, we may state that following are the requirements of an effective give-and-take of ideas and feelings:

1. **Simplicity:** In practical life, most communication has to be simple, direct and without ornamentation. You have to keep in mind the receiver's level of understanding and his mind-frame when he receives the message. Pressed for time, he would prefer a simple statement to a complicated one. To simplify, one may use tabulation, graphics, charts, etc. keeping the words to the minimum.
2. **Face to face communication:** It is generally to the sender's advantage to get face to face with the receiver. This helps to get an immediate feedback and respond to it. Hence interactive media save time and give instant results. When a salesman is talking across the counter, when a spokesman is addressing a news conference, the message acts two-way. Hence face-to-face communication may be used wherever possible to the optimum advantage.
3. **Use of feedback:** The sender or originator of a message should prepare himself to receive the feedback. Then he knows what reaction the message is producing in the target audience. If a new product is launched, surveys may be conducted to know how people feel about it. If an ad is issued, you have to test whether it is working the desired way. Is the message clear? Is it reaching the right audience in the right manner? The quality of reception? (see also chapter 3) This is to be assessed and considered in further planning.
4. **Listening with understanding:** When you are at the other end of the communication, you have a responsibility as a listener and receiver of messages. You have to be attentive and make an effort to concentrate. To grasp the message fully, you have to attune yourself to it. You have to keep an open mind and receive the message without criticising it, approving it or disapproving it until you have heard it fully. Good listening requires patience and self-discipline. Good listeners help the speaker to become a better communicator. Devoted and sympathetic listening draws the best out of the speaker. That is why listening is called an art. Also, while listening you have to make mental (or written) notes of the message. Then, at the end of the listening session, you can have a ready summary of what the speaker said.

5. **An environment conducive to communication:** An environment of trust needs to be created for effective communication to take place. Trust is created by communicating one's sincere interest in the receiver. The one who is managing the environment has to frame the right policies and take appropriate steps to achieve this. The management must understand what is creating "noise" or barrier to communication. It has to take steps to remove the barriers. For example, the audience may not be properly introduced to the credentials of the speaker. Or at the time of receiving a message the receiver may be closed or hostile to the sender. It is necessary to set the stage for the communication.
6. **Non-verbal communication:** Your gestures and posture must be in harmony with the spoken message. You have to learn the technique of expressing yourself well through body language. The speaker should reflect a positive attitude. You should receive the non-verbal communication, too.
7. **Use of the "You" factor:** The communicator should minimise the use of *I, me* and *mine*, and maximise the use of *you* and *yours*. This has to be in spirit as well as words.
8. **Awareness of the audience's bias:** The communicator should be aware of the audience's pre-conceived ideas and should try to set the record straight. Talking in a mixed gathering, he has to be specially careful that he does not generalise or stereotype individuals or groups. If, for example, some smokers are present in a gathering, he has to exercise care in making remarks about smoking. The same for a group of mixed nationalities.
9. **Overcoming differences of language:** The same word may convey different meanings to different people because of their varied linguistic backgrounds. For example, the proper English usage for writing an exam is "to take an exam." But under the influence of Hindi, one tends to say that the examinee is "giving an exam." In such cases, it is better to say, "appearing for an exam." Also, pronunciation of words has to be acceptable to the audience. The text as well as the context of the message should be understood. The use of unconventional and technical words should be cautious, and sometimes they need to be explained. The same goes for short forms which are too numerous these days, with new ones coming into circulation every day. The best practice is to go over the essence of the message and make sure that it is understood.

Benefits of Effective communication

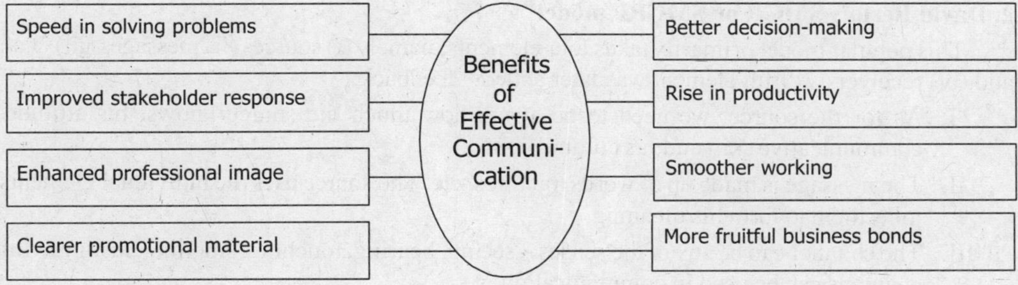

1.6 COMMUNICATION THEORIES AND MODELS

A theory of any phenomenon seeks to explain how it works. It is a set of statements and general laws relating to it. In the case of communication, we have a number of theories mainly presented as models for an easier understanding.

From the ancient Greek philosopher Aristotle to twentieth century scientists, many have proposed models of communication. Ancient India also has its own outlook about it.

There are four major assumptions relating to communication:

(i) Communication is a process which has no beginning or ending – it begins and ends arbitrarily (at random).

(ii) Communication is of the nature of a transaction with many causes and many effects on different people. Some of these are unintended.

(iii) Communication has numerous dimensions. Its sources, audiences, attitudes, tones and influences are multiple. The messages affect both the sender and the receiver.

(iv) Communication serves numerous purposes for different parties that directly or indirectly participate in it. Each party has its own interest angle.

1.6.1 A Survey of Theories/Models of Communication

To begin with, Aristotle in his *Rhetoric* (which means the art of speaking and writing for persuasion) says that rhetoric is made up of the speaker, the speech and the audience. This forms the base of modern theoreticians.

1. Lasswell model of communication

Lasswell, an American political scientist, seeks to describe communication by asking –

Who
Says what
In which channel
To whom
With what effect?

According to Lasswell, communication has three jobs to do:

(i) observe the surroundings (ii) make meaning out of it (iii) transmit culture from one generation to another.

2. David Berlo's SMCR or SMCRF model

This popular model primarily takes four elements, namely (i) sources (ii) messages (iii) channels and (iv) receivers. A fifth element was later added – feedback.

I. As for the source, we need to be aware how much the source knows, his attitude, his communicative skill and his cultural context.

II. The message is made up of words, pictures, etc. The source uses the individual elements and joins them to form his meaning.

III. The channel can be any of the senses – seeing, hearing, touching, smelling, tasting. Multiple channels can be used in communication.

IV. The receiver, too, is characterised by his/her knowledge, attitude, receiving skills and culture. In the event of a major variance between source and receiver, communication may fail.

Berlo says that communication is ongoing and dynamic. A piece of communication is a bucket with many bits from many sources – and this bucket is dumped on the receiver. This is also called his *bucket theory*.

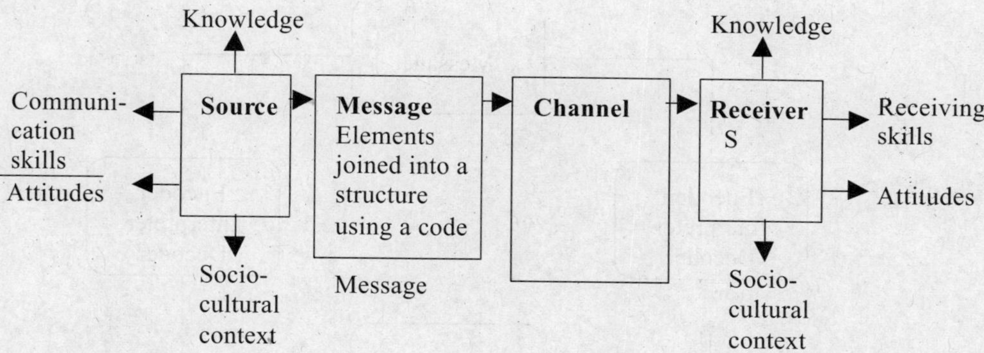

3. Shannon and Weaver model

Their theory, presented as a model, has five key components in ideal communication:

(i) An information source, creating a message
(ii) A transmitter, converting the message into a signal which can be sent
(iii) A channel, which can carry the signal to the receiver
(iv) The receiver, who reads the signal and takes it to the end-user
(v) The destination, the final user of the message

This theory adds the sixth, unintended component of noise, present in actual situations, causing interference in the reception of the message.

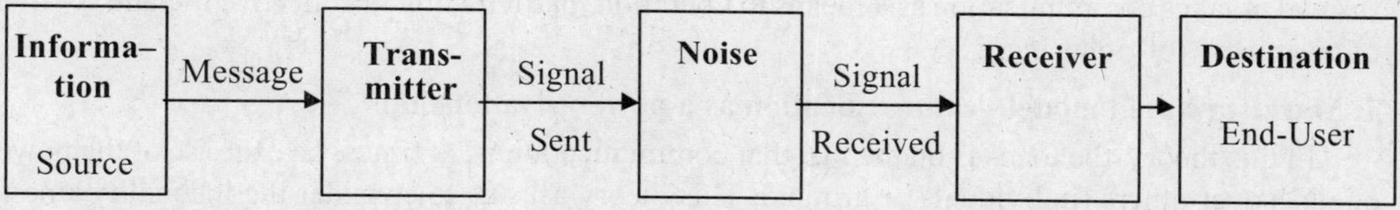

In this theory, noise is stated as the main problem in communication. Noise is of three types (see also "Barriers to Communication"):

(i) Technical problems (e.g. weak antenna of TV)
(ii) Semantic barriers ("wish him" taken as "poison him" under the influence of Hindi)
(iii) Problem of effectiveness (an ad jingle in a dull tune)

To this theory, Kirk and Talbot make a supplement, stating three kinds of noise (for which they use the word *distortion*).

(i) **Stretch distortion**: In this, information is systematically changed.
(ii) **Fog distortion**: In this, a message is partly lost due to surrounding interferences (e.g. air-conditioner's humming)
(iii) **Mirage distortion**: In this, a word or a signal that is not there is received.

The Shannon and Weaver model was used in India's planning of communication. It was considered that encoding and decoding are the vital acts and need the most attention.

4. Osgood and Shramm circular model

In their model, communication is taken as an eminently two-way process, with both parties sending and receiving by turns, interactively.

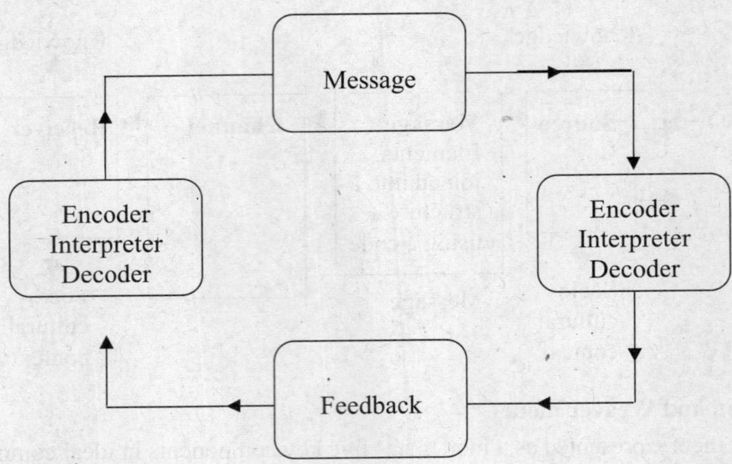

5. Carey's model – communication as a ritual

James Carey, an American anthropologist, gave this model. A ritual is a custom, a traditional practice. This model rejects the theory that communication is a means of social control. Instead, it states that media like TV recall and re-enact myths, values and meanings of life. Communication is seen simply as creating shared beliefs, representing the beliefs and celebrating them.

6. Paulo Freire's theory – communication as dialogue

This model rejects Aristotle's model which sees communication as a transmission of a message. Instead, it takes communication as a means to liberation, participation in collective life and creation of awareness (of rights etc.).

7. Marxism-based model - communication as a power-relationship

In this theory, the focus is on the fact that communication is, at times, an exercise of the power one has over others (individuals or groups). This theory asks us to consider the inequality among classes, castes, economic and social groups. Communication is a reflection of the power-relation in a family, a factory, or between senders and receivers of mass communications.

8. Indian communication theory

Indian sage Bharat Muni has written on Indian poetics, and calls **sadharanikaran** the key process in communication. This term is close to the Latin word *communis* from which comes the word communication.

Bharat Muni says that right communication is between **sahridayas** (i.e. those whose hearts are attuned to each other's). To be sahridayas, the sender and receiver have to have a common culture, common learning and be adapted to each other.

Bharat Muni's **rasa** theory states that the human mind has nine **permanent moods (sthayee bhavas)** and these can be aroused to create nine rasas – i.e. types of aesthetic delight. The rasas include **bhayanaka rasa** (fierce mood), **hasya rasa** (jocular mood), **karun rasa** (compassionate mood)...etc. The message, by producing the desired mood (rasa) in the audience, achieves sadharanikaran (unity of spirit).

This theory emphasises the receiver's mental conditioning by which he/she can be in tune with the message. Sadharanikaran does not mean to persuade the other party, but stresses the joy of sharing.

In the Indian tradition, communication is a mental search for meaning whose aim is self-knowledge, freedom and reaching the Truth. While Indian model focuses on the interpretation by the receiver, Western models stress expression.

A theory of communication derived from Buddhism stresses the impermanence, the changing nature of communication in the fluid world.

9. Islamic theory – communication for building brotherhood

According to the Islamic theory, umma or community is the main thing in communication as against Western models which deal mainly with the individual receiver. The Islamic theory considers communication as a tool of building relationships in a community. We remember the opposition in the Muslim countries to Salman Rushdie's heretic novel. We note that Rushdie is a product of Western education and is patronised by the Western press, and his approach is seen as unpalatable to Muslim communities.

1.7 AUDIENCE ANALYSIS

To send out a meaningful communication, the sender needs to know the audience or audiences he is dealing with. Otherwise one lands with a situation where one has spoken but not told. If it is a buyers' market, with a choice of products to the consumer, the need to know the audience is even more urgent.

Modern management researchers have identified five types of audiences:

(i) **Primary audience:** This is the audience that will decide the fate of your communication – to act on it or not to act on it. The housewife who selects the washing soap is the primary audience to a soap ad.

(ii) **Secondary audience:** These are the people who comment on the message and implement the decision once it is taken. The husband who buys the soap from the market is the secondary audience.

(iii) **Initial audience:** This is the person or persons who are the first to receive the message and then pass it on to someone else to deal with. The general manager may be the one to receive and address a complaint to the sales manager. He is, then, the initial audience.

(iv) **"Gatekeeper" audience:** These are the people who have the power to stop the message before it reaches the addressee. The secretary to chairman is a gatekeeper audience.

(v) **"Watch dog" audience:** This includes all alert bystanders who see a message conveyed and if necessary, react favourably or otherwise. Woman activists, as a watch dog audience, may object to some posters.

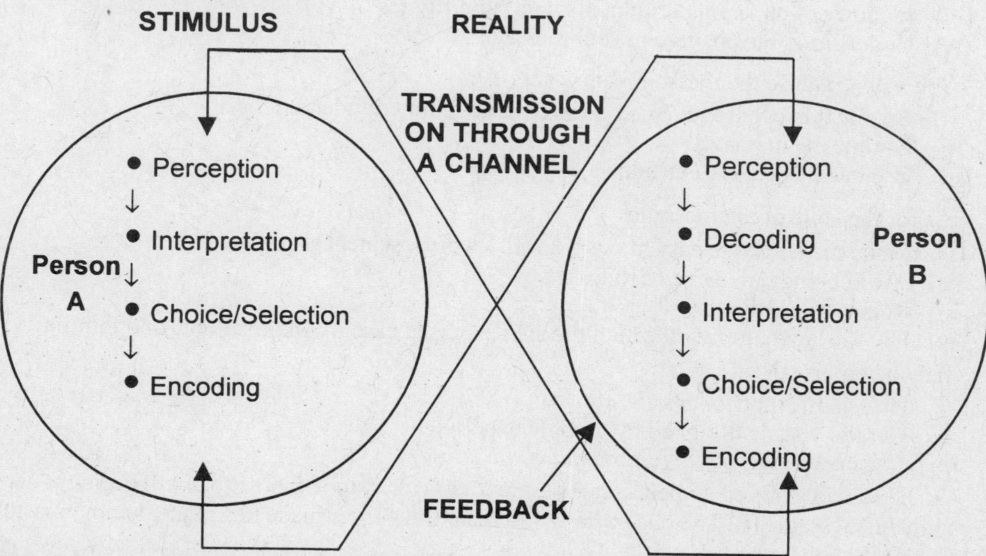

Source. Kitty O. Locker Stephen Kyo Kaczmark, Business Communication : Building Critical Skills, McGraw Hill, Irwin Boston, 2004.

Now one can see that the communication must pass through the filter or screen, reach where it is meant to, convey the correct sense, be acted upon, and withstand the scrutiny of the alert.

The importance of audience analysis: If you have been sending messages for a large number of people, then you probably know that "many men, many minds". Some like an emotional appeal, some an intellectual or scientific. That is why advertisement of a food product says: "Taste may be the reason, vitamins the excuse – or vice versa." This is a clever device to attract all kind of consumers.

Knowing your audience

To know an audience is to know what motivates the members of it. In Shakespeare's play *Julius Caesar,* Antony has to speak to the Romans after Caesar's murder. The Romans at that time dislike the dead king. Antony has to gain sympathy for Caesar and create antipathy for the killers. He starts by befriending the listeners. He then makes an ironical remark about how people forget the good in others (here Caesar), and partially praises the murderers! He does not want to shock the listeners. He then shows how good a friend Caesar was to Antony… and eventually shows how generous Caesar was to the citizens of Rome. Antony manages to reverse the mob opinion against the murderers and gets the Romans to hunt for them.

This is a masterpiece of persuasive communication based on common human psychology. A businessman may manipulate minds much the same way. He starts with an appeal to the values which the audience likes even if he has to create new values.

The audience may like the virtue of economy (limited spending), yet the businessman may play on human psychology to sell luxury goods that simplify life and make it comfortable. He appeals to a value (comfort) which is often deeper than the value of saving money.

Two-wheeler makers compete with each other by emphasising different values in their target audience: the riding joy, the speed and acceleration, the fuel efficiency, the prestige of owning the number one product, and so on. The audience mood changes from one to the other as it receives different messages.

So, after the businessman has made a study of what moves the audience, he adapts his message to it.

Audience analysis guides you to:

(i) Protecting the receiver's ego
(ii) Blending logic and emotion with suitable images of each
(iii) A choice of appealing arguments, facts and figures
(iv) Underlining the positive in your message.

You may organise the message this way:

(i) Be direct except to give bad news (e.g. declining dividends).
(ii) Outline the message.
(iii) Use headings and subheadings as you go.

As for the style of the message:

(i) Make the language easy at every level – words, sentences, quotes.
(ii) Avoid being defensive or rude.
iii) Remove negativity.
(iv) Use the languages with which the audience is at ease – conversational and familiar.

Advice on visuals:

(i) Use charts, models, photos etc.
ii) Get the visuals designed by graphic experts.
iii) Use appealing colour combinations.

In the case of a mixed audience, it is best to give priority to (i) Those that will decide to act or not to act on the message. (ii) The ones who will screen it. A film is made to suit the common taste of the public and the censor board.

1.8 SELF-DEVELOPMENT AND COMMUNICATION

While one develops oneself as a person, one also becomes a better communicator (listener/ speaker/writer/reader); and when one tries to become a better communicator, it helps in an all-round growth of one's personality. As such, to understand the relationship between self-development and communication is at the very heart of our subject-matter in this book. Business communication is not an end in itself but a means to achieving professional and personal fulfilment.

Dimensions of self-development

For the sake of a better understanding, we can look upon the human personality as made up of the physical, the intellectual, the emotional and the spiritual side.

Physical betterment means staying healthy and strong by regulating one's food habits, exercise schedule, rest and recreation. It also requires adequate medicare.

Intellectual betterment includes acquiring a good memory and imagination and knowledge of the world with which one is concerned: one's specialisation (economics/ management/ physics/ teaching etc.), driving, civic laws, general knowledge, use of gadgetry, etc.

Emotional betterment aims at staying cheerful and sociable by maintaining good relationships. It requires positive thinking. A good emotional life is the key to overall progress, hence career drivers need to note this.

Spiritual betterment basically means cultivating detachment and an unruffled temper in the ups and downs of life. Prayer, meditation, religious books and discourses help in this, and so does contemplation of the meaning of life.

How self-development helps in better communication?

A balanced and well-adjusted person has a good chance of becoming an effective communicator.

- Such a person listens well and notes the hidden meanings too.
- His/her body language - a conscious and unconscious instrument of communication - supports his/her other messages.
- He/she takes a profound interest in all aspects of life and helps others with their self-development.
- His/her group behaviour is pleasant and teamwork productive.
- He/she can generate useful ideas from a calm mind.
- His/her holistic perspective on life helps in the quality growth of an organisation and makes him/her a natural leader in course of time.
- To such a person people open their hearts in trust and offer cooperation.

Good communication as an aid to self-development

A conscious effort to evolve one's communicative personality results in the person's overall uplift. Just consider the essentials of good writing: clarity, conciseness, courtesy etc., and the necessaries of effective listening: genuine interest in others, concentration, an open mind etc. As one improves one's communicative skills, one has to overhaul one's entire personality. After all good communication comes from the centre of a person. Communicative excellence builds up a sound personality in so many ways:

It begins with good listening. This helps to build sympathetic understanding of others. One comes out of oneself and gets liked by others.

When one acquires a good speaking ability, one's confidence goes up and one learns to speak rationally as well as persuasively. One develops an insight into human psychology and eventually a masterly understanding of human nature.

- Better selections for reading and a good reading speed help the individual to commune with great minds, skip the irrelevant and acquire an idea bank of his own. "Reading makes a full man."
- Good writing requires, above all, exactness. We know great ancient thought from the well-written books of the past. By cultivating good writing habits, one develops a wise personality. In Sanskrit *kavi* means both a poet and a wise man.

In this way, self-evolution as a communicator leads to a cultivated mind and spirit, and roundness of personality.

Tips on self-development

A thinking person always evaluates his place in the world and tries to make it better and better. Here is how:

1. **Self-review:** Every day and from time to time, he reviews his speech and actions and tries to find out where he has gone wrong or fallen short. Self-review helps him to overcome his weak areas.
2. **Good management of time:** He manages his time well, beginning with his hours of waking up and going to bed. He plans his work and works his plan. This planning is for a day, a week, a month, a year and the distant future. His estimates become realistic and efficiency sharpens.
3. **Developing a calm mind:** "A sound mind in a sound body." A man on the path of self-improvement tries to acquire a health which would enable him to meditate. Swami Vivekananda says that the way to the meditation hall is through the football field. That is, first physical health, power, teamwork – and then meditation.
4. **Communing with great minds:** He chooses his books and discourses optimally – just the right combination to develop all four aspects of personality. Something on health-building and removal of diseases; something about the various arts and skills useful in life; great creative literature; and spiritual texts - if possible of all religions.
5. **Building up courage:** A self-improvement fan tries to overcome his fears, whatever they may be, by meeting situations head-on in a planned manner. He also has the initiative to take up good causes. He is proactive – originator of actions.
6. **Humility and gratitude:** Newton pronounced that even with his unequalled place as a physicist, he had just a pebble on the shores of knowledge. Life is short, art is long. This teaches humility. Further, a self-improver learns to be thankful to all who have made him what he is. A wise person is known to thank even his opponent where this is due.

1.9 SWOT ANALYSIS

In modern management studies, SWOT is a useful buzzword – an analysis of one's **S**trengths, **W**eaknesses, **O**pportunities and **T**hreats. A SWOT analysis is required in the regular course of a person's or a company's life, and especially at the start of an enterprise. For this, one can overview the past and consider others' opinions, too. One has to be one's own final judge and follow the gut feeling. SWOT analysis helps to know one's standing and choose the correct areas for development and growth.

Case study 1 (an individual)

Let us consider Mr. X who wants to be a chartered accountant.

Strengths	Weaknesses
Accountancy and business in the family Good colleges and libraries around Consistent first class upto HSSC	Gets up too late Watches TV too much Bad handwriting and grammar
Opportunities	**Threats**
Can earn a good income as a C.A. Can get career satisfaction	May not use his full potential May know correct answers but present them poorly

The remedy for such a person is to regulate his habits and take charge of his time. He needs to hitch his wagon to the stars (keep a high aim) and do some motivational reading. He needs to take a course in grammar and go to a handwriting workshop. Since he is a borderline case for becoming a CA, he has to remove his fears and develop confidence through test series. At the same time, family successes in accountancy should be used to learn the practicalities. But they should not make him complacent (self-satisfied).

Case study 2 (an organisation)

Four friends come together and think of starting a legal firm. Their SWOT chart is:

Strengths	Weaknesses
Know one another since childhood All are graduates in law with a first class Have good communicative skills	They live in a town and must migrate to a city Their religious backgrounds differ Have poor understanding of modern means of communication (computers etc.)
Opportunities	**Threats**
Good law firms are few in the region, hence good scope It would give them financial and career satisfaction.	A possible financial collapse, since migration to city would cost a lot Religious misunderstandings

This team has to work in coordination in the town itself, build up a good financial base, underplay religion and learn the use of modern gadgetry.

A. Questions based on critical understanding. Comment in about 30 words.

1. **Communication does not simply involve sending of a message by a person.**

Ans. Communication is a two-way process, not merely the sending of messages one way. It involves listening, understanding and providing feedback to complete the communication. It involves encoding and decoding according to the message received.

2. **Encoding the matter is an important element of communication.**

Ans. What you wish to communicate can be said in many ways. It has to suit the audience, and has to be encoded accordingly. It refers to preparing the matter for communication indeed in a suitable language along with supporting, signs, symbols, etc.

3. Communication is a social activity.

Ans. Man alone hardly needs to or can communicate - unless it is thinking or monologue. But when he is with others of his kind, in society he can - and, in fact, must - communicate. Social life is necessary for communication. Communication is a must for social life.

4. Feedback enhances effectiveness of communication.

Ans. Feedback ensures that communication becomes a two-way process and the sender knows through the receiver's response whether he has received the entire message and grasped its intent.

5. Decoding is necessary for interpretation and understanding of message.

Ans. In communication, the sender chooses certain words and/or non-verbal elements to encode his message for the receiver. Hence, the receiver has to decode it to understand its intended meaning.

6. Feedback makes communication a two-way process.

Ans. Feedback effectively links the sender with the receiver ensuring a two-way process, facilitating questions and clarifications by the receiver to understand the message exactly as meant by the sender.

Comment on the following:

1. Communication is multi-dimensional.
2. Conveying information is the first and foremost function of communication.
3. Ideal communication is a two-way process.
4. Technological advancement has contributed to the growth of communication.
5. A host of reasons can lead to barriers in communication.
6. Semantic problem in communication is due to weak communication channels.
7. Feedback must always be interpreted carefully.
8. Decoding is the process of interpreting a message.
9. Feedback is the message sent by the decoder to the encoder.
10. The receiver and the decoder are one and the same person.

B. Questions for revision

1. Explain briefly the process of communication.
2. Explain how the following contribute towards effective communication:
   (i) Politeness
   (ii) Clarity of purpose
   (iii) Feedback
   (iv) Attentive listening
   (v) Control of emotions.
3. "Communication is the sharing of understanding." Discuss this and bring out the process of communication.
4. What are the barriers to communication?
5. List some tips for effective communication.
6. Discuss the role of feedback in the communication process.
7. Explain the importance and benefits of communication.
8. Discuss how the growing importance of human relations has affected business communications.
9. Elaborate on the factors contributing to the importance of communication.
10. Discuss the key elements of the communication process.
11. Explain, with diagrams, any two theories of communication.

12. Name of five types of audiences. What is the relative importance of each?
13. Outline the requirements of growing as a person.
14. Self-development and development of the communicative personality are mutually supportive activities. Discuss.
15. What do you understand by SWOT analysis?
16. Make a SWOT analysis of a person who wishes to be a doctor and has the following features:
    (a) Great interest in technological products
    (b) Voracious general reader
    (c) Frail health, unable to stand hostel life
    (d) Feels aversion for vomit and such things
    (e) Very good percentages in exams
    (f) Father is a Class I government officer
    (g) Lives in a village
    (h) Bad handwriting
17. Make a SWOT analysis of a workshop for fabrication of steel furniture that wants to expand.
    (a) Currently located in a multi-story industrial complex
    (b) Land available in industrial estate in plots of 4000 sq.ft.
    (c) Reputation as giver of precision and quality
    (d) Can provide own stake of Rs. 5 lakhs for a loan of Rs. 15 lakhs
    (e) Minimum investment required for moving to industrial estate is Rs. 40 lakhs
    (f) For factory management, it depends on a trusted old employee
    (g) More galas likely to be available in the existing industrial complex
    (h) Owner lives closer to the industrial estate but far from the existing industrial complex.

■■■

CHAPTER

2

Forms of Communication

What should you know?

- 2.1 Introduction – Classification of Communication
- 2.2 Verbal Communication – Written, Oral
- 2.3 Non-verbal Communication
- 2.4 Dimensions/Directions of Communication
- 2.5 Formal and Informal Communication
- 2.6 Modern Forms of Communication – Fax, Internet/email, Videoconferencing

2.1 INTRODUCTION – CLASSIFICATION OF COMMUNICATION

For communication to be effective, the communicator has to be very careful in the choice of the media (plural of *medium*). Media here means the methods adopted by the communicator to convey his message. This choice of media depends on several factors, such as the urgency of the message, the time available, the costs involved and the intellectual and emotional level of the receiver.

The following diagram shows various media and means of communication:

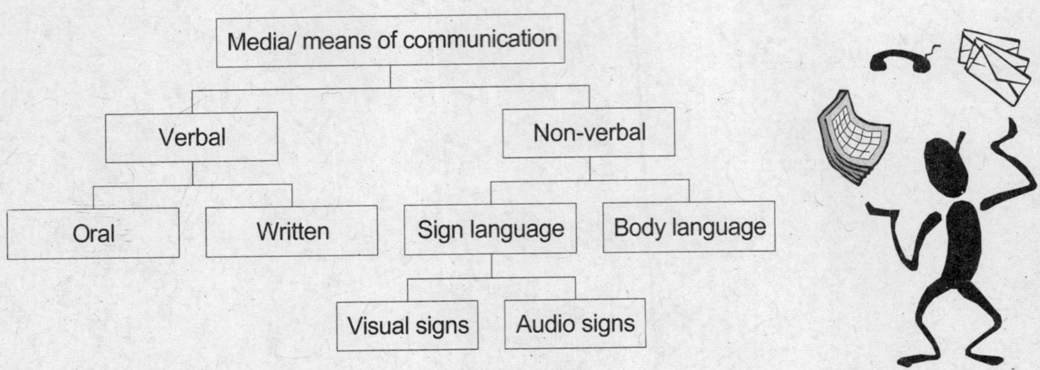

2.2 VERBAL COMMUNICATION – WRITTEN, ORAL

The word verbal means 'connected with words and use of words.' Any communication using words is verbal communication. Words are the most precise and powerful sets of symbols. Words denote as well as connote meanings. That is why all serious or formal communication is usually in words. Words, as we are all aware, can be written or spoken. Thus, verbal communication can further be divided into two types:

(a) Oral (b) Written

(a) Oral Communication:

"A wound inflicted by speech is more painful than a wound inflicted by a sword."

As the term itself suggests, communication through the spoken word is known as oral communication. Of the working time spent in verbal communication, 9 % is in writing, 16 % in reading, 30 % in speaking and 45 % in listening. In oral communication, words should be chosen very carefully so that what they connote has the precise shade of meaning. The sender of the message or his representative is usually the speaker, while the receiver or his representative, the listener. Listening is also an important aspect of oral communication.

Factors in oral communication

- The speaker
- How he speaks
- What he speaks
- To whom he speaks
- Whether he receives a feedback

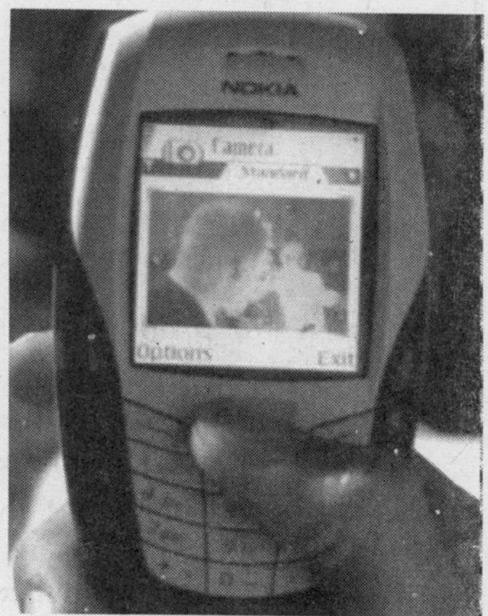

Pre-requisites of oral communication

- Clear and proper pronunciation of words
- Clarity and exactitude
- Conciseness
- Right tone
- Right pitch
- Right style and vocabulary

Merits of oral communication

(*i*) **Saving of time and money:** Oral communication saves money as well as time. No money needs to be spent for producing oral communication since it involves only the spoken word. Oral communication is, therefore, economical. Secondly, there is hardly any delay from the time when the sender sends the message and the receiver receives it. The words are received and understood as soon as they are spoken. Oral communication, therefore, saves time, too.

(*ii*) **Immediate feedback:** The feedback in most oral communication is immediate. The words are received as soon as they are spoken, and the receiver can also give his reaction immediately. The speaker can gauge the mood and the response of the listener. The immediate feedback is an advantage for the speaker.

(*iii*) **Saves paperwork:** Paperwork is minimal since communication is in the form of spoken words.

(*iv*) **An effective tool for exhortation:** When the communication is oral, you can try to persuade the listener. Doubts can be cleared immediately.

(*v*) **Builds a healthy climate:** A friendly atmosphere is created when you communicate orally since there is less formality. You can also make modifications in the communication immediately on the basis of the feedback and response from the listener.

(*vi*) **Best tool during emergency:** Oral communication is the quickest tool during an emergency. It is the best method of communication when an immediate and fast response is critical.

Demerits of oral communication (limitations)

(*i*) **Greater chances of misunderstanding:** Unless it is recorded, you cannot refer to an oral message again. There are, therefore, greater chances of a message being misunderstood or misinterpreted. In fact, there is also a chance that the message may not be understood at all.

(ii) **Bad speaker:** Only an individual who can satisfy all the requisites of effective oral communication can produce good results. More often than not, a bad speaker may send the wrong message. When speaking, one communicates through the articulation, voice modulation and body language, too. A message may be misunderstood if there is a disharmony among these components. Also, as mentioned earlier, what the words connote and what they denote should be in harmony, else the message may lead to a conflict in understanding.

(iii) **Ineffective for lengthy communication:** Oral communication is not useful for lengthy communication. Because of human limitations, there is every likelihood that something important will be missed out.

(iv) **Lower retention rate:** Oral communication suffers from the drawback of a low retention rate. A listener may absorb only some part of an oral message since the attention span differs from person to person. People also tend to forget an oral message quickly.

(v) **No legal validity:** Oral communication lacks proof of record. There is no permanent record or proof of what has been said. An individual who has given a message may deny it later; similarly, an individual who has been given an oral message or instruction may say he never received it. Hence, oral communication has very little value from the legal point of view.

(vi) **Difficult to fix responsibility:** Since a message is transmitted orally, it is difficult to fix responsibility. This may also lead to carelessness in the implementation of a message.

(b) Written communication

A message constitutes written communication when it is put in "black and white." It is a formal type of communication. The sender of the message or his representative constitutes the writer. Written communication is usually considered binding on business organisations and is often used as evidence. Technological advancement has enlarged the gamut of written communication through email and other such facilities.

Factors in written communication

- The writer
- The content
- The language used
- The purpose of the communication
- The style adopted - formal or friendly
- The receiver

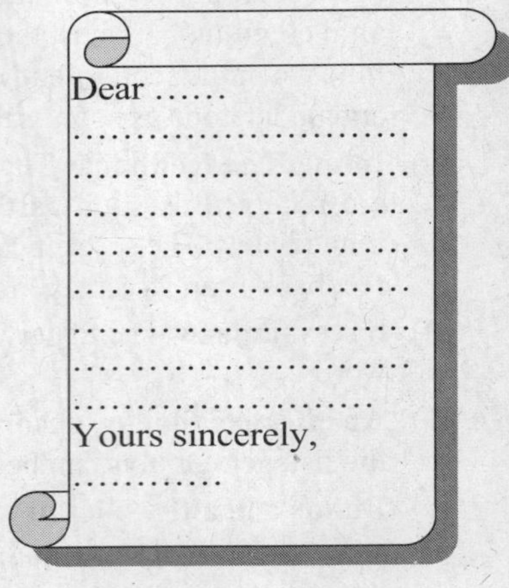

Pre-requisites of written communication

- How much to put in writing
- What to leave out
- When to stop
- When to convey
- To whom to convey
- By what means to convey

Merits

(i) **Precise and accurate:** Written communication is generally prepared with great care and precision. The very prospect of writing makes a person conscious. You have to be very serious and organised while communicating in the written form, because written communication is open to verification.

(ii) **Easily verified:** Since written communication is on paper etc., it can be read and re-read. It also offers itself to verification. There is also, thus, less chance of someone twisting the message to his or her own advantage.

(iii) **Permanent record**: Written communication constitutes a permanent record. It also acts like evidence. It proves very useful for future reference as it can be preserved for years. For example, old orders and decisions can serve as the basis for new ones.

(iv) **Suitable for lengthy and complicated messages:** Lengthy and complicated messages can be understood better when they are in the written form rather than in the oral. There is less chance of misinterpretation and misunderstanding. Also, the language used is less subject to change.

(v) **Responsibility can be easily fixed:** In written communication, responsibilities of sender and receiver can be fixed easily. People have the tendency of shifting responsibilities for mistakes, but this is difficult if the onus is obvious in black and white.

(vi) **Has legal validity:** Written communication is acceptable as a legal document. Written communication has been used as evidence since time immemorial.

Demerits

(i) **Slower method of communication:** Written communication can be time-consuming since it may take even two or even three days to reach the receiver (by letters, for instance). By contrast, oral communication is immediate.

(ii) **Further delay if clarifications are required:** Written communication hampers quick clarifications. The receiver may write back for clarifications and wait for a reply, making the process tedious. Even if clarifications are not needed, there is still a delay between the time the sender writes a message and the receiver receives it.

(iii) **Leads to too much of paperwork:** Since written communication is basically done on paper, one may tend to use it as an escape mechanism Paper-free offices remain a dream.

(iv) **Always a possibility of ambiguity or lack of comprehensibility:** It is quite possible that the receiver is not able to comprehend the exact meaning of a written message that he has received. The clarity of a written message also depends upon the skill, or the lack of it, in the sender. If the message has not been written properly, it will not be understood, either.

(v) **Costly in terms of money and man-hours:** Writing letters is a costly process not only because you need to spend money on postage, but also because several persons are involved in the process of sending out a letter from an organisation. Their time costs an organisation money. While oral communication can be short and quick, written communication, because of its very nature, tends to be lengthy.

(vi) **No flexibility:** The written word is not subject to instant change after communication. Therefore, conveying an afterthought may prove very lengthy, and, at times, even impossible.

(vii) **Literacy essential:** It goes without saying that in written communication, the sender as well as the receiver should be literate. In fact, we may wrongly presume that they are so. In many Asian Countries, where literacy is low, a written message will be meaningless for large masses of illiterate persons. Literacy also means literacy in the language of the message. The receiver should know the language in which a message has been written. It is no use receiving a message in English if you are not conversant with that language.

Notwithstanding its limitations, it can be safely concluded that written communication remains the spine of an organisation. Almost all formal communication is in the written form.

Visual Aids

A visual aid is an illustration in tabular, graphic, schematic or pictorial from. Visual aids help communicators to get their message across more effectively to their audience. Visual aids help by making the material more interesting, clarifying and simplifying complex subjects and highlighting important points for better retention by the audience.

A checklist for creating effective visuals is given below:

- Visuals should be simple and easy to understand and the design and layout should contribute to the overall understanding of the subject.
- Visuals should depict the data accurately and important points should be emphasised.
- Visuals should be appropriate for the intended audience.
- Care should be taken that the type-face and fonts are clear and readable and the captions short and informative.

2.3 NON-VERBAL COMMUNICATION

Scientific analysis has shown that body movements and gestures constitute 55% of effective communication. Hence, non-verbal communication merits great consideration.

Non-verbal communication involves things such as gestures, posture, physical appearance etc. It takes place without written or spoken words. Non-verbal communication is those messages that are expressed by means other than linguistic. While you can refuse to speak or write, it is impossible to avoid behaving non-verbally. Non-verbal communication is classified here in two different ways:

I.

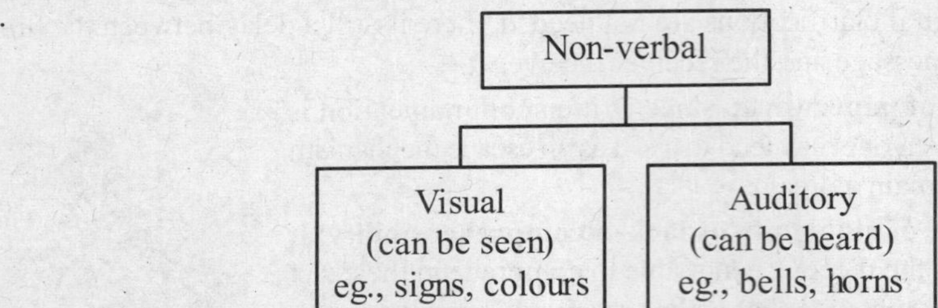

II.
- Body language or **kinesics** – body movement, facial expressions, posture, etc.
- Vocal characteristics – **paralanguage**
- Space - **proxemics**
- Surroundings
- Silence

2.3.1 Kinesics

The study of bodily movements that form a part of non-verbal communication is known as **kinesics.** It is an integral part of our communication. Existence as a receiver is supposed to observe non-verbal communication 55% of the time. Our body consciously as well as unconsciously, conveys messages, moods, attitudes, etc. in the same way as language uses sets of symbols to convey meaning.

(*i*) **Facial expressions:** The face is said to be the mirror of the mind. Whatever we feel is reflected on our face. The face can convey energy, anger, grief, sincerity and a host of other feelings and emotions. A smile means friendliness, while a frown means anger. A creased forehead shows worry while a raised eyebrow shows surprise. Hence, it is very important to exercise a check and control over our feelings. Although this is a difficult task, you can get positive results with continuous efforts.

(ii) **Gestures:** Gestures are small body movements that transmit some message. It can even be the transmission of specific information. Some gestures may be conscious while others may be involuntary. Some gestures have an almost universal meaning, such as a headshake for a "no" or a handshake as a "hello". Then there are other gestures that may have regional meanings. Strictly speaking, gestures are a part of body language because our head and hands tend to communicate by themselves in their own way.

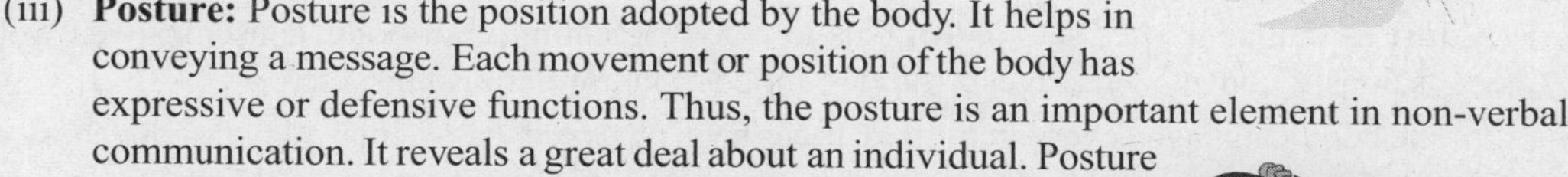

(iii) **Posture:** Posture is the position adopted by the body. It helps in conveying a message. Each movement or position of the body has expressive or defensive functions. Thus, the posture is an important element in non-verbal communication. It reveals a great deal about an individual. Posture concerns the overall bearing of the body. It includes the angle of inclination and the position of the arms and the legs. A raised head indicates openness, while a tilted head indicates curiosity. However, one should remember that none of these postures have any specific meanings of their own. They acquire meanings in association with other symbols and in the context of communication.

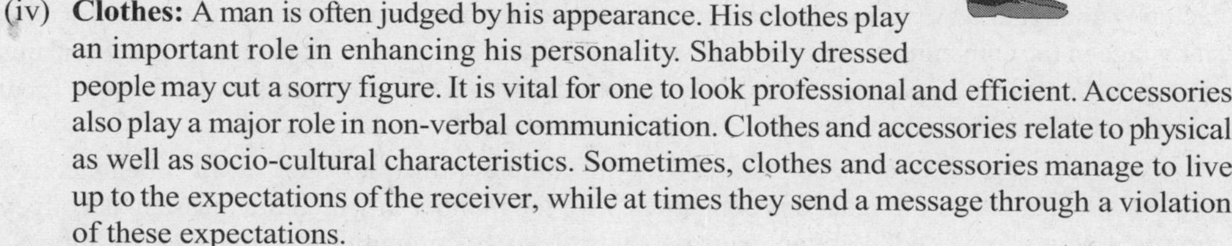

(iv) **Clothes:** A man is often judged by his appearance. His clothes play an important role in enhancing his personality. Shabbily dressed people may cut a sorry figure. It is vital for one to look professional and efficient. Accessories also play a major role in non-verbal communication. Clothes and accessories relate to physical as well as socio-cultural characteristics. Sometimes, clothes and accessories manage to live up to the expectations of the receiver, while at times they send a message through a violation of these expectations.

(v) **Eye contact:** Eyes are the windows to the soul. Eye contact constitutes a very important factor of face-to-face communication. Through eye-contact, the speaker gets signals whether the channel of communication is open. Discomfiture or nervousness results only in a brief eye contact; on the other hand, a long and fixed gaze shows interest. Depending on our feelings, we have smiling eyes, angry eyes, painful eyes, evasive eyes, and so on.

(vi) **Silence**. Silence speaks louder than words. It lays down the relationship between communicators and their attitude towards each other. Silence shows the inability to converse further. A student who has not done his homework will stay mum when the teacher asks him for it.

Indicators of Non-verbal Communication

Positive	**Negative - Submissive**	**Negative - Aggressive**
Smile	Floundering voice	Harsh voice
Open posture	Defensive arms / legs	Wagging finger
Interested expression	Slow speech	Fast speech
Moderate eye contact	Fretting expressions	Supercilious expressions
Accurate pitch and volume of voice	Deceitful looks	Immoderate eye contact

Body Language

Body language stands for the way the body communicates without words, through the movement of its parts.

The nodding of our heads, blinking of our eyes, waving of our hands, shrugging of our shoulders, etc., are expressions of our thoughts and feelings. All these movements are the signals that our body sends out to communicate. That is why this area of study has been called **body language**.

Just as language uses sets of symbols to convey meaning, our body, consciously as well as unconsciously, conveys messages, attitudes, moods, status relationships, etc.

The body language is very important. It has been observed that we may play fast and loose with words, but our body speaks out the truth. Even if we try to hide the truth or anything that we want to suppress, our body, our eyes, our gestures may speak out loud and clear.

2.3.2 Paralanguage

The world of communication that involves signs, signals, pitch, tone and fluctuations to convey meaning is **paralanguage**. Para means 'like' or 'akin'. Paralanguage means "like language," but not actually a language. Anything that performs the task of communication as a language without being a language in the conventional sense of the word, falls within the purview of paralanguage. Paralanguage is used to describe a wide range of vocal characteristics which help to express and reflect the speaker's attitude. It is non-verbal because it does not consist of words.

Verbal communication is concerned with the content of the message – *what* is being conveyed? On the other hand, paralanguage is concerned with the manner in which the message is conveyed – *how* is it being conveyed? Paralanguage depends on voice, intonation, pitch, pause, volume, stress, gestures, and signals. Through pitch and volume variation, stress on words, etc. one's voice can convey enthusiasm, confidence, anxiety and the speaker's mental state and temperament.

Voice: Voice is the first signal that we receive or use. A good listener can gauge a lot from the voice itself. There are various categories of voices. A voice can be sweet, soft, musical, cultivated, pleasant, nasty, clear or indistinct, among other things. The voice can help reveal a speaker's background, mental state, education, sex and temperament.

Intonation: Intonation is the modulation of the voice and the shift in stress. Intonation is a part of effective communication. For example, a message with serious content should not be delivered in a high tone, but in a sombre tone.

Pitch: Pitch is the vocal slant of the voice. It is very important because it reveals the speaker's frame of mind. An unusually high pitch may reflect agitation. An unchanging pitch may be boring or monotonous, decreasing the listener's span of attention. The pitch may also help us understand the speaker's social position. A person in a position of authority uses a higher pitch than a subordinate. The flaring of tempers usually results in a change in the pitch.

Pause: A pause emphasises a message. A pause is to speech what a comma is to prose. A pause at the wrong place may lead to miscommunication. For example, the difference between '**fruit trees**' and '**fruit, trees**' is vast.

Volume variation: The speaker should adjust the volume of his voice depending on the size of the audience. Larger the audience, the louder the voice should be. Volume variation makes the speech effective. Sometimes changing from loud to soft and from soft to loud has the desired effect.

Mixed signals: Mixed signals occur when the tone, pitch and facial expressions of the speaker do not match the words that he is speaking. This confuses the listener as to the exact motive of the speaker. For example, an individual may congratulate another, but his tone may be cold. In this case, the listener will not be sure whether the speaker is really happy or is merely fulfilling a formality. Praise delivered in a sarcastic tone conveys mockery.

Proper word stress: Communication can be made more effective by putting proper emphasis or stress on the right words.

Overall impression: A message is understood by the listener not only by the content, but also by the manner in which the speaker conveys it. The speaker's bearing, attitude, dressing style, physical appearance, age, gender, accent and the quality and tone of the voice also affect the message that gets communicated. For a message to be effective, the overall impression given by the individual should be in consonance with the message that he wants to convey.

Advantages of paralanguage

(i) No oral communication is complete without paralanguage as it is closely connected to language itself.

(ii) To a large extent, paralanguage indicates the position and situation of the speaker, whether in an organisation or in society.

(iii) It also reflects the speaker's personality and background to a great extent.

(iv) Paralanguage is indicative of the mental state of the speaker. A discerning listener can derive the right conclusions from the pitch, tone and speed of a message. This can often be very useful.

Limitations of paralanguage

(i) Paralanguage is 'semi' or 'like' a language. It is not language by itself. Therefore, not all the advantages associated with actual language can be attributed to paralanguage.

(ii) Paralanguage involves the drawing of conclusions on the basis of a number of peripheral (side) attributes. Such drawing of conclusions need not always be right. In such a case, they may also serve to create undue bias. This, in itself, makes paralanguage misleading or confusing at times.

(iii) Also, as speakers may come from different backgrounds, cultures and situations, the conclusions from paralanguage may be difficult to draw, especially to convey a message in its entirety.

2.3.3 Proxemics or territory or space

Proxemics is another important type of non-verbal communication. The term, proxemics is derived from the word *proximity*, which means closeness. Proxemics is used with reference to space or territory. A lot of communication takes place non-verbally through the sheer manner in which we use the space around us. Scholars have also attributed a lot of non-verbal communication to the colour, design, layout and utilisation of the space around us. This is also proxemics.

The space around us can be broadly classified as under:

Intimate space: Most body movements take place within 18 inches around us. It is our most intimate circle of space. Only very close people or family members can enter this space, be it through a whisper, a pat on the back or a handshake. It means that the less the space between the two persons communicating, the more intimate is the nature of communication.

Personal space: Personal space extends from 18 inches to four feet where we have normal conversation with friends, colleagues and associates. It is used in informal talks and impromptu discussions in which one may not be averse to taking important decisions.

Social Space: This can be anywhere between four feet and 12 feet. It reflects a formality of relationship. It also reflects a lack of spontaneous behaviour. An individual's responses are more collected and well thought-out. Social space reflects reason, planning and control, usually associated with business communication within a formal relationship.

Public Space: This starts from a distance of 12 feet. One has to raise one's voice to be heard. There is a lack of personal feelings and an added sense of detachment.

Paralanguage	Proxemics
Reflects feelings and attitudes of the speaker through a wide range of vocal characteristics.	Feelings and attitudes are reflected by the way people use space around them.
Paralanguage gives important clues about the speaker's educational, national/regional background and mental state.	Proxemics helps us to understand relationships and interaction patterns between people.
It is a systematic study of how an individual verbalises.	Proxemics is also concerned with the use of space by groups of people.

2.3.4 Surroundings

How you organize the surroundings also contributes to the communication. The room where you meet your visitors may be dazzling or simple. It may be gaudy or sober. The decor of the place, the furniture, the artistic pieces that adorn your office, tell about yourself and your taste.

2.4 DIMENSIONS/DIRECTIONS OF COMMUNICATION

Every organisation has a multidimensional or multidirectional communication. The directions in which communication is carried out are:

(i) Downward
(ii) Upward
(iii) Horizontal or Lateral
(iv) Diagonal or Crosswise

2.4.1 Downward Communication

Traditionally, the emphasis in business organisations has been on downward communication. This is because of the hierarchical nature of organisations where all communication basically and naturally flows from top to bottom. It is the communication that comes from superiors and flows down to the subordinates.

Methods of downward communication

Downward communication can be written as well as oral. The oral communication is mostly through information channels. The written downward communication takes the form of orders, circulars, policy statements, memos and procedural documents.

Example, a CEO (Chief Executive Officer) or a General Manager issuing instructions or sending letters to various departmental heads.

Objectives

1. To give specific directions about a job
2. To explain procedures
3. To apprise subordinates of their performance
4. To explain the significance of a job given to a subordinate with respect to the organisation's goals

Limitations

(i) **Distortion:** Downward communication is often marred by distortion or contortion of the message. Any piece of information loses a bit of its accuracy whenever it passes from one person to another. In fact, some directions or instructions may not even be understood. This often affects the accuracy of the information. By the time it reaches the receiver, the very crux of the communication may be lost.

(ii) **Loss of information:** There is every likelihood of information getting lost in the huge labyrinth that a business organisation often is. Information in a written form is considered safer, but even this is likely to get lost.

(iii) **Delay:** Downward communication may take a long time to reach the person concerned. The communication has to go through various levels before reaching the grassroots. This makes downward communication time-consuming. Often, this delay in downward communication frustrates the top managers who have issued the communication.

(iv) **Under-communication and over-communication:** Downward communication may also be hampered by under-communication or over-communication by the intervening superiors. The superiors may talk too much at times, and too little at others. They may, thus, dilute or modify the communication.

(v) **Built-in resistance:** Downward communication reflects an authoritarian setup. It prevents subordinates from participating in the decision-making process. It gives them a feeling of being talked down to. Subordinates may, therefore, oppose the decision or not welcome it wholeheartedly.

2.4.2 Upward Communication

As the term suggests, this channel of communication pushes information upwards. It starts from the people at the lowest level of an organisation and reaches the top. An open-door policy, social gatherings, reports, direct correspondence, counselling, etc. are some common methods of upward communication. Managers have now recognised the importance of this channel of organisational communication. Until now, it was felt that the right to communicate had been vested only in the top management.

Methods of upward communication

(a) **Periodical meetings**: These are regular meetings with the staff and subordinates conducted to invite suggestions, opinions or other ideas.

(b) **Written representations:** An example of upward communication is a written representation given by employees to their superiors as regards what they feel about the work environment and suggestions regarding improvement.

(c) **Informal gatherings:** Parties and get-togethers provide opportunities for the employees to share their feelings and have an interaction with the superiors.

(d) **Suggestion schemes:** The employees are encouraged to give suggestions on the practices and the systems being followed in the organisation. For this purpose, a suggestion box may be kept.

Objectives

(i) Feedback: This channel provides the management with the necessary feedback. On the basis of the feedback, the management can ascertain whether the subordinates have understood a given set of directions properly.

(ii) Outlet for held-up emotions: The employees get an opportunity to vent their problems and grievances when they communicate with the management.

(iii) Positive suggestions: Quite often, this channel brings forward some very useful suggestions from the employees, which can be implemented for the organisation's benefit.

(iv) Harmony: Upward communication creates a congenial atmosphere and brings the management and the employees closer to each other. It creates a positive psychological factor as employees feel involved.

Limitations

(i) Most problems in upward communication are psychological in nature. Most higher-ups still do not like to be 'told' anything about or against their own decisions or wishes.

(ii) The employees are also hesitant to walk up to managers and initiate upward communication.

(iii) A common belief among employees is that it may not really be in their interest to communicate their problems to superiors.

(iv) Sometimes managers may not accept certain unpleasant facts. This may lead to the distortion of this channel of communication.

(v) Subordinates may become too bold and directly approach the top authority with their complaints. This proves harmful as the relations between the workers and their immediate superior get strained.

(vi) Upward communication may also be used by sycophants for personal gains. Such employees may try to endear themselves to the superiors by passing on selective information. Genuine information may, thus, get suppressed or distorted.

2.4.3 Lateral or Horizontal Communication

This kind of communication takes place between departments or people on the same level in an organisational structure. It is one of the most frequently used channels of communication.

Face-to-face discussions, telephonic talks, periodical meetings, memos, etc. are the ways of carrying out this type of communication. It is very important for the smooth functioning of every organisation as it promotes understanding and coordination between various departments. Embarrassing situations can arise when there is a lack of proper horizontal communication.

For example, the production and the marketing departments must interact with each other because marketing tactics and production planning go hand-in-hand.

Objectives

(i) To create a friendly atmosphere in an organisation

(ii) To cut across departmental barriers

(iii) To ensure quick feedback

Limitations

(i) Lateral communication may give birth to gossip. It can be used for rumourmongering and spreading false information.

(ii) Good ideas may get suppressed because such communication often comes without authority or sanction for implementation.

(iii) Lateral communication can be effective only if there is proper coordination.

2.4.4 Diagonal or Crosswise Communication

Diagonal or crosswise communication envisages a *horizontal flow* of information as well as interaction across different levels of an organisation's hierarchy. Communication flows across different levels in an organisation among people who may not have direct reporting relationships. Diagonal communication is used to speed up the flow of information. It makes effective efforts for achieving organisational goals. A great deal of communication does not follow the organisational hierarchy, but cuts across well-drawn lines. Channels of such communication are general notices, informal meetings, formal conferences, lunch hour meetings, etc.

Objectives

(i) To help in proper coordination

(ii) To communicate effectively whether laterally, horizontally and diagonally

(iii) To improve mutual understanding

(iv) To boost the morale of lower level staff through interaction across all the levels in the organisation

Limitations

(i) There is a fear of encroachment in diagonal communication. The superiors may feel bad when their subordinates are given importance, and may even end up feeling bypassed.

(ii) The superiors may resist suggestions just because these have come from subordinates. This comes out of a subconscious feeling of not having been part of the consultation process.

(iii) Diagonal communication can lead to a network that is extremely complex. An absence of accepted procedures may lead to internal chaos. The fallout can then be external displeasure.

Comparison between Upward and Downward Communication

Basis of comparison	Downward communication	Upward communication
Direction	Downward communication flows from higher to bottom level.	Upward communication flows from bottom to higher levels.
Speed	Its speed is fast, empowered by authority.	Its speed is slow.
Purpose	Its purpose may be to give orders for implementing plans.	Its purpose is to provide feedback and give suggestions.
Nature	Its nature is authoritative and directive.	Its nature is informative and that of an appeal.
Examples	Its examples include orders, circulars, notices, etc.	Its examples include reports, suggestions, grievances, etc.

2.5 FORMAL AND INFORMAL COMMUNICATION

Communication can also be classified according to the degree of ceremony or formality it has. Thus we can divide communication into two broad categories:

(a) Formal channels

(b) Informal channels

2.5.1 Formal channel of communication

A formal channel of communication is the means of communication normally controlled by people in positions of authority in an organisation. Hence, it has also been referred to as an organisation's 'main line of operational communication'. All the reports, records and other forms that supply working information to various parts of an organisation are included in the formal channel of communication. These channels of communication do not function automatically. A good business organisation will ensure that these are carefully planned and designed to its needs.

Advantages

(i) **Effective:** Formal channels are considered the more effective of channels of communication. With organisations constantly growing in size, formal channels help to bridge the gap in the communication process. It is a readily available means to reach through to every corner of an organisation, which would otherwise be difficult.

(ii) **Prevent bogging:** In formal channels, the rules are well laid. For example, a worker communicates with the supervisor, the supervisor with the manager, and so on. Thus, only necessary information gets filtered and sent to the top. It prevents the top-level management from getting bogged down with the irrelevant nitty-gritty (the practical details) of information and leaves it free for bigger decisions and overall management.

(iii) **Better monitoring:** An organisation can design formal channels to suit its specific needs. This can help monitor organisational activities. It can ensure that problems are solved without too much delay.

(iv) **Good atmosphere:** Good formal channels of communication reflect professionalism. They help consolidate the organisation. They also keep the managerial personnel in control.

Disadvantages

(i) **Deter free flow of information:** Formal channels deter a free flow of information. Formality demands that the information flow take a specific route only. This inhibits the natural flow of information.

(ii) **Time-consuming:** Formal channels of communication often lead to delays. The information may not directly reach the person for whom it is meant. It will often have to take a circuitous formal route where the intervening links may be meaningless. As a result, formal channels of communication can become time-consuming.

(iii) **Affects decision-making:** Filtering and monitoring of information at lower levels is a double-edged sword. While it has its advantages, it may also prevent vital information from reaching the top management. This may change the perspective while making decisions.

2.5.2 Informal Channel of Communication / Grapevine

The informal channel of communication is often discouraged or looked down upon in an organisation, and is not officially sanctioned. It is popularly referred to as **grapevine**. This is because it runs in all directions irrespective of the formal structure. The origin of the term *grapevine* can be traced to the way the botanical vine grew over telegraph wires, making telegraphic messages go in unintended directions. In business life, grapevine owes its existence to man's gossippy nature. Humans tends to speak loosely or lightly with their associates wherever they may be. Time to time they feel the need to get freed from the necessity to stick to logic or truth.

As people go about their work, they have casual conversation with their friends in the office. These conversations deal with both personal and business matters. This results in the generation of a rumour mill, which is a grapevine.

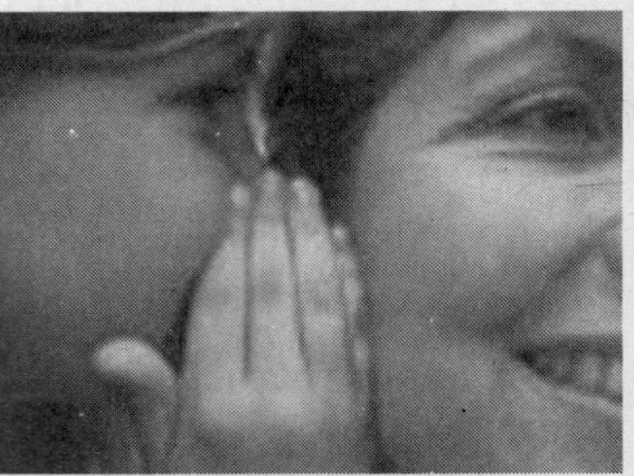

Grapevine is classified into four categories
Single strand: Each one tells another.
Group or gossip chain: One tells all persons in his/her group.
Probability chain: Each randomly tells a number of people.
Cluster chain: Some tell selected others.

Grapevine satisfies the social needs of members, leads to more relaxed human relations (partly through the release of fantasy), serves to fill the possible gaps in the formal communication and links even those people who do not fall in the official chain of command.

Other characteristics of grapevine are:

- It is more people-oriented then issue-oriented.
- May not be totally authentic and dependable.
- Grapevine transmission flows in all directions in an organisation.
- Grapevine information travels very fast.
- Its responsibility cannot be fixed.

Factors leading to grapevine

A rumour mill becomes active when the following factors exist in an organisation:

(i) A lack of sense of direction, especially in times of crisis. The more the uncertainty, the greater the rumourmongering.

(ii) The formation of favoured groups of employees by the management. This breeds insecurity among other employees leading to rumours.

(iii) A lack of self-confidence amongst employees leads to the formation of groups. These groups often run rumour mills.

Advantages

(i) **Speed:** Speed is the most remarkable characteristic of this channel of communication. It is possible to transmit information remarkably fast since there are no formal barriers and no stopping. A rumour, thus, may spread like a wildfire.

(ii) **Feedback:** The feedback through this channel is much faster than a formal channel of communication. The channel is like the pulse of an organisation. The reaction to the decisions, policies, directives and directions often reach managers faster through this channel than through the formal one.

(iii) **Parallel function**: The informal channel does not have official sanction, but is an inevitable parallel to the formal channel. It works as a supplementary channel of communication in an organisation. Good managers have been known to use the informal channel to their benefit for transmitting information otherwise unfit for formal channels.

(iv) **Support system:** A grapevine is an informal support system developed by employees within an organisation. It brings them closer and gives them immense satisfaction.

Disadvantages

(i) **Less credible:** A grapevine is less credible than a formal channel of communication. It cannot be taken seriously as it involves only the word of mouth. It is, therefore, likely to be contradicted.

(ii) **Selective information**: Informal channels usually fail to carry the complete information. As a result, the receiver does not get the essence of the whole message. Mischiefmongers or vested interests may use the channel for transmitting selective information.

(iii) **Creates trouble:** A grapevine can foster trouble within an organisation as there is no control over the information sent, received, its portrayal and perceptions. Information gets distorted. A grapevine can be synonymous with the spreading of false or wild stories.

(iv) **Leakage:** Information may get leaked at the wrong time. The term 'open secret' in an organisation can often be attributed to such leaks.

Effective use of informal channels of communication

(i) The higher authorities should ensure that employees are well informed of the working of the organisation. This will reduce the tendency for distortion.

(ii) Activities that update knowledge should be frequent. This will prevent the generation of rumours.

(iii) The higher authorities should not indulge in favouritism.

(iv) A manager should conduct regular meetings with the employees.

(v) The manager should make efforts to identify popular employees who can serve as leaders for other employees.

(vi) As far as possible, employees should be involved in the decision-making process.

(vii) Managers should not indulge in loose talk.

(viii) A manager should be a good listener.

(ix) A manager should try to get regular reviews about his style of work.

2.6 MODERN FORMS OF COMMUNICATION – FAX, INTERNET/EMAIL, VIDEOCONFERENCING

The technological advances of the past few decades have made it possible to transmit printed messages, pictures and even live performances to all corners of the world with speed . With a single touch, you can send communications to a number of destinations. Not only large business houses but even medium and small ones use them in their day-to-day working. Among such means are fax, internet/email and videoconferencing.

2.6.1 Fax

Just as the conventional telephone carries voice, a fax or facsimile machine carries printed messages (words and pictures in photocopy form) from the sender instrument to the receiver instrument.

The sender of a fax message prepares the copy on a sheet (generally no larger than A4 size) which can be fed into the fax machine. He dials the destination number, gets the fax tone and feeds the message into the machine. The printed message is converted into electronic signals as the paper rolls through the fax machine. This message is received in the same form at the other end on the paper roll that is attached to the machine. Fax machines may have these additional features:

(A) Remote activation: The owner may use a remote control device to operate the machine.

Despite power failure :

(B) The fax machine may be made to function even during a power failure.

(C) Memory: The message sent may be retained in the memory of the machine. At the receiving end, in the absence of paper, the message may be recorded in the machine for developing a printout afterwards.

(D) Answering machine: At the receiving end, there need not be an operator to receive incoming messages. They are automatically received.

Advantages

(A) Fax enables an accurate transmission of a document including pictures and handwriting. Colour faxes are also a possibility.

(B) Fax can be sent through a computer, in which case it is restricted to the messages created on the computer.

(C) A fax message can be confirmed on telephone to ensure its authenticity.

(D) Faxes are admissible as proof in the court. In this respect they are superior to email.

(E) With repeat dialling facility, a busy number can be reached as soon as it becomes free.

Disadvantages

(a) It is expensive compared to email and post.

(b) Sometimes the reception is blurred due to channel defects or mechanical failure at either end.

(c) At the sender's or the receiver's end, the document to wrong people may be exposed. Hence it is often difficult to maintain secrecy in sending and receiving a fax message.

(d) At the receiving end, the message is printed at the receiver's cost. In case unwanted messages pour in, the receiver has to bear the cost.

Specimen fax messages

There are new conventions about drafting and laying out a fax message. Their is a tendency to minimise the vertical space of the letter. If a business letter is to be sent by fax, it is formatted in one of the following way:

Specimen fax no. 1

ABC Corporation

1, M.G.Road, Nagpur
Telephone: 0712 2537890, Fax: 0712 2520781
Email: abc@crystal.com

FAX MESSAGE

To LMN Inc., Mumbai
From Joseph De Cunha
Fax no. J/123
Subject Shortfall in your consignment
Date 4th July 2011
Page/s 1

We would like you to take immediate note of the shortfall in your consignment dated 1st July 2011 to us which was supposed to contain 40 stainless steel basins but contains only 30. We trust you will check up with your despatch section and make good the shortfall at the earliest. Please confirm by fax.

Joseph De Cunha

Purchase Manager

Specimen fax no. 2

Apex Importers-Exporters

1244 Dock Yard Street, Mumbai.
Telephone: 022 32109213, Fax: 022 21132204
Email: apeximp@indiatimes.com

Fax Message

To Kiran Jhaver Inc. **From** Raj Desai
Fax No. AIE/233 **Subject** Extension of L/C
Date 30 June 2011 **Pages** 2, including this one

As requested by you, we have arranged to extend the L/C dated 1 January 2011, which was due for expiry on 30th June, to 31st July 2011. A copy of it is being sent alongside.We hope you will take advantage of this and ship the garments within this date. In the event you are unable to do so, we will be constrained to cancel the order. Please stay in touch and advise the progress in shipping the order.

Raj Desai
Dy. Managing Director

2.6.2 Internet and e-mail

Internet is an international computer network that links computers from sectors such as government agencies, business houses, educational institutions and individuals. It receives information, stores it and allows it to be read on satisfying certain conditions. Internet Service Providers (ISPs) allow one to create the e-mail ID free, hoping to recover the cost through the ads to which the user is exposed during the use of email. A typical email address reads jagannathjoshi@rediff.com. Some other ISPs are bsnl, yahoo, hotmail, and gmail.

Here, rediff is the ISP. Note the use of only lower case (small) alphabets email in IDs.

Every time the user wants to send messages or check the incoming mail, he can reach his ID by typing a password which makes the mail account private. However, once you have submitted to the mechanism of email you do not know who might read this "private" information far away. As such email does not guarantee 100% secrecy.

Advantages

(a) Email is by far the cheapest and fastest means of sending printed information (verbal as well as non-verbal). At one click of the button, hundreds of pages of information can be sent to hundreds of email addresses worldwide (to be noted by receivers upon checking the incoming mail or inbox).

(b) No paper is required. Messages can be created directly on the computer, and added on from different computer files, CDs, floppies, etc.

(c) This facility is now available in many regional languages of India.

(d) It is informal and allows the sender to remain anonymous (since he can use any name as his email ID. For instance J.K. Singh can use udankhatola as his email name).

(e) Organisations and publishing houses take cognisance of messages coming via email. Newspapers and magazines print letters that come via email.

(f) As long as you carry your password with you, you can open your email account on any computer in the world which has this facility. You remain unemcumbered even with a mobile handset. You can just enter an internet café, pay the rent and use the email. Email is extraordinarily portable.

(g) You can have an address book in your email account, record the incoming mails, edit them and so on.

(h) When you reply to an email message, the sender's message is automatically sent back to him for ready reference.

(i) As human need and imagination guide, more innovations are possible.

(j) Email can enable an ongoing electronic conference. People across the world can "meet" on internet and confer on a topic of common interest.

(k) The receiver need not respond at once as on the telephone but can take his time. Emailing helps to avoid a direct interface.

(l) In an organisation, a subordinate may quickly and directly reach a superior on email. Email makes an organisation more democratic (as individuals have more chance of being heard by the proper person even if he is several levels higher).

Disadvantages:

(a) Email, because of the potential anonymity, remains an informal channel of communication.

(b) Excess use and flooding of unwanted messages (especially from advertisers) is a major drawback of this system. Unless one takes care to block unwanted ads, one finds one's inbox full of offers which may be doubtful and insincere. Wading through chunks of email is one of the biggest problems for those who depend on email for their communication needs.

(c) One may not be private while using the computer for emailing. To that extent the secrecy is lost.

d) In case the receiver is unable to open his email account as soon as a message is received, the message cannot work for him.

Guidelines for the use of email:

Email is a new and peculiar means of communication, bringing in its own conventions:

(1) Your email message may be read by more persons than intended. So you have to take care.
(2) An email message must have all the elements of good composition such as brevity, clarity, courtesy.
(3) You may use the spellcheck mechanism of the computer to ensure correct spelling.
(4) The email format on the computer provides for sending and mentioning cc (carbon copy) and subject line. These may be written for the receiver's convenience.
(5) If a single email contains messages for various sections of an organisation, they may be separated at the composing stage.
(6) You should not use all capitals in writing a message as this looks awkward and rude.
(7) When responding to a message, only the essential part of it may be quoted and the rest deleted.
(8) You may create the message in a different programme (such as wordpad or notepad) and transfer it to your email.
(9) If you proofread on the computer screen, be extra careful.

Specimen email messages

Specimen email 1

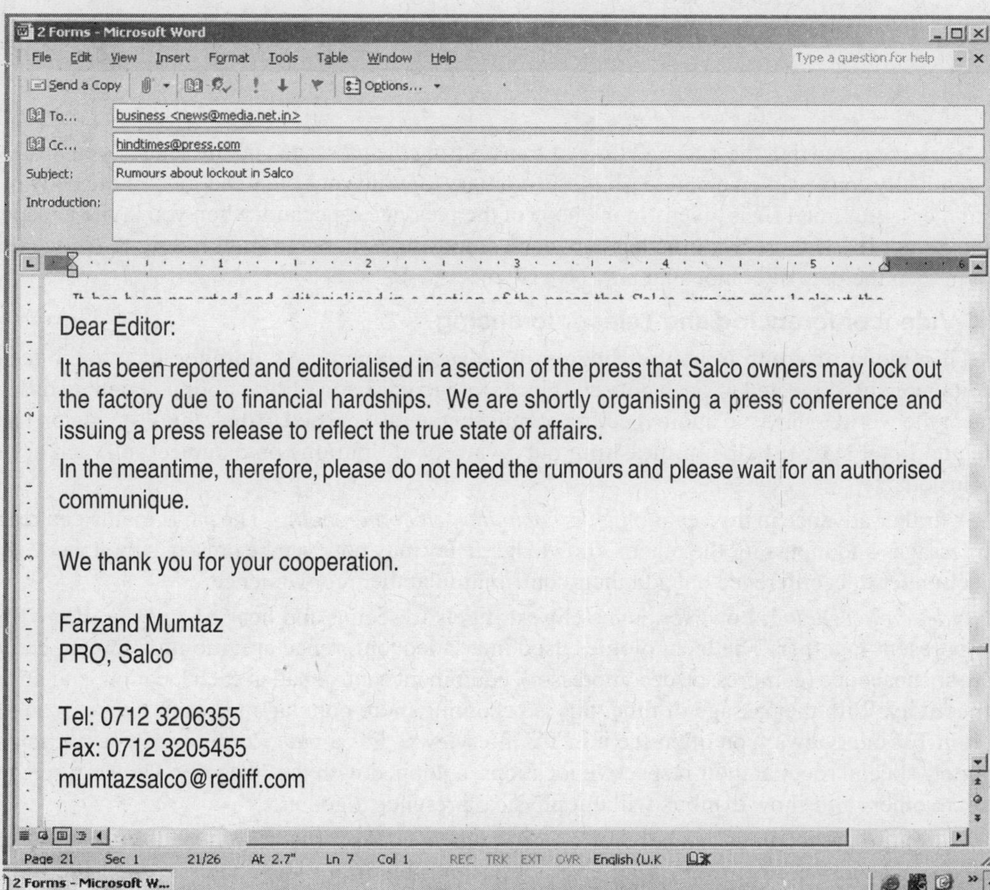

2 Forms - Microsoft Word

To... business <news@media.net.in>

Cc... hindtimes@press.com

Subject: Rumours about lockout in Salco

Introduction:

Dear Editor:

It has been reported and editorialised in a section of the press that Salco owners may lock out the factory due to financial hardships. We are shortly organising a press conference and issuing a press release to reflect the true state of affairs.

In the meantime, therefore, please do not heed the rumours and please wait for an authorised communique.

We thank you for your cooperation.

Farzand Mumtaz
PRO, Salco

Tel: 0712 3206355
Fax: 0712 3205455
mumtazsalco@rediff.com

Specimen email 2

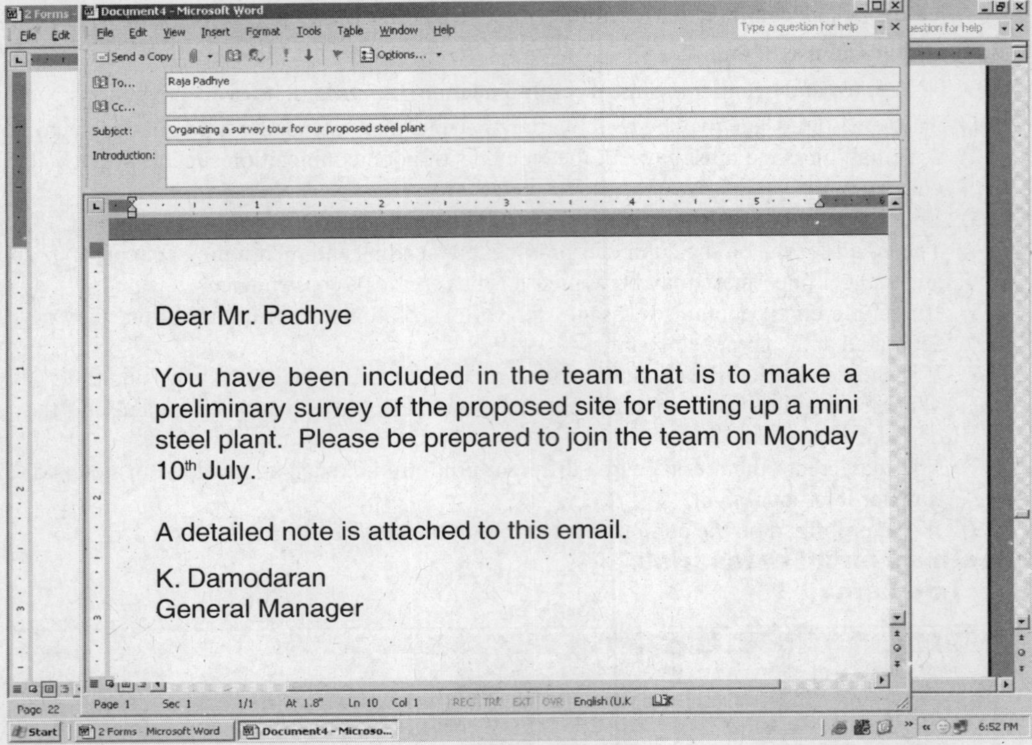
Document4 - Microsoft Word

To... Raja Padhye

Cc...

Subject: Organizing a survey tour for our proposed steel plant

Introduction:

Dear Mr. Padhye

You have been included in the team that is to make a preliminary survey of the proposed site for setting up a mini steel plant. Please be prepared to join the team on Monday 10th July.

A detailed note is attached to this email.

K. Damodaran
General Manager

It may be noted that the date and time of transmitting the message and the sender's email ID are automatically conveyed on email. Still it is customary to write your email address in the body of the email message. Email ID is given in the body of the message especially when you invite a response at a different ID. If there is a time lag between composing a message and sending it, for whatever reason, then the date of composing may be written.

2.6.3 Videoconferencing and Teleconferencing

This mode of communication begins in *teleconferencing*. A number of telephones are simultaneously connected to one another. Teleconferencing is a facility enabling people in different parts of the world to have an audio meeting or multilogue (as opposed to dialogue), saving on transit time and hotel stay. It helps in thrashing out a variety of opinions on a subject to reach a faster conclusion.

A further advance in this technology is *computer teleconferencing*. The participants can react to the messages and inputs for the others' knowledge. They may not even be present simultaneously for the computer teleconference but add their contribution at their convenience.

Videoconferencing, however, is the closest it gets to seeing and hearing one another without being present together. The technologies used in a videoconference are: monitor screen, camera, microphone, codec (compressor-decompressor), equipment control pad at each location, and internet connectivity. With the passage of time, this is becoming more popular and easier to use. You often see it in TV interviews. You often see it in TV interviews. For a videoconference, the participants get into a special room at their respective locations, equipped with the gadgetry. They can see, hear, speak to others and show exhibits without physical presence together.

The entire proceedings can be recorded on video tapes. As someone has jocularly put it, except for the snacks and coffee, everything else is transmissible in a videoconference. At present, the privilege of the richer business houses, videoconferences are set to gain wider popularity. Video classrooms are another possibility in this field, where an expert faculty member may teach a number of classes in a number of towns simultaneously and answer the participants' queries.

A. Questions based on critical understanding. Comment in about 30 words.

1. Sign language cannot be a complete substitute for a verbal communication in all cases.

Ans. Sign language, which includes visual signs and audio signs, has its limitations. It can communicate only elementary and simple ideas. It is better to combine it with verbal communication.

2. No one can be held responsible for informal communication.

Ans. Informal communication is unstructured and haphazard. It moves across departmental lines, bypasses superiors, and flows around lunchrooms, down hallways or wherever people get together in groups. Therefore we cannot fix the responsibility for informal communication.

3. Body language always speaks the truth while speaker may play with words to hide the truth.

Ans. Facial expressions, eye contact, gestures, postures, movements of body parts, etc. tell the truth when one is trying to convey contrary ideas by playing with words. However, good actors can hide the reality by giving false expressions and movements.

4. Communication need not be made in words alone.

Ans. We do not communicate by words alone. There exist many non-verbal modes of communication, such as visual signs, paralanguage, body language, etc.

5. The space around us is also used as a source of communication.

Ans. Communication can be made through space around us. The distance you keep while communicating reflects feelings and attitudes and thus affects communication. A serious study of this dimension is called 'proxemics' or space language.

6. Grapevine communication has its own utility in disseminating information.

Ans. Information can be disseminated to some extent by using the grapevine mechanism. This helps to assess preliminary reaction of people in the organisation. Thus it is not useless, and has its own utility.

7. Information overload is as bad as information gap.

Ans. Information overload also creates a number of problems (as information gap does) The receivers have difficulty in selection and screening, and so on.

8. Channel choice and medium of communication are not important.

Ans. False. Even the most carefully constructed message will fail to achieve results if it does not reach your audience. The choice of communication channel and medium should not interfere with the message. E.g., if a written document is the best choice, you have to make it physically appealing and easy to understand.

9. While communicating with the subordinates, a manager should maintain a distance.

Ans. A tactful manager will not stand aloof from his subordinates, he would rather mix freely without giving the impression of cheap popularity. This will enable him to interact with subordinates and get proper feedback.

10. Face-to-face communication is sometimes better than written communication.

Ans. Face-to-face communication is better as one can read the body language and the response of the receiver is immediate. The doubts can be cleared instantly in face to face communication.

11. Grapevine encourages rumourmongering.

Ans. Grapevine is an informal form of communication. Since there is no responsibility in it, it is not reliable. Thus it tends to spread rumours.

12. People communicate more through body language than words.

Ans. Bodily movements, facial expressions, and gestures which constitute body language account for more than 55% of communication.The verbal component accounts for just 7% or so, with the remaining 38% attributed to the volume, tone, inflection etc.

13. Proxemics is the study of space language.

Ans. See question 5

14. Written communication has a longer life than oral communication.

Ans. Written communication can be documented and recorded. You can retrieve it at a future date. This is not so for oral communication. Thus written communication enjoys a longer life.

15. Kinesics is the study of body movements.

Ans. The study of bodily movements that form a part of non-verbal communication is known as 'kinesics.' It is a part of our communication, as a receiver generally observes non-verbal communication 55 % of the time.

16. Paralanguage is close to verbal communication.

Ans. Paralanguage is used to describe a wide range of vocal characteristics. They help to bring out the speaker's attitude. It is non-verbal because it does not consist of words.

17. Eye contact is of paramount importance in face-to-face communication.

Ans. In face-to-face communication, proper eye contact reflects the feelings of the speaker and is helpful in making effective communication.

18. Anger is the worst enemy of communication.

Ans. Effective communication requires control of emotions. In case of anger, a person loses his reason and blurts out something undesirable.

19. Face is the index of the mind.

Ans. If a person is happy or unhappy, its reflection is found on the face. Face is the index of the mind. Most people show their inner feelings on the face. The face also shows a person's nature.

20. Non-verbal communication is more reliable and more efficient than verbal communication.

Ans. True. Non-verbal clues like expression, eye behaviour, gestures and postures, vocal characteristics, personal appearance, use of time and space provide over 90% of the meaning of communication. By paying attention to non-verbal clues you can detect the true intentions of the speaker .

21. Written communication can be preserved in sharp contrast to oral communication.

Ans. Written communication can always be documented in a form that has credibility and can be put to future use. Oral communication can definitely be recorded but it requires pre-arrangements and the records generated may not have credibility and legal sanctity.

22. No oral communication can be effective without proper listening.

Ans. Listening plays a vital role in communication. A typical manager needs to listen at least as much as he needs to talk. Too many people fail to realise that real communication goes in both directions. *Seek first to understand than to be understood.*

23. Written communication is a creative activity.

Ans. This is because writing is an art as well as a skill. To be creative is to adapt your response exactly to the current situation, not to repeat what you saw in some other, seemingly similar situation. It requires a lot of practice and creativity.

24. Paralanguage is not very reliable.

Ans. The voice quality, speaking speed, pitch, tone etc., which are components of paralanguage, can affect the message a lot to the extent of changing the meaning.

Comment on the following:

1. Issuing orders and instructions is at the heart of downward communication.
2. A communicator has to be prudent with his choice of the media.
3. Kinesics is integral to communication.
4. Grapevine is a credible and reliable channel of communication.
5. Paralanguage is close to verbal communication.
6. Informal channels of communication cannot be used effectively.
7. Communication is a game of listening only.
8. As communication is a two-way process, preparing in advance is a waste of time.
9. Reading the body language at the time of listening is conducive to better communication.
10. Semantic barriers arise due to language problems.
11. Grapevine is a credible and reliable channel of communication.
12. Semantics is the study of meaning.
13. The basic purpose of communication is to issue orders to subordinates.
14. "Life is a communication-centred activity. If we cannot communicate effectively, we cannot live effectively." Explain the statement and describe the various aspects of body language.

B. Questions for Revision

1. "Communication in an organisation is multi-directional." Discuss the statement by explaining briefly the different types of channels of communication based on directions of communication.
2. Distinguish between downward and upward communication networks.
3. Make a comparative study of horizontal and diagonal communication.
4. State the major limitations of paralanguage.
5. Discuss the importance and limitations of upstream communication.
6. Discuss the various dimensions of non-verbal communication.
7. How can a message be conveyed more effectively through voice?
8. Prepare a checklist for creating effective visual aids.
9. What do you mean by body language? Discuss its various aspects.
10. Compare sign language and body language.
11. Explain the advantages and disadvantages of written communication.
12. When can communication be said to be total?
13. Make a comparative study of formal and informal channels of communication.
14. Can body language be muted?
15. Define proxemics. How does it help in the comprehension of a message?
16. Classify the different channels of communication.
17. Compare and contrast oral and non-verbal communication.
18. What are the features of fax and email that make them effective tools of speedy communication?
19. Enumerate the benefits of videoconferencing.

CHAPTER

3

Listening as a Tool of Communication

What should you know?

3.1 INTRODUCTION – LISTENING SKILLS

"The better you listen, the luckier you will get." - ***Kevin Murphy***

"A good listener is not only popular everywhere, but after a while he knows something." - ***Wilson Mizner***

"Let every man be quick to hear, slow to speak." - ***New Testament***

"One of the best ways to persuade others is by listening to them."- ***Dean Rusk***

Conversation: "Are you going to the market?"
"No, no, I'am going to the market."
"Oh, I thought you were going to the market."

Conversation: "The duchess was saying that you are a charming conversationalist.
What is your secret?"
"Well, the whole evening she was talking and the whole evening I was listening."

From the above clips, it is clear that there is much power in listening. Good listening is necessary for success. A good listener is more liked, more influential than a one-way speaker. Every successful businessman is a good listener.

Good listening is essential in business. But this listening is dynamic rather than passive. One responds in harmony with the speaker and guides him/her in the direction that is mutually beneficial.

Listening is one thing and hearing another. Hearing is the physical process of sound falling on one's ears. But listening involves the brain, draws attention to the subject-matter and makes sense of the talk. Hearing is through ears and listening is by mind.

Intelligent listening requires openness of the mind, focus, constant mental classification – and association of the message heard, and taking notes – mental or written.

The process of listening

This process has five stages – sensing, interpreting, evaluating, remembering and responding.

Sensing: Sensing means to get in tune with the speaker, as we tune a radio. The listener is prepared and knows that he has to listen. If the listener is not sensing, one may simply promote listening by asking, "Are you listening?"

Interpreting and evaluating: Listening is meaningful when a person converts the words coming to him into ideas. The ideas make sense or no sense. The listener keeps what is useful, separates what is useless, and keeps a note of what is unclear or incomplete. The speaker may emphasise one thing, the listener may consider another thing important. A complainant may worry about his troubles; the PRO may want to know basically who erred in the organisation.

Remembering: Listening serves a greater purpose if the message is recorded for its useful life. To aid one's memory, one may take notes or create mental pictures, for example when an address is being explained. But written notes may sometimes put the speaker on the alert and halt his communication.

Responding: The listener may respond on the spot by making appropriate remarks: "I see," or "Is it so?" or "Okay." This reassures the speaker. The listener may ask questions to bring out the required nformation and complete the picture from his point of view. Responding also means to act on the message received and to let the speaker know this.

3.2 APPROACHES TO LISTENING

Listening can be classified from a mere show-off to the wholehearted act.

1. **Pretending to listen:** In such listening the listener faces the speaker, across the table or on the phone line, as long as he speaks and then switches off without registering the message. This is mere hearing and not listening.
2. **Selective listening:** This is the case when one edits the message as takable and not takable. In the case of an important message, selective listening leads to partial fulfilment of the instructions
3. **Superficial listening:** This is the case when the listener takes in only the words but not the spirit of the message. (Some writers classify this as "attentive listening but this is an ironical term. In the normal sense attentive listening is good, while in this technical sense, "attentive listening" means a mere show off of listening. Another such ironical technical term is "precious writing", which means overuse or inexpert use of decorative words.)
4. **Emphatic listening:** This term conveys full emphasis on the act of listening and taking in the entire message in word and spirit. The listener takes in the tone, the pauses, and the body language related to the words. Emphatic listening is necessary to move from one's preconceived stand. The listener's openness makes him ready to be influenced.
5. **Dynamic (mutually creative) listening:** Here, listening is a creative process in which the listener contributes to the meaning that is being conveyed. He adds his energy to that of the speaker to generate "synergy." Collective acts are achieved through dynamic listening. It helps to bring out the best in the speaker.
6. **Intuitive listening:** Intuition, hunch or sixth sense is the power that is above reason. It leads to a direct insight into the truth. For an intuitive listener, a mere hint, an undertone or a silence is enough to read the other person's mind. Intuition is nurtured when one listens to high quality music or finds natural or meditative solitude. Deep listeners have the power to develop a hunch about what is said. A good mother knows a child's mood by intuitive listening.

3.3 BARRIERS TO EFFECTIVE LISTENING

1. **Poor hearing:** If one's sense of hearing is defective, listening is impaired. On becoming aware of it, one should get medical help.
2. **Listener's chain of thoughts:** The mind is almost always active, thinking its own thoughts. These may become rapid and loud from time to time, marring one's receptivity.
3. **A too heavy message:** Use of jargon or overcompression of ideas may make an oral message too heavy for the listener.

4. **Rapid or accented talk:** One has this experience when listening for the first time to certain foreign radio stations. While the broadcast is clear to the regular listeners and those at home with the speakers' accent, for others there is a bar to listening.
5. **Listener's self-importance or prejudice:** If the listener has put himself above the speaker, there is no receptive attitude. There is a "know-all" air in the listener and little regard for the speaker. Also, if the listener conceives a prejudice against the speaker, or has prejudices on the topic of the message, the listening is hindered.
6. **Misunderstanding about the role of a listener:** Some listeners may not be aware of what their role in a particular situation is. They may think that it is the speaker's responsibility to explain everything properly. They may belittle their own role as that of a one-way receiver. They may think that the role of the speaker gives the other party an overriding importance.
7. **Cultural gap:** If the speaker and the listener have different cultural habits, the listening may be incomplete. The listener may assign different importance to a word or phrase than is meant. While orientals are used to an elaborate style of addressing a gathering, westerners are often quite brief about it. But this can be distracting to an easterner.
8. **Preoccupations:** Some people listen while eating, drinking or doing handiwork. In such cases the attention is divided. A busy manager, for instance, may try to listen while filing papers or opening the mail. This may mar the listening.
9. **Ego:** If the receiver considers himself superior and is not willing to listen, this ego problem acts as a stumbling block in the listening process.

3.4 TIPS FOR EFFECTIVE LISTENING

In practice, effective listening means getting the entire message spoken. It may be "emphatic listening" or any listening better than it. In business one has to listen in formal as well as informal situations, to get information, opinions, etc. The listening style is to be adjusted to the gravity of the occasion.

To be an effective listener is to overcome the barriers to listening. As one's importance grows in an organisation, the need for proper listening increases. In some positions it is unusually high – e.g. for a PRO or complaints redressal officer. On the other hand, effective listening is a natural ladder to success. Listening is made effective in different ways when,

(a) you are in a higher position and,
(b) a lower position or a member of a large audience.

Here are some general tips for this:

1. **Position yourself mentally:** Stop talking, put aside your little chores, and come to grips with the speaker.
2. **Make the speaker comfortable:** Give emotional encouragement to the speaker by a welcome attitude to the message. Show that you want to listen. A smile, an eye contact or an encouraging phrase like "Please go ahead" or "Tell me all about it" may do.
3. **Tune in to the spoken message:** Adjust your mental attitude to the subject and the message even if it is surprising or new. Be receptive and be positive about it. This is empathy – to feel as the speaker feels.
4. **Be patient:** The speaker may have a long story to unwind. It may sound overly long. He/she may be longwinded about it. He/she may not find words quickly, be halting in speech, wandering in the mind. He may be unorganised. All these situations require a patient response if the speaker is important to your business.
5. **Do not interrupt:** An interruption may break the speaker's chain of thought or annoy him/her. Sometimes you had better listen to it all even if you know it. A show of your knowledge may reduce the speaker's importance.

6. **Concentrate with effort:** Some managers have a radio playing in the background while holding a discussion. The listener must mentally switch out the song etc. and switch in the talk. This requires an audio filter in you. With concentration this is possible.
7. **Check your temper:** If the listener is rude or angry, the vital input may stop. Differences can be expressed politely; mistakes can be withstood with generosity.
8. **Be soft in expressing criticism:** Criticism is disapproval of the other person's acts or words, maybe of his whole personality. Most people would welcome criticism if it comes as a suggestion. "That was silly of you" can be replaced by "But you could have done it otherwise, you still can do it otherwise."
9. **Appreciate and encourage:** As an individual listener you may smile or utter words of praise. "Wonderful" or "Well done" can be inserted while listening. As a member of a mass audience you may cheer the speaker. As a proactive listener you may become the cheerleader.
10. **Ask questions:** Questions help you to direct the talk the way you are interested and helps the speaker to organise his message, edit it to the point. Questions can also be a form of encouragement.
11. **Be sincere in your reactions:** As a busy and practical manager you do well to express your opinion honestly, without a false gloss to it. People who express themselves honestly (though tactfully) are eventually better liked. Sincerity of course requires self-confidence.
12. **Close on a cordial note:** Reconciliation is the aim of all human transactions. Hence, after you have differed and argued, let the conversation end on a pleasant note. In diplomacy this is of paramount importance – to keep the gates open for further talk. "Let's agree to disagree" can be your motto.

QUESTION BANK

A. Questions based on critical understanding. Comment in about 30 words.

1. To be a good listener, vary the way you listen to suit various situations.

Ans. True. Different situations demand different listening skills. In listening for the essential message (content listening), the emphasis is an understanding and retaining what the speaker is saying. In empathetic listening, we try to understand the speaker's emotions and needs and respond accordingly. In critical listening, we tend to evaluate the speaker's message for logic and credibility.

2. There are several essentials of good listening.

Ans. Listening is a skill that needs to be mastered. For developing good listening skills, one must cultivate a positive attitude, concentration, direct eye contact, and supportive body postures.

3. There are several barriers to listening.

Ans. The various factors which act as a deterrent to the listening process are poor hearing : listener's chain of thoughts, a too heavy message, rapid or accented talk, listener's self-importance or prejudice, misunderstanding about the role of a listener, cultural gap, preoccupations, ego.

4. Emphatic listening is helpful in business.

Ans. In emphatic listening the listener takes in the words and spirit of the speaker. He listens with an open mind, with the emphasis on receiving the speaker's input. Thus, by knowing the other party, a businessman can promote his interests.

5. A speaker must allow for the cultural differences in the listener.

Ans. When the two parties conversing are from different cultures, speaking and listening have to be attuned to each other. The speaker must know what his message would mean to the listener with his/her cultural background.

B. Questions for revision

1. What are the psychological barriers to listening?
2. Name the various types of barriers to listening with a brief description of each. (400 words)
3. How can a manager become an efficient listener? In what way does it pay him in his career?
4. What are the different types of listening? Which type of listening is the best?
5. Distinguish between: (i) Hearing and listening (ii) Critical listening and comprehension listening

■ ■ ■

CHAPTER

4

Group Communication

What should you know?

4.1 INTRODUCTION – MEANING AND DEFINITION OF GROUP

In common terms, a group can be defined as the coming together of two or more people with a common purpose who stay joined over a period of time. Within an organisation, the same definition can be extended to mean an officially bonded segment of workers or employees who share a common goal.

A group is a cluster of two or more individuals who interact with each other on a relatively enduring (long-term) basis, identify themselves as a part of a distinctive unit and share certain common interests, values, goals and activities. A group possesses four characteristics: (a) collection of two or more people (b) interaction among members over a period of time (c) common interests or goals (d) people see themselves as members.

Just like an individual, a group, too, has its own personality, which is known as **group personality**. Members of a group get many opportunities for interaction. Interaction in its broad sense means communication between people and activity together. Thus, communication plays an important role in determining a group's personality.

Types of Groups

1. **Small Group:** It is a compact cluster of a very few individuals.
2. **Large group:** It is a collection of a few small groups.
3. **Primary group:** It is almost synonymous with a small group.
4. **Secondary group:** It is nearly the same as a large group.
5. **Formal group:** It is a work unit established as part of an organisation and its structure.
6. **Informal group:** It is a voluntary, unofficial formation of people of an organisation.

Characteristics of Group Personality

1. A group usually consists of two or more individuals. One individual cannot form a group.
2. Groups must possess a stable structure. A group can change as can its components, but there must be some level of consistency of either tenure or function. Stability is an important characteristic of a group.
3. A group is usually associated with a common goal or interest. Therefore, members of the same group usually share the same interests.
4. It is also important for the members of a group to perceive themselves as a group. That they can identify themselves as a group and distinguish members from non-members is a basic characteristic of a group.
5. A group basically denotes collective power. There is a strong binding force, which often translates into pressure to get things done or to get problems solved
6. Groups have their own prejudices as an individual does, and these get stronger when members come in contact with each other. Moreover, a group generally resists change.

4.1.1 Group Dynamics

Group dynamics is a field of study concerned with research and analysis of various forces and patterns of the formation of small informal groups in organisations. It includes such aspects as composition, interaction, and behaviour of informal groups. It also covers the study of behaviour of work groups in organisations.

Group dynamics as a discipline is concerned with the promotion of understanding on the following aspects:

1. Why and how groups are formed.
2. What forces are operative in the structure of groups.
3. How groups grow, decline, and die.
4. How they make decisions and solve problems.
5. How they achieve unity and handle conflict.
6. How they change and adapt themselves.
7. How they influence task performance and member satisfaction.

4.2 ADVANTAGES AND DISADVANTAGES OF GROUP DECISION-MAKING

4.2.1 Advantages

"Two heads are better than one."

"The more the merrier."

1. **More information:** A group is better equipped as far as information is concerned. An individual cannot have all the information that is available to a group as it consists of several individuals.
2. **Diversity of views:** A group always has the advantage of varied views. This is because a group always has more than one members, and since every member is unique, there is bound to be a variety in their views also. This is also the reason why there are varied approaches to solving a problem. As group decisions tend to cover a greater area, they provide a better insight for decision-making.
3. **Greater acceptability:** The views expressed by a group have more acceptance than those from an individual. This is because the decisions are not imposed, but are part of a larger consensus (general agreement). A group decision is automatically assumed to be more democratic, and the decision of an individual can be perceived as being autocratic (dictatorial).
4. **Expert opinions:** There may be some group decisions that require expert opinion. The group can either include experts or can call them from outside to form a separate group to take a decision on a particular issue.

5. **Degree of involvement:** The members of a group feel involved with a given problem. This minimises their resistance. It strengthens an organisation and facilitates decision-making.
6. **Encourages people's participation:** A group usually provides a platform for people to present their ideas. Group dynamics is more likely to draw out participation from people who may otherwise be hesitant to talk or interact. It encourages people to take an initiative as they feel part of the decision-making process. Usually there is no individual onus (burden) in the event of failure, which makes it easier for people to come up with suggestions and solutions to problems.

4.2.2 Disadvantages

1. **Time-consuming:** A group involves several individuals. Getting them organised, planning and coordinating their meetings, defining and explaining to them the purpose of a meeting and the goals, and finally reaching a solution or arriving at a decision can be quite cumbersome. Making decisions in a group can, thus, be time-consuming. The time loss involved in group dynamics cannot be ignored.
2. **Lack of onus:** It is difficult to fix responsibility in a group. In an organisation, it is often essential to fix responsibility before a problem can be solved. It is difficult to do so if anything goes wrong with a decision made by a group.
3. **Individual domination:** Quite often, discussions in a group are dominated by a few members. Although a group discussion means a collective discussion, some people usually manage to usurp (draw to themselves) a position of informal leadership owing to their personality or style of participation. This position can also be because of the position held within the organisation or simply because of self-confidence generated by previous experiences. Sometimes only a few individuals dominate and the others fade away in a group, thereby defeating the very purpose of group discussion.
4. **Compromise decisions:** The need to arrive at a group decision sometimes results in a compromise. The solution offered is not essentially the best. It is, instead, a compromise acceptable as a mid-point to all concerned. There are different demands and social pressures, and members may agree to a proposal without really evaluating it. Such support may not be wholehearted.
5. **Expensive:** Group decision-making is quite expensive in terms of time, money, energy and man-hours. There is also a theory which says that the larger a group gets, the less is the individual contribution from each member.
6. **Groupism:** The very word has negative connotations. Some members of a group may start harbouring a feeling that they are different from the others. This actually leads to informal groups within the larger formal group, which may generate negative sentiments towards other groups or people outside the group.

4.3 DISCUSSION

A discussion is possible for an individual only if he is part of a group. The origin of the word *discuss* is the Latin word *discutere*, which means 'to shake' or 'to strike'. Discussion begins with the sharing of views, information, etc. within a group. Thereafter, all this communication is shaken or stirred (as in a debate) through exchanges to enable the group to arrive at a decision.

Ingredients of a discussion

Here are the three ingredients of a discussion:

1. **Purpose:** The first ingredient is the purpose of holding a group discussion. The aim of a group discussion is to arrive at a satisfactory conclusion. A group discussion usually helps to decide the next course of action. Random talk without arriving at a decision is not a discussion. It is, therefore, important to clarify the purpose for which the discussion is being held. Once this has been done, the discussion is likely to stay on course.

2. **Planning:** Planning is a crucial element. People decide the aim of the discussion. A group discussion that aims to arrive at some decision cannot just have random expression of ideas. The discussion has to be planned in such a manner that every step takes the group closer to its goal. As such a group must have a leader or initiator. Such person or persons prepare an agenda, inform the members about the discussion, fix the time, date, and venue for a meeting. At the discussion, they ensure that the members do not wander from the basic agenda and purpose.
3. **Participation:** The participation of members is the life of any group discussion. Members of a group have to be drawn out. It should not be dominated by a few. Although this does tend to happen in most group discussions, the silent members' intelligent listening also helps. A group discussion is held to invite maximum participation. Every member must, therefore, contribute his or her share of information, opinions, etc. Only then can the discussion be meaningful and effective.

Role of leadership in the conduct of group discussion

A discussion should be held in a free atmosphere and democratic manner. For this, every group discussion has to be piloted by a leader. In the absence of a leader it may run here and there. A leader gives proper direction and moderates diverse views, resolves differences among participants and helps the group in coming to a logical conclusion. Hence a leader is essential for a group discussion.

4.4 TECHNIQUES OF GROUP DECISION-MAKING

There are various techniques of group decision-making. The techniques include **committee meetings, command meetings, brainstorming sessions, nominal group technique**, and **Delphi technique.**

4.4.1 Committee Meetings

A committee can be defined as a group appointed by the parent organisation, which meets to investigate a problem, and, later, to formulate its report and recommendations. Constituting of committees is a common practice in organisations to solve a problem or approach a situation. There are various kinds of committees in an organisation. Some examples are **executive committee, advisory committee** and **standing committee**. Each committee has a well-defined role to play in the organisation. The members of these committees may come and go. They may periodically change or rotate according to the constitution of the organisation. The parent body that constitutes a committee also lays down its powers.

Types of committees

1. **Standing committee:** A standing committee is usually a small representation from the main body, empowered to make management decisions. It is a permanent committee. The committee shares the leadership function, too. Its job is to ensure that an organisation runs smoothly, since every decision cannot be made by convening a meeting of all the members of the organisation.
2. **Advisory committee:** An advisory committee is usually a body of experts that assists in decision-making. The committee is usually consulted when an expert opinion or specialised information is needed for organisational functioning. The members are usually nominated at regular intervals specified by the constitution. While they can be drawn from within the organisation, members of an advisory committee can also be outsiders included specially for the purpose.
3. **Ad hoc committee:** An ad hoc committee is just what the name suggests – for a special

purpose, hence temporary. Ad hoc committees are formed for a specific mission or period, and are dismantled after they do their duty.

A committee has the following jobs to perform:

(a) Collect data.
(b) Inquire about the attitudes and opinions of the members.
(c) Arrive at a decision after considering all the options.
(d) Have an accurate record of the decisions made.

4.4.2 Command Meetings

As the name suggests, command meetings are supposed to be dominated by the manager who issues instructions to his subordinates. Such meets are held specifically to allow a manager to share information with his subordinates. The crucial element of collective responsibility disappears in such meetings as the communication is mostly one-way. The onus (responsibility) rests totally on the superior or the manager.

Command meetings need to appear friendly and not domineering. While the manager is there to share information, the very idea of 'command' makes the workers act like the opposition.

Command meeting	Committee meeting
Is a meeting between manager and subordinates.	Is of a group appointed by parent organisation comprising experts for decision-making.
Manager alone is responsible for decision -making. It is autocratic.	Takes systematic and logical steps which involve all members in the decision-making process. It is participative.
Main objective of the manager is to share information, state policies or give directions.	Objectives could vary – advisory/problem solving/decision-making etc.

4.4.3 Brainstorming Session

A brainstorming session is a process of generating ideas. It encourages all alternative approaches and withholds criticism. The theory of brainstorming was first developed by an advertising agency in 1939 in the United States. Brainstorming as a word is associated with outlandish, unusual and maverick (independent minded) ideas. However, the idea behind brainstorming is to allow the brain to wander freely. Therefore, all ideas are welcome, irrespective of how out-of-the-way or impractical they may sound initially. It is basically a device that has been used to overcome the need to follow set patterns within an organisation. Several complex situations have been solved through a brainstorming session. In a brainstorming session,

(a) No idea is criticised.
(b) New ideas are welcomed.
(c) The emphasis is on the quality of ideas.
(d) Outlandish or *avant-garde* (advanced) ideas are equally, in fact, more welcome.

Brainstorming is an effective way of generating brilliant ideas. In a brainstorming session, members of the group who are assigned the task of solving a problem sit at a table. The group leader states the problem and the members express their opinions freely. A brainstorming session needs to be chaired by a person of wide understanding and imagination , low ego, and good control over the proceedings. The members toss ideas around. No idea is discouraged or abandoned initially. Every idea, every suggestion is recorded without any criticism. The members are encouraged to think creatively and differently from the normal. Once the suggestions have been made, each idea is analysed and assessed for its potential to solve the problem. A collective decision is then made as to the solution or solutions to the problem. For example, a suggestion made some years ago to ease traffic congestions over weekends was to show good movies on television. Cable television had not arrived in India then, and the movies kept the people at home, leaving the streets deserted. Now, of course, the coming of cable television has changed that.

4.4.4 Nominal Group Technique

The nominal group technique is just what the name suggests. People do meet as a group, but their interpersonal communication is restricted. Even if they are present as a group, they operate individually. The following steps are taken in this technique:

1. Each member writes his ideas independently on the problem or the issue concerned.
2. All the ideas are collected and recorded.
3. The group then discusses the ideas.
4. Every member ranks the ideas individually.
5. The idea with the maximum marks is the final decision.

This technique helps a group to interact formally without stifling independent thinking.

4.4.5 Delphi Technique

This technique resembles the brainstorming technique, except that it does not require the physical presence of the members of a group. In fact, the technique was evolved to allow members of a group to arrive at a decision without having to meet actually. Members sitting at different, sometimes far-flung, places arrive at a consensus through Delphi. The technique is implemented through questionnaires sent to its the members. The problem is discussed indirectly through the questionnaire.

Initially, the problem or the decision is identified. A questionnaire is then evolved to solicit answers that will help arrive at a decision. There can be a choice of solutions, opinions etc. or just a clearcut solution. There is little chance of the answers being influenced as members are away from each other and there is no direct contact between them. There is also no loss of crucial participation through inactivity or overdomination as every member replies independently.

The responses are collected and compiled. After going through the results, the trends or solutions become apparent. Else, further clarifications on some issues may be sought.

This can lead to further questions that are likely to help clear the issue even better. The churning and rechurning of questions finally leads to compilations that reveal the majority opinion or help arrive at a decision.

The Delphi technique has some major advantages as well as disadvantages. It saves space and money as it does not need all members to get together at one place. It also ensures that there is no colouring of opinions due to the dominance by some members. Each member is in a position to express his opinion without the fear of being rebuked or ridiculed. The answers, and the solutions are, therefore, likely to be more sincere.

The technique has some inherent disadvantages. It can be quite time-consuming. It is unsuitable when a fast decision is needed. It involves the cumbersome process of contacting a member not once but several times and getting his or her reply. It also calls for great intelligence in formulating the questions so that the necessary solutions are obtained. The whole exercise is, otherwise, reduced to a mere burdensome formality with hardly anything to show at the end.

Nominal group	Delphi technique
Members meet face to face.	Members do not meet and may be situated far and wide across the country or even different countries.
Problems solved through idea generation and individual presentation & individual ranking.	Problem-solving through well-designed series of questionnaires.
Each member writes down his ideas and then presents them to the group.	Each member anonymously completes questionnaire.
Final decision taken on the basis of the idea with the highest aggregate ranking	Final decision is taken when a consensus is reached.

4.5 MEETINGS, NOTICES, AGENDA, MINUTES

4.5.1 Meetings

A meeting is a coming together of (generally) three or more people to exchange information in a planned manner and discuss issues set out before them to arrive at decisions, solve problems, etc.

A meeting can be **formal** or **informal**. As regards a formal meeting there are set rules for convening it and conducting it, with a written record of its proceedings. It requires a **notice** which is a call, an invitation to attend it. It has an **agenda** or list of things to deal with, and the outcome is systematically written in the form of **minutes**. An informal meeting can be without any written notice, for instance a staff union meeting in the lunch room to discuss a picnic.

A meeting has a **convenor** who calls it, and a leader or **chairperson** who directs it.

Types of meeting: Meetings are broadly of three types –

(i) **Informative**, where the purpose is to give information to the participants about a new scheme, product, etc.

(ii) **Consultative**, in which the members are consulted to solve a problem.

(iii) **Executive**, in which decisions are taken by those empowered to do so.

In practice, most of the meetings serve more purposes than one. Some additional classifications of meetings are – meeting for negotiation purpose, meeting for giving instructions, etc.

Purpose of a meeting

The purposes of holding meetings are listed here in a skeleton form:

To reach a common decision/agreement
To solve a problem
To understand a situation, exchange ideas and experiences
To inform, explain, present ideas
To give and get feedback on new ideas
To give training
To plan and prepare for action
To resolve differences and misunderstandings
To generate enthusiasm and seek cooperation
To review past performance and evaluate it
To create a feeling of continuity and solidarity in a body's working.

In this mechanical age, union is strength, and united work is done by means of meetings. It is estimated that worldwide, millions of meetings are conducted every day, and their number and usefulness is on the rise. That is why although many negative remarks are made about the use of meetings, on the whole we find that meeting is a useful device of collective decision-taking and action.

4.5.2 Advantages and Disadvantages of Meetings

Advantages

(i) **Save time**: Since one can meet a number of people at a time interactively, a meeting can save time.

(ii) **Addressing groups**: One can divide the audiences according to their background and need, and address them group by group.

(iii) **Cope with information explosion**: New technology and new regulations are coming thick and fast. Meetings enable us to cope with this situation.

(iv) **Social and emotional support**: Members get personal support from each other when they meet and exchange ideas.

(v) **Feeling of being consulted**: Members get the feeling that they have been consulted and this is useful in getting their intelligent and willing cooperation.

(vi) **Democratic functioning**: Democracy aims at achieving all people's welfare by all people's involvement. This is possible through meetings.

(vii) **Idea development**: Ideas are systematically cross-fertilised, analysed and improved by a group.

(viii) **Defusing troublemakers**: By the collectivity of constructive forces, troublemakers can be isolated in a meeting and positive action got going. The opponents of a plan get a forum to voice their opposition, which can be overcome before a group of supportive people.

(ix) **Bolder decisions**: Collectively we can take more adventurous decisions because of united strength.

(x) **Various interest groups represented**: In a meeting many interest groups can be represented and minorities can also be given due attention.

(xi) **Preventing mistakes**: A meeting helps to avoid mistakes by a collective and many-angled focus on issues.

Disadvantages

1. **Time-consuming**: Meetings require a number of people to come together at the same time and place. This costs time because other work has to be set aside for the sake of the meeting.
2. **Inability to arrive at a decision**: Just as "two heads are better then one," it is also true that "too many cooks spoil the soup." Multiplicity of views and personal stubbornness of members may prevent a meeting from taking a decision which a chief executive may take alone.
3. **Lack of seriousness**: Many meetings suffer from the drawback that members come unprepared and feel that the others will do the thinking and talking. They feel they can take a free ride. "Everybody's job is nobody's job."
4. **Inexpert chairing**: Just as an airplane is steered by a pilot, a meeting is piloted by the chairperson. His lack of skill and personal failings/biases may fail a meeting.
5. **Expensive**: Meetings are expensive to arrange – they require a place, paperwork, prior communication, and travelling by the attendees.
6. **Open to disruption**: A meeting is prone to being disrupted by an element that is opposed to its objective. There are times when one passenger's refusal to adjust himself delays the entire flight. The same for meetings. The spirit of give-and-take may be missing in some participants

4.5.3 Conduct of a Meeting

In conducting a meeting, one has to ask these questions:

(i) Why should one have it?

Can the job be done by telephonic consultation? If so, a meeting can be dispensed with. If a meeting is found necessary, its purpose, its objective has to be clear. Is it a legal requirement, a routine or a necessity of the time?

(ii) Who should attend it?

Only the essential parties should be called, and all required persons should be called. Sometimes there are outsiders to the organisation that are called to a meeting – the auditor, the solicitor, etc. The call to attend has to be clear and timely and under proper authority.

(iii) When to hold it?

The time has to be fixed according to the occasion and the convenience of the members. Further, the duration should be sufficient but not too long.

(iv) Where to hold it?

One has to select a place suitable for holding it. The place may have to be prepared for the meet.

(v) What to discuss and how?

To achieve the objective of the meeting, the convenor has to visualise the specific points over which there is to be a discussion. Again he/she has to set out the manner of discussion – informative, consultative or persuasive.

4.5.4 Role of the Chairperson in a Meeting

1. **Take overall charge of the proceedings**: Once the convenor has (generally in consultation with the chair) set out the agenda of the meet, the chairperson has to see that the agenda and the objective are fulfilled in the meet.
2. **Make sure he is competent**: He should accept to chair the meet only if he feels competent to run it. The chairperson's post is often rotated.
3. **"Don't do it yourself"**: The chairperson is there mainly to encourage a discussion, not supply it all. His skill lies in making the members feel that they have collectively decided issues.
4. **Use of directive verbs**: The chairman can use stimulating verbs to make members give out the necessary inputs at the meet: *substantiate, evidence, shorten, reword, classify, define, explain, elaborate, illustrate, review, describe, summarise, rephrase, simplify*...
5. **Use names**: He can get more from the members by using their names for addressing them to generate intimacy (according to the prevailing culture and custom) .
6. **"Be a traffic cop"**: The chairperson has to direct the traffic of ideas. He should not be defensive (a goalkeeper) nor a preacher (lecturer).
7. **State the purpose**: At the start of the meet he should state the purpose and again at the introduction of every new item of the agenda, so that the members are clear as to what they are supposed to do – examine, suggest or accept.
8. **"Don't reveal your preference"**: The chairman should reserve his own opinion for the end.
9. **Restrict the talk to the issue**: Members may be talkative, they may be stuck-up. The chairman has to stop the one type and encourage the other.
10. **Follow procedure**: An organisation – or the law – may require that a certain procedure be followed. The chairman needs to know it and implement it.
11. **Maintain time**: The meet should start on time, cover the agenda with proportionate time to all issues, and close on time. In practice, the early items get too much time and the last items are rushed.
12. **Speak no more than 20% of the time**: He has to link the various items and direct the members. For this he is the lead talker. But experience tells that in the name of fairness, 20% is the limit for his talking.
13. **Respond to the mood**: This is really the crux of the task. The chairman can set the mood, and if some event or some member's talk has set a wrong mood, he has to transform it. He may use humour, even a diversion, and extend all of his personality to keep the mood right. Decisions are taken when the members are ready for them.
14. **Intervene in disputes**: If members dispute among themselves, the chairperson has to step in and bring them on the track.
15. **Arrange for proper recording**: The proceedings of a meet have to be factually recorded. The chairman has to ensure this during the meet. The job should be with a competent person and he may have to be supervised. He should sit near the chairperson.
16. **Attend to those present**: He has to focus on those who are present and not those who are absent. This applies especially for starting a meet with a low attendance. Of course, the meet may require a quorum (necessary minimum attendance).
17. **Deal with spot issues**: He has to have the expertise and the presence of mind to tackle issues that arise during the meet, especially when the meet is open to new issues with his permission.

18. **Say "no" with tact**: Using analogies, quotes, precedents, common sense, and goodwill, the chairman has to tackle unwanted issues. (A senate member once proposed, "The war is over, we should reduce the army to half." The chair replied, "And we should at the same time resolve that the enemy should also reduce his army to half.")
19. **After the meet**: The chairman should see to it that timely follow-up action is taken to fulfil the obligations arising from the decisions taken. He should get the minutes written and checked, and, if necessary, circulated.

4.5.5 Role of participants in a meet

1. **Do homework**: Once the purpose of a meet is known, the attendee has to visualise his/her role and gather information and inputs for use in the meet to make it productive. He/she may consult other members to allocate roles.
2. **Be punctual**: We in India have to specially stress the need to be on time. Our trains, buses and airplanes will run on time when we learn to be punctual for routine meets.
3. **Participate actively**: A member should listen carefully (so that he may be able to summarise what is being said). He should plan what to speak and say it concisely and precisely.
4. **PREP formula**: He should be rational and forceful. PREP means –

   State your **P**osition

   Reason it out

   Give **E**xamples

   Restate your **P**osition
5. **Showcase your talent**: A meet is an opportunity to showcase one's talent and get credit for giving useful ideas.
6. **Take initiative**: There may be occasions when a member may propose a motion or second a motion when it sounds right. This requires quickness. Francis Bacon says, "Conference makes a ready man."
7. **Follow rules**: He should speak when permitted to. He should avoid cross-talk.
8. **Take responsibility**: When tasks are being assigned, a member should come forward to take up suitable responsibilities. If a task is assigned to him/her, then a willing acceptance is also a sign of dynamism.
9. **Disagree agreeably**: All differences should be expressed with courtesy and a friendly feeling.
10. **Help to steer the meet**: If the meeting is going off the track, he/she may remind the chairman to keep it on course.
11. **Stay related to previous discussion**: Any contribution to the meeting must be made in the context of the previous discussion. An idea that is already proposed need not be repeated, but one can amend it or improve it.
12. **Be involved**: The member should, in his higher self-interest, be involved in collectivism. A good participant becomes a good leader – just as a good soldier makes a good general.

4.5.6 Tips for the Conduct of an Effective Meeting

An effective meeting is everybody's baby, not just the chairperson's or the convenor's. We reap what we sow.

1. **Clarity of purpose**: The purposes of the meet should be clear and the approach should be well outlined. Then the discussion can be goal-oriented.
2. **Suitable chairperson**: The chairperson should suit the occasion. England chose Churchill as a wartime prime minister but not when peace was established.
3. **Good briefing**: All members should have a good briefing and encouragement to contribute to the meet.

4. **Ensure punctuality**: Since everybody's time is involved, the chairperson should take steps to ensure punctuality. There should be rewards for it and punishments (even if subtle ones) for not maintaining it out of sheer habit.
5. **Time management**: To start and end on time and to do justice to the agenda, the chairman should plan time well. The individual items on the agenda may be allotted fixed time to balance the time allotment.
6. **Have a strategy**: Since one-day cricket has come, we have been hearing of strategy a lot. A meet conductor should have a pre-planned strategy for how to tackle certain people, certain issues, and certain anticipated situations.
7. **Clear decisions**: The decisions should be clear and the allotment of duties according to ability and willingness. There should be a clear commitment from members.
8. **Democratic spirit**: Democracy is for everybody's equitable development. Let everyone contribute, be represented, be addressed in the decisions of the meet.
9. **Encourage listening**: Listening is encouraged when things are of interest to everyone. But different motives appeal to different people. Non-listeners face the possibility of rejection and censure.
10. **Resolve conflicts**: A clash of views should be resolved. Instead of skirting issues, one may meet them face-on.
11. **Explain positive and negative sides**: The chairperson or a knowledgeable spokesman should explain the good in an idea as well as the bad. Issue-based politics is the best. A rational and critical, knowledgeable and non-emotional approach is to be encouraged.
12. **Use disagreements**: If a disagreement arises in the proceedings, it may be a source of a better idea.
13. **Non-personal remarks**: The member need not go into the personal life of others when the meeting is about issues, not anyone's personal life.
14. **Give a multiple choice**: To give the members the feel of having chosen and decided, it is useful to give them various options and arrive at the best.
15. **Self-fulfilment**: The meeting should be fulfilling in terms of quality of decisions and quality of participation. In a friendly atmosphere, with impartial chairmanship, this feel is easier to develop. The members need to have their emotional satisfaction.
16. **Get final solutions**: Instead of half-way solutions or compromiscs, decisive solutions need to be taken.

Pitfalls

In the conduct of a meeting, we have to guard against:

(a) A delayed start
(b) Bogging down in minor issues
(c) Overshooting the time limit
(d) Interruptions
(e) Monopolising by a member or a subgroup
(f) Cross-talk
(g) Tangential talk
(h) Emotional flare-ups
(i) Weak or biased chairing
(j) Absence of key players
(k) A too ambitious agenda
(l) Meeting as a substitute for thinking and action (a kind of pouring of problems on a group and finding a scapegoat)

Checklist for the conduct of good meetings

As an arranger of meetings you may find this checklist helpful.

1. The chairs, tables, etc. should be well arranged.
2. If the members are to have nameplates, badges etc., these should be arranged.
3. Stationery items like pins, clips, sticking tape, paper, pens, etc. should be provided.
4. The public address system should be tested.
5. For visual projection, the apparatus should be tested.
6. Display items should be ready and, when necessary, fixed.
7. The hall should be neat and free for easy movement. No wires on the floor where one may trip.
8. Arrangements have to be there for snacks, water, etc., if required. Some believe that "No meeting without eating."
9. Making sure the members have received notice. Making sure they come prepared. The timing of your telephone to them is important.
10. Outside experts need special handling. Arrangement have to be made to receive and escort them.
11. One has to see to the lighting, ventilation, acoustics (sound spread) and temperature of the place of the meet.
12. Organising a large meeting is itself a committee job. One has to see that the co-arrangers are well-briefed and communication lines are open with them.
13. After the meet, the follow-up action should be prompt. The success of a meet and praise for it may turn us so self-satisfied that we may become idle.
14. One has to pursue the action plan by forming a chain of supervision. This would take away the most important criticism that applies even to well-conducted meetings – all talk and no action.

4.5.7 Notice of a Meeting

When a meeting is to be convened, a notice is required to be sent to all who are to attend it. It should satisfy these conditions:

1. It should be under proper authority.
2. It should state the name of the organisation.
3. It should state the day, date, time, and place. Also, sometimes, how to reach the place.
4. It should be well in advance. Some require seven days' notice, some 48 hours'.
5. It should state the purpose and, if possible, the agenda.
6. It should carry the date of circulation and convenor's/secretary's signature.
7. It should go to all persons required at the meet.
8. It should mention the TA/DA etc. payable and the arrangements for this.

In practice, it is necessary to ensure that the notice has *reached* in time. This may be done telephonically. Dispatch section and post are prone to delays. We often find that between the date of a letter from a major public organisation and the post mark on the letter, there is a gap of 10-12 days. A notice that should reach seven days **before** a meet should not reach seven days **after** the meet.

Specimen notices

1.

Seven Hills Housing Cooperative Society

Sundar Nagar, New Delhi

NOTICE OF MEETING

11th September 2011

The 44th meeting of the Executive Committee will be held at 8.00 p.m. on Sunday, 22nd September 2011 in Sanket Auditorium. The agenda is given below.

44.01 Minutes of the previous meeting
44.02 Appointment of a new watchman
44.03 Celebration of Kojagiri
44.04 Donations for flood relief
44.05 Permission to sell flat
44.06 Defaulting members
44.07 Purchase of a generator
44.08 Any other matter with the permission of the Chair.

You are requested to attend the meet.

Rajnath Mistry
Executive Secretary

cc: To all members

2.

Itwari Kirana Dealers Association

Resham Oli, Nagpur
NOTICE OF MEETING

To: All members

Notice is hereby given that the Annual General Meeting of the members of IKDA is scheduled to be held on 1st November, 2011 at 4.40 p.m. at Hotel India Sun, Central Avenue to consider the following business:

- To receive and adopt the Income and Expenditure Account, Balance Sheet, and Report of the Auditors for the year ended Diwali 2011.
- To elect President, Vice President, Honorary Secretary, Treasurer and Executive Committee Members for the current year.
- To prepare a representation to the NMC* about the actions of the Anti–Encroachment Squad.
- To discuss any other matter for which at least SEVEN days' advance notice is given and which is approved by the Chair.

By order of the Executive Committee

Nagpur
20th October 2011

Arun Maloo
Honorary Secretary

*Nagpur Municipal Corporation

4.5.8 Agenda

As stated earlier, an agenda is the list of items to be considered at a meeting. It is also called **business** or **order of business**. It comes from the Latin word *agendum* (singular) which means 'a thing to be done.' But agenda (the Latin plural) is used as a singular noun. It is the route map of the meeting. The specimen notices above already contain a hint of how it is written. The agenda may be a part of the notice or may be attached as an annexure. The convenor/secretary prepares it in consultation with the chairperson and gets his approval. The items of agenda should cover all that is necessary to be considered at that time. Meetings take time and effort to arrange, hence the agenda has to be well thought out. The items may be devised from –

(a) Previous minutes
(b) Suggestions received
(c) Actions and events since last meeting
(d) Correspondence of the organisation

The agenda contains routine items as well as special ones. Here are some guidelines for listing the items:

1. Apologies from absent members (need not be written previously)
2. Condolences if any (may or may not be written previously)
3. Reading and approval of minutes of the last meet
4. Matters arising out of previous meet's minutes (this need not always be mentioned)
5. Urgent and non-controversial items
6. Matters requiring closer discussion and debates
7. Any new, on-the-spot items with the approval of the chairman
8. Date of the next meet.

The last item in a meeting is a vote of thanks to the chairman but this need to be mentioned. The items are mentioned briefly or elaborately according to the practice or need. The style used is as follows:

- Appointment of auditors
- Induction of new members
- Reading of minutes
- Felicitating so-and-so on the award of Padmashri to him/her

OR

- To read and approve the minutes of the previous meet
- To consider the advertisement draft
- To organise a blood donation camp
- To appoint sub-committees for sports competition and music competition

The agenda should be manageable within the time at disposal. Some clubs have a time limit for the duration of a meeting (e.g. 90 minutes), which automatically dictates the scope of discussion.

Specimen agendas

1.

Suyash Cooperative Society

Pune

AGENDA for the 44th Meeting dated 1.9.2011

1. To confirm minutes of the 43rd meeting (1.8.2011), copy enclosed
2. To sanction loans to eligible applicants (copies of applications to follow)
3. To review the working of the Canteen Committee
4. Any other matter with the approval of the Chair
5. Next meeting

3.

332nd Meeting of Ajinkya Coop. Society
Lucknow
AGENDA

(a) To read and approve minutes of the 331st meet dated 15th August.
(b) To extend the lease to Mayur Orchards.
(c) To reconsider the decision to purchase a second-had car (taken in the meeting dated 15th July).
(d) To conduct a health camp.
(e) Any other matter with the Chair's approval.

4.5.9 Minutes

The minutes of a meeting are the record of the discussions/decisions therein. They have an official status, they are useful in law, and in some cases required by law to be written. Minutes are final when they are approved by the members of the group to which they relate, genérally in the next meeting, and signed by the chairperson.

Even if there are emotional moments in a meet, the minutes are written in an unemotional manner, are cool, factual, impersonal, impartial. Moreover, such are the demands of time on most people that the minutes should be concise, boiled down to the essentials. Only some organisations require that they record the detailed discussions as well (i.e. who said what and what were the reactions… until the decision was reached). Normally, the body of the minutes records –

(a) The motions and amendments thereto
(b) The proposer and seconder of motions
(c) The details of voting, if any
(d) Recommendations
(e) Decisions/ resolutions
(f) Tasks assigned to individuals, sub-committees

The overall minutes should give –

1. The name of the organisation/ unit
2. Day, date, time and place
3. Number in order (e.g. 33rd meeting of…)
4. Names of chairperson and secretary
5. Names of members present
6. Names of the absent
7. Attendees by special invitation, e.g. auditor, caterer, etc.
8. Record of the transactions (on the guidelines given above)
9. Signature of secretary and, after approval, that of the chairman.

Tips for writing minutes

The minutes are written generally by the secretary from the notes taken during the meet. He/she can use the agenda as the framework for writing them and use short forms, shorthand etc. to take quick and accurate notes. He may have to ask members to repeat their words to get them right.

He should note down all the particulars needed for the fair copy of minutes. The items of the minutes can be written under short headings such as are used in the agenda.

(As for reading them, some committees circulate them in advance and take them as read. Otherwise the reader should read them loudly, clearly, and quickly.)

Stylewise, they use one of these constructions:

- It was resolved that the minutes of the previous meeting be approved.
- It was decided that a sub-committee be set up to consider…

- Resolved that a blood donation camp be held on 15th August. (The verb is used in the subjunctive mood: "be done, be appointed",etc.)

Alternatively, the description is given in the past tense:

- **Minutes of last meet**: The secretary read out the minutes of the meet dated... and they were approved.
- **Donation received**: The chairman informed that he had received a donation of Rs. 50,000 from ex-member Mr. Gopal Rathi.

At the time of approval, the chairman asks, "Do you accept the mintues as they stand?" OR "Any matters arising out of the minutes?"

Your ability to write good minutes can earn you a prize position in an organisation. Also, if you hold a position and do not know how to write minutes, you may face embarrassment.

Specimen minutes

1.

Archana Literary Society, New Delhi

Minutes of Meeting dated 1st August 1999

Place and Time of Meeting	Residence of President Dr. Mansha Khan at A-12 Connaught Circus, 3.10 p.m.
Roll Call	Members present: Dr. Mansha Khan (Chairman) Mrs. Padma Raut Col. Devrajan (Secretary) Ms. Dilnawaz Kantawala Mr. Bharatendu Jain Mr. Prabhat Kumar Khatri Mr. Amrit Bose Mrs. Amrita Bose
Members absent :	Dr. Rajan Chhabra
Approval of Minutes of the Last Meeting	The minutes of the meeting dated 25th June were read by the secretary and confirmed.
Treasurer's Report	The treasurer Mr. B. Jain, circulated his report of the earnings and outgoings of the fete held on 10th July, which was accepted.
Briefing for All-India Poetry Meet	The President Dr Mansha Khan briefed the members about their roles in the forthcoming All India Poetry Meet at the Red Fort on 26th January 2000.
Induction of New Members	The membership applications of four applicants – Dr. D. K. Dawani Ms. Snehlata Sharma Mr. L. K. Gosai and Mrs. Geeta Harivanshi were accepted. The application of Prof. F.F.Guha was held in abeyance owing to invalid recommendation.
Sub-committee for Publication Unit	A sub-committee of three members – Mr. Devrajan Mr. Amrit Bose Mrs. Amrita Bose was set up for launching a publication unit.
Date of Next Meeting	The next meeting was scheduled for 15th September.

Col. Devrajan
Secretary

2.

SBI Zonal Office Employees' Welfare Organisation

Aurangabad

Minutes of Executive Committee Meeting

Meeting no. : 15	Time: 9.15 a.m.
Date: Sunday, 1 January 2011	Place: Staff Welfare Hall
Present: ABC (Chaiman)	NOP
DEF (Secretary)	QRS
GHI	TUV
KLM	

Absent: None

Sr.no.	Item
1.	Meeting called to order at 9.20 a.m.
2.	Minutes of the 14th meeting dated 20th November 2006 read and accepted.
3.	DEF proposed and TUV seconded and ABC was renominated chairman for the year 2011 unanimously.
4.	Sankrantri get-together decided to be held on 15th January. Sub-committee to be headed by NOP, with GHI and QRS as members.
5.	Meditation camp decided to be organised in the first week of February under the guidance of Swami Swarajanand. DEF to head the organising.
6.	Next meeting to be held on 31st January.
7.	Meeting ended at 10.05 a.m. with a vote of thanks to the Chair.

DEF
Secretary

4.6 Conferences

To confer means to consult, and a business conference is the coming together of people who have a common business aim with a view to consult, advise or recommend. Compared to a meeting, a conference is informal and often much larger. Its purpose is less well–defined than that of a meeting. An organisation may hold regular conferences (say annual) where the delegates get together to exchange their views, discuss their experiences and pool together their ideas. Sharing is the prominent feature of a conference.

Examples of conferences are — life insurance advisors' conference, scooter dealers' conference, small businessmen's conference, paint manufacturers' conference, etc. The delegates are enriched by the presentations of formal speakers as also by the informal discussions. For a committee to be effective it should have about seven members whereas a conference may have 15-20 participants or more.

Advantages of conferences

- Views and experiences are exchanged.
- Different sides of a common problem are presented.
- The management may meet and consult with special groups such as dealers, clients, trade union leaders.

- Expert speakers may advise and illuminate the delegates.
- New developments and new strategies can be presented.
- Doubts can be cleared.
- Employees get motivated through participation.

Disadvantages of conferences

- When employees are invited to a conference, their self-importance may overshoot and the management may appear dependent on their views.
- If an employee is called to a conference above his level of understanding, he may feel out of place.
- If the leader of the conference is ill-prepared, he may not do justice to the issues.

Types of conferences

On the basis of purpose, conferences may be classified thus:

1. **Informational conference:** In this type of conference, the object is to give information to the juniors. New policies, new technologies, reorganisation etc. can be conveyed down the line. This is a type of downward communication.
2. **Conference on a suggested solution:** A problem or situation facing the company is discussed with a possible solution. The management generates a discussion on the suggestion to know its merits.
3. **Problem-solving conference:** Here there is no ready solution but ideas are invited from the participants and thrown open for discussion.
4. **Conference for budgeting/ forecast/ estimate:** When a company wants to set a target and wants the employees' cooperation, such a conference is called. Taking into consideration the company's overall goals, the budget/ forecast/ estimate is discussed. Since the employees are involved in the forecast, they can talk of their respective environments. Also, it is easier to get their cooperation and commitment after such a conference.
5. **Conference for training:** Training is an ongoing activity in a progressive organisation. Conferences are called to train executives in new areas of expertise. A bank may arrange for a training conference on industrial rehabilitation for its field officers.

4.7 SEMINARS, SYMPOSIA, AND WORKSHOPS

These terms are applied to different types of group oral communication. The choice of a term from amongst seminar, symposium, and workshop is based on the activity conducted.

4.7.1 Seminars

In a seminar the important thing is the specialised study by one speaker or many speakers, presented before interested and learned listeners. A chairman is there to conduct the proceedings and make expert remarks. In a seminar there may or may not be pure listeners. The presentation is followed by a discussion. The participants interchange and cross-fertilise ideas. The topic is viewed by the participants from their respective angles and doubts are cleared.

4.7.2 Symposia

A symposium, as the term signals, necessarily requires a group of speakers who are experts on a certain theme and illuminate different sides of it. There is an audience for a symposium, for whose benefit it is held. The speakers use written notes and graphics to present their study. The audience, which is exposed to different views and sometimes differences of opinion, is encouraged to ask questions.

There may, for instance, be a career symposium for students where various speakers talk about the opportunities and demands of different lines open to the students.

4.7.3 Workshops

The term denotes practical activity, and a workshop is a discussion group in which the participants not only imbibe new ideas from expert speakers but also take hands-on (practical) training. If there is a workshop for sales representatives, the delegates may be asked to form smaller groups and play the roles of sellers, buyers, etc. If there is a workshop for trainers, the participants may conduct mock training sessions and their performance may be evaluated and useful individual tips given to them by expert observers. Thus the aim of a workshop is to inform, train, and facilitate practice. Since the participants have to take on new roles, vigorous question–answer sessions are a feature of workshops.

Q.1 Comment on the following statements in about 30 words each.

1. Brainstorming sessions encourage alternative approaches of ideas.

Ans. Brainstorming is an idea-generating process that encourages alternative approaches and uninterrupted expression of ideas. In brainstorming, the group leader states the problems and then group members 'freewheel' as many alternatives as they can put forth. It encourages creativity and quality of ideas.

2. Command meeting is different from committee meeting.

Ans. A 'command meeting' is a highly controlled meeting between a manager and his subordinates. In a command meeting, the manager alone is responsible for decisions whereas in a committee meeting, decisions are taken collectively.

3. Delphi technique of decision-making is different from brainstorming technique.

Ans. Delphi technique is different from brainstorming technique in the sense that it does not require the physical presence of group members. In brainstorming, group members meet and generate ideas freely.

4. Group decisions are not always good. OR Decisions taken by groups are not always superior to those by individuals.

Ans. Group decision-making suffers from domination by a few members, long futile discussions, high expense, and difficulties in fixing responsibility. Hence such decisions may be of a poor quality.

5. Brainstorming is a good technique of new idea generation.

Ans. Brainstorming implies free and open generation of ideas where participants are encouraged to think beyond conventional lines without screening and criticism. It therefore generally results in the generation of unthought –of ideas.

6. A leader is indispensable for group discussion.

Ans. Though discussion should be held in a free atmosphere and democratic manner, a leader is necessary to rudder it. A leader steers the discussion and controls it. Hence a leader is indispensable for group discussions.

7. A discussion cannot be effective without a group leader.

Ans. The group leader plays an important role in conducting a discussion. He coordinates and controls the participants, steers the discussion, and facilitates in decision-making.

8. Delphi technique promotes creative thinking.

Ans. Delphi technique facilitates decision-making without the physical togetherness of other members. Therefore decisions can be taken without any fear of criticism, helping the participants to be creative.

9. The subordinates do not have a say in a command meeting.

Ans. Command meetings are controlled by the manager dominantly, who orders the subordinates as to what they should do. Thus the subordinates do not have much say in a command meeting.

10. Decisions taken by a group are better than those taken by an individual.

Ans. A group is better equipped in terms of information, ideas, expert opinions and experience. Thus, under optimal conditions, decisions taken by it tend to be better than those taken by an individual.

11. Participation is the very life of a meaningful and effective discussion.

Ans. Without participation of members there cannot be any effective discussion. Many men, many minds. Every group member brings in his own experience and point of view. Together, they form a complete whole.

12. Delphi technique is not suitable where a speedy decision is needed.

Ans. Delphi technique involves the lengthy process of reaching out to the members and getting their replies. This may require contacting them not once but many times. Also, it requires time for formulating questionnaires. Hence, it is unsuited for fast decisions.

13. The terms seminar and symposium can be used interchangeably.

Ans. The two terms cannot be used interchangeably as a seminar is an oral presentation by one or more learned speakers for an expert audience, while a symposium is an enlightening succession of talks for educating an audience that need not be of experts.

14. Meetings are a sheer waste of time, it is individuals that decide.

Ans. This need not be so. As the roots of democracy deepen in the corporate world, meetings acquire more importance. They involve all participants for all participants' welfare, and their benefits outweigh their occasional drawbacks.

15. A meeting is wholely the chairman's baby.

Ans. No more so than teamwork is the captain's baby. As the team gets maturer, the chairman in fact becomes less and less essential. The chairman steers the meet, but every member has to play his/her role actively and responsibly. Dumping everything on the "group" is to deny competence to oneself.

16. Minutes are written as the secretary wills them.

Ans. Minutes of a meet HAVE to be impartial and impersonal – or they cease to be believable or even acceptable. Minutes are read at the next meeting and require to be approved. Diligent and alert members make their own notes of important issues and cross-check if events are faithfully recorded in the minutes.

17. Any collection of two or more persons will constitute a group.

18. An organisational structure provides for formal and informal groups.

19. Communication network of an informal group is very effective.

20. In a group, the members unwillingly fall into the trap of conformity.

21. A mere aggregation of individuals is considered a group.

22. Group decision-making and problem solving is considered superior to individual decision-making.

23. Group decisions are difficult and time-consuming.

B. Questions for revision

1. Explain briefly the ingredients of a discussion.
2. Explain briefly various characteristics of group personality.
3. Outline the role of leadership in the conduct of a group discussion.
4. Explain the procedure of conducting a meeting in a large organisation.
5. What is Delphi technique?
6. What is consensus? How does it differ from unanimity? (Hint : Unanimity is oneness of opinion.)
7. Write short notes on : (a) formal groups (b) brainstorming (c) group dynamics.
8. Discuss various techniques of group decision-making.
9. Compare command groups and committee groups.
10. Define the concept of group. Discuss various types of groups that are formed in an organisation.
11. Explain the concept of group dynamics.
12. Write short notes (50 words each) on:
    (b) Conference
    (c) Seminar
    (d) Symposium
    (e) Workshop
13. Bring out the distinctive features of a seminar as contrasted with a symposium.
14. Weigh the pros and cons of holding meetings in an organisation. What is the optimum course?
15. Define the purpose of meetings with examples.
16. The chairman can sink or salvage a meeting. Comment.
17. How can a participant showcase his talent at a meeting to further his chances in an organisation?
18. An effective meeting is a high mark of spoken and written communication. How?
19. What is the importance of the minutes of a meeting? How to write them?

C. Drafting exercises

1. Write the notice for convening a meeting of Internet Café Owners' Association to discuss the situation arising from irresponsible use of email by unknown persons.
2. Draft a notice to call a meeting of Customer Service Committee of JKL Bank which includes bank staff and members of the public. The issue – modernisation of banking service.
3. List the items of agenda of a meet of hairdressers to review the working of their profession.
4. Make up a hypothetical agenda for a meeting of Ladies Club of Devpur, devising items that give substance to the meeting.
5. Draft the minutes of a meeting of Ayurvedic Doctors' Association using the style "It was decided…."
6. Write the minutes of a meeting of Students' Union from the following agenda:
    (a) Reading of minutes
    (b) Approval of accounts
    (c) Appointment of solicitors
    (d) Participation in refugee camp
    (e) Steps to improve quality of computer education
    (f) Holding a personality development programme
    (g) Any other matters with the chairperson's permission

    The minutes should record the condoling of the death of the Vice Chancellor

■■■

CHAPTER

5

Business Letter Writing

What should you know?

5.1 Business Correspondence
5.2 Essentials of a Good Business Letter
5.3 Structure of a Business Letter
5.4 Format of a Business Letter
5.5 Tips for Clear Writing/Craft of Business Letter Writing

5.1 BUSINESS CORRESPONDENCE

Business letters are the life-breath of business. Despite the availability of telephone, conventional mail is still very popular. People like the feel of a good old "letter" in hand. It also increases the reach of a business house.

A letter is written to reach where you cannot reach yourself, and say what you cannot say yourself personally. Thus a letter plays the role of your representative or ambassador. All the qualities of a good ambassador – the polish and the courtesy, the knowledge and the convincing power - have to be there in a good business letter.

The competition in today's business world is described as "unreal"— too hard to believe. Those who have survived the competition and made it to the top are the ones who mastered, among other things, the art of writing good letters. Moreover, it is found that nearly 70% of the world's international business correspondence is in English. It follows some conventions which have to be learnt. These may of course change from time to time and from country to country. We have to make ourselves up-to-date in this matter.

Types of letters

1. Personal (to a friend or within the family)
2. Social (invitations, death notices, etc.)
3. Official (from government or its corporations, etc.)
4. Business (trade enquiries, orders, complaints, import-export correspondence, etc.)
5. Miscellaneous (letters to the editor, etc.)

1. **Personal letters:** These being letters to friends and family, express emotions or give news in an informal manner. They are often handwritten and have little restriction of style and format. Sometimes one uses a card with a printed message or greeting and adds something of one's own.

2. **Social letters:** These are in the form of invitations (to a wedding, a dinner, etc.) and follow a certain format, sometimes with ample use of the imagination. Death notices are also sent in a standardised format.
3. **Official letters:** They originate from government offices, corporations, etc. and move within the narrow restrictions of law. Hence they sound very formal. A distinct and limited vocabulary is used in such letters.
4. **Business letters:** These are letters from business houses to their customers or other business houses or to statutory bodies; they are also from individuals to business houses. The aim of these letters is to increase one's business prospects, and hence tact and persuasive power is used in writing them. Examples of business letters are, a sales offer from a company to its consumers, a job application, a letter informing of a new share issue, etc.

   These letters being the main study at hand, a classification of business letters is given below:

   (i) Enquiries and replies
   (ii) Quotations, estimates, and tender notices
   (iii) Orders and letters informing oftheir fulfilment
   (iv) Circular letters
   (v) Letters requesting payments
   (vi) Sales letters
   (vii) Complaints (claims) and replies (adjustments)
   (viii) Goodwill letters - greetings, thanks, congratulations etc.
   (ix) Credit and status enquiries
   (x) Import-Export letters
   (xi) Correspondence with banks
   (xii) Correspondence with insurance comapnies
   (xiii) Job-related letters
   (xiv) Correspondence with public authorities
   (xv) Internal communication.

5. **Miscellaneous letters:** These include letters to the editor, open letters to famous persons, letters by non-government organisations, etc.

Importance/advantages of business letters

Here is an analysis of the reasons why a business letter is valuable.

(i) **Drafting at convenience:** A letter can be composed at leisure and over a period of time, revised and edited before presentation. In this respect it differs from an oral presentation. It can be read by the recipient at his leisure, and he can make his own markings on the message received. It is a challenge to the communicator and his writing skill – a challenge which may reap handsome rewards. Successful businessmen are good communicators with a mastery of writing business letters.

(ii) **Reaches far and wide:** Within town or out of it, within the country or abroad, a letter reaches the target with much convenience. Through letters, a businessman can reach thousands of persons located at thousands of places.

(iii) **A record for purpose of law:** A written record is useful in law and for clarifying matters in the event of a dispute. Oral deals can be "airy" while a written record is solid evidence. That is why oral or telephonic discussions are confirmed through letters.

(iv) **A record for reference:** A letter can be kept by the recipient for reference at a later date and for drafting a reply. Instead of relying on memory alone, one can see the matter in black and white. A letter can be read in conjunction with other documents or with a chain of previous letters.

(v) **Solidifies a business bond:** A decent letter helps to establish a business relationship which can be developed further with future deals. An oral conversation is heard only once, whereas a letter may be read many times, over days and months. Ongoing letters to customers, dealers etc. keep the relationship warm.

(vi) **Helps to expand business:** Apart from the convenience of reaching remote places, letters enable the writer to explore new prospects in new territories. Sales letters can go in large numbers and do wonders for the sellers.

(vii) **Saves money in communication:** Personal conferences and meetings are expensive to arrange. If the same job can be done through a letter, it is better to do so. Letters are cost-effective in one more way: They save the hassles that may arise in a faulty oral presentation. Phrases frequently required can be saved and used again and again.

(viii) **Convenient for giving unpleasant news:** Sometimes unpleasant news can be given with tact in a letter, e.g. a sweet *No*. On some occasions, the receiver's oral reaction may be an outburst. A letter can explain the full situation of the "no," which helps to cool tempers. A letter also gives the recipient the time to think before reacting, which is a major courtesy.

In short, a letter is a neutral third party, a messenger for you, offering its own advantages over other means of communication.

How to give neat looks to a business letter

In public speaking, there is a saying: dress before address. Similarly, in letter writing the neatness is seen before the matter. A sloppily presented letter has to work, maybe, twice as hard to achieve its business goal.

(i) **Stationery and paper:** The envelope and the paper on which the letter is typed should be worth the name of the firm, even a little better if possible. Standard paper size is A4, but a firm may get its letterhead printed on smaller size paper also. The print layout should be artistically designed. The letter should have as few folds as possible. If a window envelope is used, the address should be clearly visible from the window (and not get covered).

(ii) **Typing:** The letter should be typed (or computer printed) with a uniform impression. Margins should be kept on all four sides, 1" to the left and right, and 1.5" at the top and bottom.

(iii) **Layout of parts:** All parts of the letter should be located in their allotted positions - the date, the reference no., the receiver's address, etc.

5.2 ESSENTIALS OF A GOOD BUSINESS LETTER

Here we discuss the principles of letter writing, which have to be mastered in the spirit. A thorough study of these can make you a sought-after letter writer and a successful entrepreneur. There are eight C's of good business letter writing : correctness, completeness, clarity, conciseness, courtesy, consideration, concreteness and convincing power.

(i) **Correctness:** The letter should contain correct information. The facts and figures need to be ascertained from the source before you commit them to paper. The spellings need to be correct, the manners correct (viz. respect shown according to the position of the recipient). The grammar and punctuation need to be according to the standard usage. In real-life business situations, many letters get wisely rejected on account of the errors they contain, because to send a wrongly worded or addressed letter is to invite embarrassment.

(ii) **Completeness:** Enough time and attention needs to be given to make the contents complete in order to fulfil the intent of the letter. The terms and conditions of sale, for example, need to be fully stated. Cool editing and comprehensive thinking is required for this purpose. All enclosures of the letter should be duly attached. The dispatcher also has a role to play in this. The letter should be numbered, dated and signed.

(iii) **Clarity:** The letter should be worded in clear language and be free from all ambiguity (double meaning). For example, in America the date 2/6/2006 means sixth February. Hence a letter going to USA should spell the name of the month. We can write "6th February 2006". Long paragraphs and uncommon words, dead phrases and foreign language words reduce the clarity of a letter. It is best to read a lot of good letters from text-books or actual correspondence to see how meaning is made clear.

(iv) **Conciseness:** Conciseness or brevity is brought into letter writing at two levels: matter and language. All extraneous information needs to be removed from the letter. Sometimes a single line of acknowledgement or thanks is enough to make an entire letter. As for language, here are some examples of how longer expressions are made concise:

Long	Short
They do not have money	They have no money.
It is a company which is very wealthy.	It is a wealthy company
There are a great many people who have tried this instrument.	Many people have tried this instrument.

(v) **Courtesy:** To be courteous is to be friendly in attitude and in the use of words. Apart from basic courtesies like saying "Dear Sir" and "Yours sincerely" there are deeper courtesies that endear a letter to its receiver.

Plain	More courteous
We have received your letter...	Thanks for your letter...
Your letter is blatantly wrong..	To set the record correct, we may submi tthat

Courtesy gives rise to courtesy.

(vi) **Consideration:** With a little recasting, a letter can sometimes become more favourable to the reader. This consideration is called "You attitude," better understood through examples (see box).

We attitude	You attitude
We are happy to inform	You will be happy to know...
We shall send the free copy if we receive...	Your free copy will be sent to you if you reply...
We will renew your subscription and send our gift ...	You can renew your subscription and receive your gift...

A "You attitude" letter generates a more positive response. However, the use of "You attitude" does not simply mean a more frequent use of the word "you." A sentence which uses "we" and "our" can also sound nice to the reader: "We would like you to have, with our compliments, a booklet..." Thus, balancing the words "we" and "you" is a finer game.

You attitude: When a reader receives a business letter, he looks for his own interest in it. Hence the importance of You attitude. It touches him directly and personally. When a letter is written from the receiver's point of view, he knows quickly and clearly what action to take or response to give. The letter should show an understanding of the recipient's situation and should address his problems.

While You attitude is recommended in general, it is particularly relevant in sales letters. It earns the reader's confidence and goodwill. You attitude does not mean just blind repetition of the word *you* and *your*, but a judicious tilting of the content in the reader's favour. The letter should eventually show how the writer is genuinely interested in the reader's welfare.

We attitude: We are proud to announce the launch of our new model.

You attitude: You will be delighted to know about our latest user-friendly new model that will serve your needs.

(vii) **Concreteness:** A business letter has to avoid approximate statements when exact ones can be given or are expected. A complaint letter can replace the phrase "loss on a large scale" by the phrase "loss of a 1000 man-hours." This can be backed up by other facts and figures. "We process loan applications speedily" can be changed to "We decide on loan applications upto Rs. 5 lakhs within 15 days."

(viii) **Convincing power:** Every letter sells an idea and is, to that extent, a kind of sales letter. To get appropriate action is the aim of the letter, for which all the skills of a good sales letter are to be applied. One has to state the benefit to the receiver and the reason why, and do so in appealing language. Consider this simple request: "Please send me a brochure of your Europe tour packages as my family and friends are interested. After Nepal and Mauritius, Europe seems a logical destination." The brochure may be expensive, but when the buying power of the letter writer and a large business prospect is offered, a brochure is likely to materialise. In a sales letter, the endorsement of a great personality, the testimony of satisfied users, or the technical specifications of a new product are the tools used for convincing.

Each "C" needs to be understood and mastered through practice. Practice makes perfect.

5.3 STRUCTURE OF A BUSINESS LETTER

Look at the skeleton letter below with numbered positions of the parts. This is a typical business letter, though we add that the practices in regard to layout differ.

1. Heading	**ABC Corporation** 1, M. G. Road Nagpur – 440 001 email: abc@vsnl.net.in Tel.: xxxxxx Fax: xxxxxx
2. Date	March 31, 2011
3. Reference	Ref. GK-2
4. Inside address	M/s. LMN and Sons 1250 Central Avenue Nagpur 440 002
5. Attention line	Attention: Shri S. P. Gupta
6. Salutation	Dear Sir
7. Subject line	**Subject: Supply of raincoats and umbrellas**
8. Body	We understand that you are distributors of raincoats and umbrellas of reputed companies. We deal in these goods and shall be glad to have your catalogue for them. A visit by your sales personnel will be specially appreciated. If your terms of sale are found suitable, we can offer you business worth Rs.20,000 to 30,000 in the coming season. We shall be happy to have an early reply.
9. Complimentary close	Yours sincerely
10. Signature block	For ABC Corporation Sd/- Partner.

1. **Heading/letterhead:** This part is often got printed by firms. The heading contains the name, address, telephone no., fax no., email address etc., and sometimes the firm's line of business. This is often a colourful part of the letter, designed by an artist.

> **ABC Corporation**
> 1111, M.G. Road
> Nagpur 440 001
> Tel: xxx xxxx Fax: xxx xxxx
> Email: abccorporation@vsnl.co.in

2. **Date:** The date of writing the letter is mentioned below the heading, without using the word "Date" as it is understood. Since American and non-American conventions about writing the day and month differ, it is best to spell out the name of the month. Hence, "31 March 2005" or "August 15, 2004" are acceptable forms of writing the date.
3. **Reference number:** Every letter sent by a firm should carry a reference number just as vehicles carry a registration number. It identifies the letter for reference and for purposes of law. It may include the file code, department name in the form of initials and an outward mail no. For example "PO/GM/4074" or "Ind/122". Government letters carry reference numbers like "ULO/Com/2000/ 2004 (T-20)". The codes are understood in the government office. The reference number should, however, be short and handy.
4. **Inside address (receiver's address):** This is written below the reference line and above the attention line, if any. It consists of the name and/or designation of the person to whom the letter is sent or simply the name of the company to which the letter is sent. For example,

(i) Mr. R. G. Ghadge
Personnel Manager
State Bank of India
Zonal Office
Kingsway
Nagpur

(ii) The US Embassy
Shantipath
New Delhi 110021

A man's name is preceded by *Mr.* or *Shri*. a woman's by *Mrs., Miss, Ms., Smt., Ku.,* etc. (There is now an increasing tendency to omit the dot and write Mr, Mrs, Ms, etc.) *Ms.* is widely accepted as a prefix for both married and single women. When a firm's name suggests joint ownership, *M/s* is prefixed, e.g. *M/s* (or *Messrs*) *Babubhai and Sons. M/s* should not be used for a limited company. If only the designation of the recipient is written, the article "The" should be prefixed, e.g. *The General Manager, The Managing Director,* etc. The recipient's title should be prefixed as the convention requires, e.g. *Dr. O.R. Kanadey, Prof. R.M.Roy*, etc.

5. **Attention line:** If it is desired that some particular person in the recipient organisation should handle the letter, his name is written below the inside address.
   Attn.: Mr. A. C. Joshi, Servicing Engineer
   For the attention of Mr G. K. Sahney
   Attention line, however, need not be a part of every letter.
6. **Salutation:** This is the equivalent of "Namaste" etc. in conversation. Some of the common salutations are:
   Dear Sir (when the addressee is a male)
   Dear Madam (when the addressee is a woman, married or single)
   Dear Sirs (when the addressee is a firm whose name is prefixed with M/s or Messrs)

Dear Shri Bhogle or *Dear Dr Panse* or *Dear Ms Naik* (when addressing by name)
Gentlemen (American system)
Ladies and Gentlemen (American system, when the letter is likely to be read by many people, or in a circular letter)
Your Excellency (when addressing a governor, ambassador or such a dignitary)
Your Highness (when addressing a head of state like prime minister or president)
Some other salutations are:
Dear Customer, Dear Subscriber, Dear Editor, etc.
Informally, one writes:
Dear Raj, Dear Sanjeev, etc.
Some people use a colon (:) while some use a comma in the salutation:
Dear Mr Chauhan,
Gentleman:
In the block style of letter writing, no punctuation mark is used.

7. **Subject line:** This line (optional) is used for indicating the theme of the letter. It is a convenience to the reader and helps him to classify the mail when he receives it. Examples:

   Subject: Enquiry about your IIT JEE training programme

   Subject: Refund of fee

   Sub : Your letter no. G-185 dated January 14 about filing tax returns

8. **Body of the letter:** This contains the message or the "real letter" for which the other parts serve as a buildup, finale and accessories. This part is to be drafted with the utmost care, since other parts are more or less routinised. The body is broken up into convenient paragraphs, which may even be numbered, especially from 2 onwards. In the block style, paragraphs are indicated by leaving a line space. Contents of the body are so planned that there is an introduction, main body, a line seeking action/response, and closing section with a phrase like "Thanks for your time and attention" or "We are at your service at all times." The chapters to follow will deal extensively with how to write the body of the letter.

9. **Complimentary or formal close:** This is equivalent to "Good bye" in conversation, and is followed by the signature of the writer. The formal close depends on the relationship with the addressee.

Opening salutation	Complimentary close	Remarks
Sir Madam	Yours faithfully, Yours truly,	This is used in official correspondence with superiors and with government departments. Write 'Respectfully' if the addressee outranks you.
Dear Sir Dear Sirs Dear Madam Gentlemen	Yours faithfully, Yours truly,	This is a standard complimentary close in business correspondence.
Dear Mr Godbole Dear Ms Gandhi Dear Dr Rao Dear Professor Saxena	Yours sincerely, Sincerely yours,	It is less formal. It is used when the writer is familiar with the correspondent.
Dear Sanjay Dear Sudha Dear VKJ	(Yours) cordially, (Yours) sincerely,	This is used in informal business letters. One can drop 'Yours' if one desires.

A firm decides its own preference in this regard.

1. Full block form: It follows open punctuation (i.e. absence of commas in the inside address, salutation, formal close, etc.), and is very easy for the typist. Every paragraph begins flush with the left margin. This style is popular in America and adopted by many business houses in India. (In this book, in the specimen letters we have generally followed this time-saving format.)

1. Heading	**ABC Corporation** 1, M. G. Road Nagpur – 440 001 email: abc@vsnl.net.in Tel.: xxxxxx, Fax: xxxxxx
2. Date	March 31, 2011
3. Reference	Ref. GK-2
4. Inside address	M/s. LMN and Sons 1250 Central Avenue Nagpur 440 002
5. Attention line	Attention: Shri S. P. Gupta
6. Salutation	Dear Sir
7. Subject line	**Subject: Supply of raincoats and umbrellas**
8. Body	We understand that you are distributors of raincoats and umbrellas of reputed companies. We deal in these goods and shall be glad to have your catalogue for them. A visit by your sales personnel will be specially appreciated. If your terms of sale are found suitable, we can offer you business worth Rs.20,000 to 30,000 in the forthcoming season. We shall be happy to have an early reply. Thanks for your attention.
9. Complimentary close	Yours sincerely
10. Signature block	For ABC Corporation xxxxxx Partner

As you can see, in the block style, all the lines are aligned to the left margin. At the line-ends in the inside address, the signature block and formal close there are no commas. This is a convenience to the typist, though the typed matter looks crowded on one side.

Hence there is the modified block form, where some of the parts are moved to the right, and some punctuation marks are added to the inside address, salutation and complimentary close.

Sample letter in modified block form:

Bharat Industrial Diamonds
145, Pancharatna
Opera House
Mumbai 400004
Tel: xxxx xxxx Fax: xxxx xxxx

Ref.: BID/6/234 15 November 2011

Roop Machine Tools,
CB-5, MIDC Industrial Estate,
Nagpur 440016.

Dear Sirs,

Subject: Your quotation dated 1 November 2011

Thanks for your above quotation. We are happy to place hereby our order for 500 pieces of grade D-50 diamonds. Please ship them by courier and documents through State Bank of India, Hingna Branch.

Please send an advance copy of the invoice by fax. You will have the payment as soon as the documents are received by our bankers.

Yours faithfully,

xxxx
Roop Raval
Managing Partner

Modified Block Form

- In this format, the date line and the closing lines are deeply indented so that the end of each line is nearly at the right margin.
- This modifies the block form by making the letter less crowded on one side.
- Punctuation marks are added to the inside address, salutation and complimentary close.

Semi-block (indented) form

In this form, apart from the punctuation marks above, the signature block is moved to the centre. At some additional work to the typist, this makes the letter more balanced and graceful.

Yash Textiles

1000, Main Road, Agra

Tel: xxx xxxx Fax: xxx xxxx

Ref.: YT/299 13 September 2011

Divine Superbazar,
102, M.A. Road,
Mumbai 400 007.

Dear Sirs,

Subject: Missing pieces in your consignment dated 28th August

We have to inform that your parcel dated 28rd August 2011 (invoice no. 1006) contains only 95 T-shirts instead of 100 as mentioned in the invoice. We hope your will please verify this with your despatch section and make good the shortfall at the earliest.

Thanks for your attention.

Yours faithfully,

R. Trivedi
Proprietor

5.5 TIPS FOR CLEAR WRITING/CRAFT OF BUSINESS LETTER WRITING

A systematic letter writer follows three steps in writing a letter:

(i) Preparation and planning
(ii) Putting the material in proper order and writing the first draft
(iii) Revision and editing to arrive at the final draft.

Let us discuss these in detail.

I. Preparation and planning before writing

At this stage, you think about the purpose of the letter and the reader. You get mentally attuned to talk to the reader at his level of understanding. You organise the facts and figures for the letter. Back references, if any, are consulted. You make a list of all that you want to say in the letter and put it in a logical order.

Further, you think of the action you would like the reader to take on your letter. You plan to present your case accordingly.

II. Actual writing of the first draft

You have to keep in mind the four factors that should shape your letter — the purpose of the letter, the reader's level of understanding, the facts, and the action desired from the receiver.

The physical structure of the contents of a letter has four parts.

(i) **The introductory part:** Here, the subject-matter of the letter is presented in an interesting manner, or the prior reference is given.

(ii) **The main body:** In this, the information you want to give is presented. If you are asking for information, you specify that. A logical build-up of the facts and figures is important. You should keep the paragraphs and sentences short but not too short. Long paragraphs are hard to read, hence it is advisable to use several short paragraphs. If a sentence runs to three lines, it is better to break it into two sentences.

(iii) **The action part:** If there is any action you would like the reader to take, you ask for it clearly in this section. Or you may tell what action you are going to take.

(iv) **Closing section:** You should end the letter in a pleasant and positive manner. This is like a courtesy before good bye. Outmoded expressions should be avoided in this section.

The old expressions are:

Thanking you in anticipation,
Hoping to hear from you soon,
Looking forward to a pleasant business association,

Modern expressions are:

Thanks for your time and attention.
I look forward to hearing from you soon.
We hope to have good business with you.
Please let me know if I can be of assistance.
Once again, thanks for writing, and we look forward to hearing from you soon.

III. Revision - checking and editing the draft

You should edit and if necessary rewrite the draft for clarity, accuracy and brevity. You should make the draft free from grammatical and spelling errors. All the parts of the letter should be neatly arranged and logically presented.

Guidelines for a letter writer

(a) **Use short sentences:** Here is an example of how we can make long sentences short.

Long: In view of the delays in transportation by rail or road, and the consequent loss in quality of medicines, we suggest that you ship the goods by air though this may be expensive on the face of it.

Rewritten: We observe that transporting the medicines by rail or road takes time and reduces their quality. As such, we request you to ship them by air even if this is more expensive.

(b) **Use familiar words:** Simple language has a charm of its own and contributes to faster reading and better understanding.

Unfamiliar: Under the present dispensation
Simpler: Under the present arrangement
Unfamiliar: The technology is obsolete.
Simpler: The technology is outdated.

(c) **Use precise words and information:** Wherever possible, vague descriptions of quantity (*much, more, most*) need to be replaced by precise descriptions. Write clearly and to the point.

(d) **Be careful in using technical terms (jargon) of a trade:** Every trade has its own special words understood by the people of the trade but not necessarily by general readers. Hence it may be necessary to reduce technical terms to a description that is understood by the reader.

Too technical: The regulator is infinitely variable.

Simpler: The regulator gives you any speed desired.

Similarly, some short forms are understood in the trade but not by general readers. They should be spelt out.

Ambiguous: Our A.M. will be visiting your site.

Spelt out: Our Area Manager will be visiting your site.

(e) **Use the first person:** Letters written in the first person are liked better than those in second or third person. Hence the use of the first person should be as frequent as possible.

(f) **Avoid needless repetition:** Clear writing is understood in one reading. Repetition shows overanxiety to make a point. Repetition is therefore to be used only in exceptional situations and to convey the most important ideas. For example, "We repeat, the last date of the offer has been **preponed** to 15th March."

(g) **Use straightforward constructions:** The sentence construction needs to be straightforward. Literary language may use an occasional inversion; however business language should avoid it.

Roundabout: Enclosed herewith are the invoice and bill of lading.

Straightforward: We enclose the invoice and bill of lading.

(h) **Follow grammar:** It is risky and inelegant to break rules of grammar. You may make a wrong impression by doing so. In colloquial usage, you may say, "Long time no see." But such an adventure in business writing is not advisable. Close attention is needed.

Wrong: One of our reporter will visit you.

Correct: One of our reporters will visit you.

(i) **Maintain unity:** Each paragraph should be devoted to one idea. A mix of ideas should be avoided.

(j) **Build a paragraph on a logical footing:** The arrangement of ideas in a paragraph should give a sense of continuity. Connector words and phrases such as *moreover, all the same, nevertheless, however,* etc. should be employed with skill.

(k) **Courtesy through You attitude:** The letter should be written in a manner that shows consideration for the reader and his concerns. This of course does not mean merely the frequent use of the word *you* but a mental orientation that is helpful to the reader.

(l) **Suit your tone to the occasion:** The tone of a letter may be formal or informal, persuasive or humorous, positive or negative according to the demands of the situation. Write naturally: "To your own self be true," says Shakespeare, and this applies to letter writing. The letter should reflect your personality, with the necessary polish.

(m) **Be accurate:** The information you carry in your letter should be truthful and verified for its accuracy.

(n) **Patterns for organising a letter:** There are some time-tested methods along which letters in general and sales letters in particular should be organised. One of the formulas is called A I D A - attention, interest, desire, action.

> **Attention:** Attract the reader's attention by touching his need.
> **Interest:** Arouse his interest in your message by appealing to his self-interest.
> **Desire:** Create a desire in his mind by a promise to fulfil his need.
> **Action:** Show what specific action you want him to take and make it easy for him to take that action.

Another formula is called IDCA, - interest, desire, conviction and action.

Interest: Catch the reader's eye by saying something interesting to him.
Desire: Proceed to create a desire in his mind for what you say.
Conviction: Offer some convincing facts to make the desire firm and good enough to be translated into action.
Action: Show what action is required to be taken.

How to construct a paragraph:

At the risk of some repetition, we stress the necessary ingredients of a good paragraph in a business letter.

Maintain unity: one paragraph, one idea.

Highlight the important sentences in the paragraph.

Avoid all that is extraneous.

Keep the paragraph short and moving forward.

A. Questions based on critical understanding. Comment in about 30 words.

1. The formal close of the letter must match the salutation in the letter.

Ans. It is essential that the complimentary close of the letter must match the salutation in the letter. For example, if the letter begins *Dear Sir, Dear Sirs or Dear Madam,* the complimentary close should be *Yours faithfully*. If the letter begins with a personal name, e.g. *Dear Mr. James, Dear Mrs. Robinson, or Dear Ms Jasmin,* it should be *Yours sincerely*.

2. A letter's appearance is a part of its message.

Ans. A business letter reflects the image of the business entity. The appearance should be pleasing to the eye. It should have an impressive layout. The quality of stationery should be good and appealing.

3. Good business correspondence promotes a company's public relations.

Ans. Business letters which are well-drafted not only communicate clearly but also serve as messengers of goodwill and contribute to positive image-building of the organisation.

4. Using verbs in active makes communication more effective.

Ans. Yes, use of verbs in active voice makes the communication very powerful. Hence, they must be preferred to passive voice. For example, instead of saying 'your contribution is recognised by the management,' it is more effective to say 'The management recognises your contribution.'

5. At the time of giving feedback 'You attitude' is important.

Ans. At the time of giving feedback, you have to talk about your reaction, your perceptions, your needs. Here, your attitude is, therefore, secondary. However, the feedback should help the company. To that extent then should be you altitude in it.

6. Written communication is a creative activity.

Ans. Written communication requires a lot of skill and practice. It is a creative activity which one can learn only through constant practice and dedication. To be creative is to produce a response according to situation, and not to repeat what was used in a seemingly similar situation.

7. **Communication is the single most essential skill in business operations.**

Ans. A businessman has to communicate with several people and several organisations. These include suppliers, customers, creditors, bankers, government departments, corporate clients, etc. Without effective communication skill, the business operations cannot be successfully carried out.

B. Questions for revision

1. Set out complimentary closes, signatures and designations for the following letters:
   (a) A letter addressed 'For the attention of Mr Gary Hatton, Purchasing Manager', from Mr Derek Holmes, General Manager.
   (b) A letter beginning 'Dear Caroline' to be signed by Ms Jacqueline Hatton, Training Manager.
   (c) A letter beginning 'Dear Miss Clark', to be signed by Miss Angela Marshall in the absence of Mr Jeffrey Garrison, Managing Director.
2. Write short notes on:
   (a) Simplicity in business correspondence.
   (b) Importance of effective business correspondence.
   (c) Characteristics of effective business letters.
3. Describe with examples commonly used layout conventions of business letters.
4. Outline the tips for clear writing of business letters and give specific reference to tips for paragraph design.
5. What principles will you adopt to structure a paragraph?
6. What do you understand by the term You attitude? How is it different from We attitude? Illustrate with examples their relative merits and demerits.
7. Enlist and briefly outline the major components of a typical business letter.
8. Explain the following with reference to effective correspondence:
   (i) Conversational style
   (*ii*) You attitude
   (*iii*) Persuasion
   (*iv*) Positive language

■ ■ ■

CHAPTER

6

Enquiries, Quotations and Tender Notices

What should you know?

6.1 ENQUIRIES

6.1.1 Introduction

A letter of enquiry is written to secure information about goods or services that you may require. In this, you state your purpose and ask for the price list, quotation, sample, etc. It is a letter from a prospective buyer to a seller.

Letters of enquiry are of the following types:

(*i*) Unsolicited enquiries: These are made at the buyer's initiative.

(*ii*) Solicited enquiries: These are made when the seller solicits (i.e asks for) enquiries through an advertisement or otherwise.

(*iii*) Requests for special terms or concession

(*iv*) Routine enquiries by existing customers in continuation of the business process

6.1.2 Guidelines for Drafting a Letter of Enquiry

(*i*) State clearly and briefly what you wish to buy and whether you want general information, a price list, a catalogue or a quotation.

(*ii*) If there is a limit upto which you can pay the price, do NOT mention that in the letter, otherwise the seller may be inclined to hike the price to that limit.

(*iii*) Most suppliers state their terms of payment and delivery, so these need not be asked for unless you want special modes.

6.1.3 Useful Phrases for Enquiry Letters

Some useful opening lines for enquiry letters are:

- *We are interested in... and would be pleased to have... .*
- *We are in need of... and shall be grateful if you send us... .*

- *You advertisement in... interests us and we would like to...*
- *I understand that you are dealers in/manufacturers of... and would request you to send us your catalogue of... .*

Some useful closing lines are:

- *Your early reply will be appreciated.*
- *In your reply please include the delivery details.*
- *Please inform how soon you can supply the goods as we require them for our immediate needs.*
- *If your goods find acceptance with our customers, we can place regular and large orders with you.*

6.1.4 Specimen Enquiries

1. Enquiry about water heaters advertised in the papers

Dear Sir/Madam

I am interested in buying your solar water heater advertised in the papers. Could you please send me your price list and any descriptive leaflet that you may have?

Yours faithfully

2. Enquiry about safes

Dear Sir/Madam

I have seen your safes in a local bank and am interested in knowing more about them with a view to buying one. Please send me your current catalogue, especially of small safes.

Yours faithfully

3. Enquiry about readymade garments

Dear Sir/Madam

We are a large department store in Nagpur and would like to know more about the readymade garments that you manufacture. Could you tell us the brand names that you deal in, the range of clothes that you market, and something about their quality? Please send us your price list as well.

Yours faithfully

A. K. Sinha
Manager

4. Enquiry about tubeless tyres

Dear Sir/Madam

I am much interested in the tubeless tyres that you manufacture, for sale through our retail chain.

Please send me your illustrated catalogue and price list.

Yours faithfully

5. Enquiry about poster paper

Dear Sir/Madam

We will shortly be requiring 50 reams of good quality white poster paper suitable for action bill and poster work generally. We require paper that will retain its white appearance when in use.

Please let us have a quotation, including cost of delivery at our premises within 7 days of your receiving the order. Please send us some samples.

Yours faithfully

6. Enquiry about air-conditioning service

Dear Sir/Madam

We would like our office to be air-conditioned. We shall be glad if your engineers make a survey of the place and submit a quotation of the cost involved.

Yours faithfully

6.2 QUOTATIONS (REPLIES TO ENQUIRIES)

6.2.1 Introduction

When you receive an enquiry, it is like walk-in business. You must answer it promptly and to your advantage. If it is from an established customer, you can state how much you appreciate it. If from a new source, it can be the beginning of a lasting and mutually beneficial business relationship.

A quotation is an offer to sell goods at a given price and upon the stated conditions. That enables the prospective buyer to know where the seller stands in the deal.

6.2.2 Guidelines for Drafting a Quotation

(i) Thank the enquirer for his interest.

(ii) Give details of price, discounts and terms of payment.

(iii) Indicate whether the price includes packing, insurance, freight etc. or they are to be charged for separately.

(*iv*) State the date of delivery.

(*v*) Give the date upto which the quotation is valid.

(*vi*) Solicit business by expressing the hope for an order. Some of the common terms used in quotations:

(a) **The prices are ex-factory/ex-warehouse**: That means the buyer has to pay for the movement of the goods from that point onwards.

(b) **FOR**: This is a standard expression meaning "free on rail/road". The cost covers the movement of the goods to the specified railway station / roadways and loading.

(c) **FOB** (free on board): This means the goods will be loaded on board a ship free of cost. The buyer is responsible for the costs thereafter such as freight, transit insurance, etc.

(d) **Ex ship**: This means the quoted price includes delivery over the side of the ship.

(e) **Carriage paid**: The quoted price includes delivery to the buyer's premises.

(f) **Carriage forward:** The buyer has to pay the delivery charges.

6.2.3 Useful Phrases for Quotations

Some opening lines for replying to enquiries are:

- *Thanks for your letter of enquiry dated... As requested, we enclose... .*
- *In reply to your enquiry of... we are pleased to send, by separate post,... .*
- *We are happy to learn that you are interested in... .*
- *We are pleased to receive your enquiry of... for... .*

Some closing lines are:

- *We look forward to receiving your valued order soon.*
- *You may contact us over the phone or by email also for any further details.*
- *We hope to hear from you soon and shall attend to your orders promptly.*
- *I hope the samples reach you soon and look forward to receiving your order.*

6.2.4 Specimen Quotations

1. Reply to enquiry about readymade garments

Dear Sir/Madam

Thanks for your enquiry dated 10th March about our readymade garments. We manufacture jeans and tee-shirts under the brand name of Tuffies.

We would like to draw your attention to the trade and quantity discounts you can enjoy, printed on the back of the enclosed pricelist. Our terms of sale are also stated therein.

We shall be happy to do business with you.

Yours faithfully

2. Reply to Enquiry no. 5 (about poster paper)

Dear Sir/Madam,

We thank you for your enquiry dated 10th July and, as requested, enclose samples of our paper. These should assure you that they satisfy the requirements that you have stated.

The prices are as follows:

Excel: Rs. 4000 per ream
Superior: Rs.3800 per ream

The prices quoted include delivery at your office. We can supply the goods from ready stock upon demand, and assure your that we enjoy a good reputation for delivery on time.

We trust the samples will satisfy you and that you will place your valued order with us soon (as the prices are likely to go up after 15 days).

Yours faithfully

3. Reply to Enquiry no. 6 (about air-conditioning of office)

Dear Sir/Madam

As requested by you, we have got our engineers to survey your office for air-conditioning and we are pleased to quote for the job as follows:

> Rs. 65,500 for installation of air-conditioners including cost of materials. (Offer valid for 15 days)

We trust you will find this a competitive offer. We take this opportunity to enclose a list of our satisfied customers.

Yours faithfully

4.

ELGI Equipments Ltd.

Regd. Office : Marol Co-op. Estate Ltd., Plot no. 48, Andheri (East), Mumbai 400059
Tel: 022-XXXX XXXX Fax: 91-22-XXXX XXXX email: elgimum@satyam.net.in

Ref: MUM/AKS/183 January 10, 2011

Bajiram Foods Ltd.
G-125, Central Bazar Road
Nagpur 440 010

Kind attn: Mr. Ghate, Works Manager

Dear Sir

Sub: Your requirement of a screw compressor

Thanks for the recent discussions at your office on the subject of our supplying a screw compressor E-155 to you. Our detailed offer is enclosed herewith:

Annexure I: Technical specifications
Annexure II: Price and commercial terms and conditions

You would be glad to know that we are one of the largest manufacturers of screw compressors with more than 20,000 satisfied customers on our roll. We have a state-of-the-art manufacturing unit at Coimbatore and we export to UAE, Singapore and USA.

We hope our offer suits you in every way. We shall be glad to answer any query of yours in this regard.

We look forward to your valued order and assure you of our best attention.

Yours truly
FOR ELGI Equipments Ltd.

Pankaj Seth
Sales Manager

PS/md

Encl: As above

5.

PVS Coal Suppliers

Regd. Office: 33, Central Avenue, Nagpur 440002
Tel:0712- XXX XXXX email: pvs@satyam.net.in

Ref: CS/777
April 15, 2011

OM Steel Industries
C-5, Royal Industrial Area
Nagpur 440016

Kind attn: Mr Mate, Works Manager

Dear Sir

Sub: Your query about supply of A and B grade steam coal

We are pleased to receive your enquiry dated 5th April on the above subject and quote our rates for the supply of coal as under:

Coal grade A
Price: Rs. 2700 PMT*
Transportation: Rs. 900 per truck

Coal grade B
Price: Rs. 2600 PMT
Transportation: Rs. 900 per truck

Terms and conditions:

1. Advance payment @Rs.20,000 per truck is required, which will be adjusted in the bill.
2. The freight charges should be paid to the driver against the delivered material. The cost of any shortage exceeding 150 kg per truck, may be deducted from the freight and the balance amount paid to us in the name of Nagpur Roadways.
3. You will allow a shortage of 150 kg per truck.

We look forward to your order and thank you for your interest.

Yours faithfully
For PVS Coal Suppliers Ltd.

Sales Manager

* PMT = per metric ton

6.3 TENDER NOTICES

6.3.1 Introduction

A tender notice (Request for Proposals or RFP) is a published advertisement, generally issued by companies or government departments, inviting the vendors or service providers to make their offers for supply of goods or services. Sometimes tender notices are also for sale of goods, especially scrap.

A tender is an offer for the supply of specified goods or the performance of a specified work at prices and under conditions set out in the tender notice. A response to a tender notice is **expression of interest** (EOI) and becomes legally binding only when the tender is accepted.

Tender Notice
○
Tender
○
If accepted, results in a contract

Generally, the inviter of tenders gives prescribed forms in which the tenders are to be made. This form takes care of the details in which the advertiser is interested. Nowadays it is customary to give a website address for details of terms and conditions as this cuts down the advertising cost.

6.3.2 Guidelines for Drafting a Tender Notice

(i) The advertiser should give his name and address at the top. The words "Tender Notice" or "Notice Inviting Tenders" or their equivalent should be written below it. The date and tender notice number should be given.

(ii) The authority inviting tenders must be stated. One of the ways for this is: "The Purchase Manager, ABC Ltd. invites sealed tenders from experienced dealers who meet the eligibility criteria for supply of the items listed below."

(iii) The following information regarding the tender must be given:
- (a) Date and time of issue of tender documents
- (b) Date and time of receipt of the tenders
- (c) Date and time of opening of the tenders
- (d) Cost of tender documents
- (e) Earnest money required to be deposited
- (f) Eligibility criteria of the tenderer (e.g. that he should be registered)
- (g) Whether a banker's solvency certificate and income tax certificate is necessary.

(iv) It is usually stated in the tender notice that the authority issuing the tender notice reserves the right to reject or accept any tender without assigning any reason.

(v) If the tender details are available on website, this fact is stated.

(vi) Signature of the authority inviting the tender.

6.3.3 Specimen Tender Notices

1.

PVS Enterprises Ltd.

Gandhi Marg, Surat

Notice Inviting Tenders

No.5/CE/2006 1 May 2011

The Purchase Manager. PVS Enterprises Ltd., Gandhi marg, Surat, invites sealed tenders from Indian vendors for supply of the goods stated below. Further details are available in the tender documents available on our website www.pvs.org from where they may be downloaded free of cost.

1. Tender reference no. : NIT/121/2011
2. Items : Handicams, digital cameras worth Rs.10 lac (estimated)
3. Tender fee : Rs.500
4. Earnest money deposit : Rs 50,000

Note:

Date of issue of tender documents : 5-5-2011 to 20-5-2011

Last date for receipt of tenders : 23-5-2011 (upto 3.00 p.m.)

Date of opening of tenders : 24-5-2011 at 11.00 a.m.

The company reserves the right to reject any or all tenders without assigning any reason.

Sd/-

Purchase Manager

2.

KVIC INVITES

Professional Marketing Agencies

Khadi & Village Industries Commission (Ministry of ARI, Govt. of India) is the apex Central Government agency for rural industrialisation, effecting annual sales of Rs. 10,193 crore of KVI products through 7000 sales outlets. In order to build and promote marketing of KVI products it is intended to engage, on product basis, a panel of professional agencies. Offers are invited from professional agencies with proven track record at National and Zonal Levels in marketing of basic consumer products particularly in the field of supply chain and distribution management, brand promotion, packing and design development, quality control and market research. Interested professional agencies may collect the brief along with application form within 7 days and submit their offers at either of the following addresses:-

Director (Marketing)
Khadi & V.I Commision,
3,Irla Road, Vile Parle(w),
Mumbai-400056.
Tele Fax: 0022-26716680

The Manager
Khadi Gramodyog Bhavan
24, Regal Building,
Connaught Place,
New Delhi-110001.
Tel.: 011-23411651
Fax: 011-23418126

E-Mail:karnailsingh@kvic.gov.in website: www.kvic.org.in

Excerpted

3.

Devpur Municipal Corporation

Garden Department
Civil Lines, Devpur

Tender Notice

Ref: TN/101/2011 30 June 2011

Sealed tenders in the prescribed form are invited for the following works from DMC's registered contractors of appropriate class who have done similar work in govt./semi-government or local self-government institutions of amounts mentioned against the works.

Sr. No.	Name of work	Estimated cost (Rs.)	Cost of tender form (Rs.)	Eligible contractor
1	Maintenance of Central Garden for a period of one year	11,92,890	12,000	Work experience of Rs. 5 lakhs
2	Maintenance of Gandhi Garden for one year	4,41,440	4,500	Work experience of Rs. 2 lakhs

Note:

1. Blank tender forms can be obtained from office of the Garden Superintendent, Devpur Municipal Corporation, Civil Lines, Devpur after producing documents pertaining to eligibility of the contractor.
2. Earnest money deposit @ 10% of the estimated cost will have to be paid in the form of DD/pay order of any local branch of a nationalised bank in favour of Garden Superintendent, Devpur.
3. Recent income tax clearance certificate, sales tax clearance certificate and a document pertaining to eligibility for the contract will have to be submitted in a separate envelope (envelope no. I) along with the tender.
4. Competent authority reserves the right to reject or accept any tender without assigning any reason therefor in the interest of DMC.

Garden Superintendent
DMC, Devpur

Schedule of dates is as given below:

1. Sale of blank tender forms : From 1-7-2011 upto 2 pm on 8-7-2011
2. Submission of filled in tender forms : Upto 2 pm on 9-7-2011
3. Opening of tender forms : At 4 pm on 9-7-2011

Adapted

4.

TATA INSTITUTE OF FUNDAMENTAL RESEARCH

Homi Bhabha Road, Colaba Mumbai- 400 005
Tel. No.: 2280 4545,fax No. 2280 4566/4610-11
Email:psmurthy@tifr.res.in www.tifr.res.in

TENDER NOTICE NO.:PUB -17/10-11

Tender are invites for the following:

Tender No.	:	TFR/PD/CM3-625/PUB
Description	:	Making Aluminium Alloy slats by laser cutting as per our specification & drawing
Due date	:	27.02.2011.
Last date	:	for sale of Tender Documents:24.02.2011.
E.M.D.	:	Rs. 20,000/-favouring Registrar, TIFR payable at Mumbai

Tender specifications can be had from the Purchase Section on payment of the tender fee(non-refundable) of Rs. 200/-by cash/money order along with a letter addressed to the Cashier, Accounts Department, on any working day between 11.00 A.M. to 12.30 P.M. and 1.00 P.M. to 3.00 P.M.

Tender in sealed envelopes duly superscribed with the Tender Number and the Due Date as mentioned above, alongwith DD/pay order of Rs. 20,000/- toward EMD should be submitted so as to reach the purchase officer by 12.00 hrs. on the due date specified. Tender will be opened in the presence of attending tenderers at 14.00 hrs. on the same day.

The Institute shall be under no obligation to accept the lowest or any other tender received in response to this tender notice and shall be entitled to reject any tender without assigning any reason whatsoever.

PURSHASE OFFICER

Excerpted

QUESTION BANK

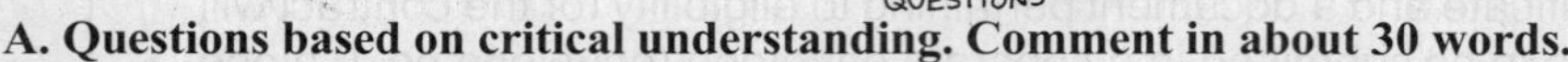

A. Questions based on critical understanding. Comment in about 30 words.

1. **A letter of enquiry is initiated by the buyer.**

Ans. A letter of enquiry is written by a prospective customer asking for information about goods or services. It asks for general information, an illustrated catalogue, price list, quotation, sample, estimate, etc.

2. **A quotation is initiated by the seller.**

Ans. A quotation is a statement about supply of goods at the price and on the terms stated in it. It is sent by the seller/supplier usually in response to an enquiry.

3. **An expression of interest and tender is one and the same.**

Ans. A tender is usually an offer to supply goods or perform some work. Similarly an expression of interest tells of the willingness to perform some task. Both the terms convey the same meaning.

4. **Tenders are submitted by buyers.**

Ans. Tenders are usually offers given by the interested seller and not by the buyer. They are given to the interested buyer in response to his published tender notice. When the tender notice is for sale of goods, tenders are submitted by buyers.

5. **Tender is given in response to a tender notice.**

Ans. A tender notice is published by corporations etc. inviting offers from prospective suppliers/ sellers who meet the requirements of the buyer. The interested supplier etc. then submits his systematic offer.

6. **A letter of quotation is a specific offer of sale made in response to an enquiry**.

Ans. A quotation is an offer to sell goods at a price and on stated conditions. It states the seller's position in regard to the supply. The buyer can then choose to deal or not deal or ask for a modified offer.

7. **You have seen an ad in a newspaper for an inverter and wish to buy it straightaway by enclosing a draft. You should write a letter of enquiry to the supplier.**

Ans. If you have made up your mind to buy a product, where is the question of sending an enquiry? You have to place an order. Enquiry is preliminary to placing an order and not legally binding. An order is legally binding.

8. **When making an enquiry, if you have a certain budget you should frankly inform the seller about it.**

Ans. When the seller's prices are not fixed but negotiable, it is unwise to let the seller know your budget ; he may be tempted to hike the quotation in case it is lower than your budget. It is better to be silent about your budget. You may of course stress the expectation of a very competitive quotation.

9. **The tender-inviting authority is under obligation to accept one of the tenders received.**

Ans. The tender notice usually has, or ought to have, a clause stating that the tender-inviting authority may reject any or all tenders in the interest of the company. As such there is no obligation to accept a tender from the lot received.

B. Questions for revision

1. Bring out the difference between a letter of enquiry and a reply to an enquiry. Illustrate your answer.
2. How is a tender notice drafted?

C. Drafting exercises

1. You are a manufacturer of shoes without a brand name. Respond to an enquiry from the police commissioner for supplying 200 pairs of shoes in standard sizes for its constabulary. State the merits of your unbranded product.
2. In response to a query from an export house, quote your rates for printing visiting cards and letterheads in four colours. Stress the advantages of ordering in a larger bulk.
3. Nagpur Industries Limited intends to purchase a heavy-duty photocopying machine. On behalf of the company draft a suitable letter of enquiry. It is important that the copier be able to reduce or enlarge easily.
4. As a manager of PVS Corporate Services, you are considering the installation of an inverter designed to supply electricity. Write a letter to Bijlee Industries asking for an estimate. Point out that you require the inverter to support ten tube lights and five fans. Ask for suggestions and advise.
5. In response to a letter of enquiry in Q.3 write a letter of quotation on behalf of JodhpurCannon Enterprises.
6. Draft a tender notice on behalf of Maldar Industries for purchase of a generator/ computers/ printers/ machinery.
7. Make an enquiry with a manufacturer of steel furniture for purchase of furniture for a college office.
8. Ask for a quotation for wall-to-wall carpeting of your office.
9. Write a letter of enquiry to a private hospital for conducting a health check-up camp in your factory for 50 employees.
10. Respond to an enquiry from an industrial house for a maintenance contract for its two water coolers.

CHAPTER

7

Placing Orders and Their Fulfilment

What should you know?

7.1 Orders

7.2 Fulfilment of Orders

7.1 ORDER

7.1.1 Introduction

In the trade cycle, once a price or quotation is found acceptable, the next logical step for the buyer is to place an order, and for the seller to fulfil the order. Here we shall study the correspondence that accompanies these transactions.

A letter of order is a legally binding contract, hence it has to be written with proper caution. If an order is sent over the telephone, it is desirable to confirm it in writing.

7.1.2 Guidelines for Placing an Order

(i) You should place an order in firm and clear language. Your You attitude to the seller requires this.

(ii) Even if stated in earlier correspondence, give a detailed, exact and full description of what goods or services you wish to have. This includes details like size, make, quality, colour, reference number (from the catalogue), identification number, etc. These should not contradict what you have written earlier and what the seller has offered. Hence a proper study of the previous correspondence is necessary while placing the all-important order. You may enclose a photocopy of the quotation which you have accepted for placing your order.

(iii) Mention the quantity you wish to buy and give a reference of the price list or state the price at which you wish to buy.

(iv) Clarify the mode of payment. If you are a regular buyer, the seller would know. If you are a buyer on credit, he may debit your account for settlement according to set norms. In other cases, follow the seller's desired mode of payment. If an advance is desired, and if the seller is trustworthy, send it.

(v) If the mode of transport – rail, road, air, courier, etc. – is settled with the quotation or price list, then you will have to accept it. In other cases, this needs to be mentioned.

(vi) The time period of delivery needs to be clarified. If you require the goods urgently, then state so. The goods are expected to arrive in reasonable time, but you should clarify what you consider reasonable time. In the case of seasonal or special-event goods, the importance of the time factor is self-evident.

(vii) State the address where you want the delivery of goods.

(viii) Normally, adequate packing is the supplier's responsibility, and may have been clarified in the quotation. However, if there is a choice or a special requirement of yours, then you should state the mode of packing of the goods.

(ix) Make sure of your position as regards transit insurance of the consignment. If it is normally insured, fine. If special instructions are required for this, give them. Incidentally, when the price is c.i.f. - cost, insurance, freight - you know that the goods would be insured.

Printed order forms:

Some companies have printed order forms. They have the advantage that -

(a) They may be numbered, making the referencing easy.

b) They make sure that all relevant information is indicated.

They may have conditions printed on the back, but a reference to them is required on the front of the form. Even with a printed order form, a covering letter is desirable as it allows you to make any necessary point and confirm the terms of your understanding.

7.1.3 Useful Phrases for Placing Orders

Useful openers for placing an order

1. *We enclose our order for 200 Ultra carburettor kits.*
2. *The accompanying order is for 30 inverters...*
3. *Thanks for your quotation and information leaflet of 2nd February in response to our email for them. We give below our order for...*
4. *I would like to place a trial order for Rite watches manufactured by Svatantra Udyog. Below are the details of our requirements.*

Useful closers for placing on order

1. *We hope to have a continued cordial business relationship with you.*
2. *I look forward to your acknowledgement/confirmation.*
3. *If the goods pick up in the market, we hope to place many more orders with you.*
4. *If the goods are sold out you may look forward to more orders from us.*

7.1.4 Specimen Orders

1. Order for TV sets

Dear Sir/Madam

We hereby confirm the order placed over the phone today and request you to supply:

10 nos. Luxem TV sets E-35 @ Rs. 21,500 each
5 nos. Luxem TV sets E-36 @ Rs. 18,900 each

Please bill with your 20% trade discount.

The TV sets are required for the forthcoming Dashehra-Diwali season, and we look forward to their early delivery as agreed.

Yours faithfully

2. Order for tyres

Sethia Traders
Y-25, Yeshwant Stadium
Nagpur 440012
Tel: XXXXXX

20th July 2011
Ref: 0-135/6

The General Manager (Sales)
JVS Tyres
Chinchwad
Pune

Dear Sir

Sub : Order for tyres

We thank you for your quotation dated 15th July and are happy to place our order for the following items:
16" x 4.5" tyres 20 nos.
18" x 5" tyres 20 nos.
19" x 5" tyres 100 nos.

Please insure the consignment at our cost. Please make sure that the goods are despatched so as to reach us within 10 days. Please send the documents through our bankers, Bank of Baroda, Sitabuldi, Nagpur.

Thanks for your interest in our business.

Yours faithfully
For Sethia Traders

Sd/-
Managing Director

3. Order in tabulated form

Dear Sir/Madam

Sub : Order For Utensils

Please supply the following items at your usual discount of 20% off listed price.

Quantity	Description	Catalogue no.	Price (Rs.)
1000	Stainless steel spoons	1245	4.50
250	Stainless steel glasses	283	10.00
230	Stainless steel plates	122	35.00

All these items are required for the marriage season and we hope you will despatch them latest by this Saturday as agreed.

Yours faithfully

7.2 FULFILMENT OF ORDERS

7.1.1 Introduction

An order must be promptly acknowledged, especially if the fulfilment is going to take some time. This may be done by -

(a) Writing a letter, or

(b) By sending a printed acknowledgement card.

7.2.2 Guidelines for Responding to an Order

The acknowledgement has the following objects:

(i) Thanking the customer and building goodwill.

(ii) Legal acceptance of the terms of the order.

iii) Reference to the date of receipt of the order.

iv) Stating when the order will be fulfilled and the likely date of delivery.

v) Putting in a clause about getting further business and continued support from the customer.

7.2.3 Useful Phrases for Accepting an Order

Useful openers for acknowledging an order:

1. *Thank you for your order no. 12858 dated 29th February, which we received today. The order is being filled immediately and may reach you by courier by March 5.*
2. *Your order for a paper manufacturing machine is being readied and will be despatched by 10th September.*
3. *We are pleased to inform you that your order for plastic drums is receiving our immediate attention. The goods will be despatched by Saturday and we note to inform you by phone when this is done.*

Useful openers for fulfilling an order

(When an order is fulfilled, the information may be faxed or emailed, but still the buyer needs the documents to receive the goods.)

1. *Your order no. 1258 of 1 March is already despatched by a TCI truck and the documents have been sent by speed post to your banker.*
2. *We are pleased to advise you that your order for medicines has been shipped by air today. The documents are enclosed to this letter.*
3. *Your order no. GK-102 is being sent by a special truck today, to arrive in Raipur within three days.*

Useful closers for acknowledging/fulfilling an order

1. *We hope to receive more business from you.*
2. *It is a pleasure to do business with you and we hope to hear from you soon.*
3. *Once again, thanks for your order.*
4. *We feel confident that you will be completely satisfied with these goods and find them very good value for money.*
5. *We hope there is a good take-off of these goods in your area.*

7.2.4 Specimen Replies to Orders

1. Acknowledgement of an order

Dear Sir/Madam

Subject : Your order for almirahs

Thanks for your order no. E-297 dated 8th August for steel almirahs.

We confirm the supply at the price stated in your letter and are arranging to despatch the goods by rail early next week. Please be sure that the goods will be upto their reputation and your satisfaction. We hope to have continued orders from you in the future.

Yours faithfully

2. Response to order for TVs

Dear Sir

Subject : Your order for TV picture tubes

Thank you for your order of 600 TV colour picture tubes. We shall deliver you order within 15 days, i.e. by 25th July, as desired by you. The documents will be sent through your bankers. You will be entitled to a 2% cash discount in case you pay within three days of receipt of the documents.

These picture tubes, we are glad to report, are based on this year's technological innovations which make a major improvement over the previous one. We trust your TVs using them will find a good acceptance with your dealers and end-users.

Yours faithfully

3. Offer of an alternative product

Dear Sir

Sub : Your order for mirrored almirahs

We thank you for your order no. 1131 dated 5 August 2011, asking us to despatch 40 mirrored almirahs.

However, we are currently manufacturing only non-mirrored cupboards. As your order is an urgent one, we would like to know whether these would suit you. As soon as we receive your confirmation, we shall arrange to despatch your order.

Yours faithfully

4. Response to cancellation of an order

Dear Sir

Sub : Your cancellation of order

We note with concern that you have to cancel your order for 30 one-day cricket suits which you had confirmed on 4th May. It so happens that by now we have already invested Rs. 20,000 in your order for purchase of material. As such, we have to ask you to reimburse us for this investment. You may collect the material we have on hand.

In case you would like us to fulfil the order in the near future, please state so. In that case, you would only have to pay the carrying cost of our investment.

Yours faithfully

QUESTION BANK

A. Questions based on critical understanding. Comment in about 30 words.

1. **A letter of order is written by the seller.**

Ans. No, an order is by the buyer. A letter of enquiry initiates a commercial transaction. In response to a letter of enquiry, the prospective seller submits a quotation. After the quotation is accepted, the buyer sends out a letter of order. The letter of order creates a binding contract.

2. **Responding to an order is an opportunity to reinforce your marketing.**

Ans. When you write to a buyer about supplying goods according to his order, you can mention what is good in your product/service and express a desire for more orders in the future. This gives him some psychological satisfaction in buying and creates goodwill.

3. **You don't have to specify the mode of transport and payment while placing an order.**

Ans. These questions may be settled with the seller's offer/quotation to you. But if you have a special requirement of yours, you have to settle it afresh . Sometimes this affects the pricing too.

4. **An order is legally binding.**

Ans. Yes, a letter of order creates a binding contract. The process of transactions up to a sale follows this sequence: first, a letter of enquiry from the buyer, there a quotation from the seller and then the acceptance of the quotation and placement of order by the buyer, which generates a contract.

B. Questions for revision

1. State the guidelines for responding to an order.
2. What important points should be included in the letter of order?

C. Drafting exercises

1. Draft a letter placing an order for a photocopying machine.
2. On behalf of the librarian, G S College of Commerce, Nagpur, write a letter of order to Venus Book Depot for the following books:

Business Finance for Beginners by Dr. V K Jain & D G Sharma. - 10 Copies
Company Law for Beginners by Dr. V K Jain - 10 copies
Income Tax for Beginners by Dr. V K Jain - 15 copies
Indirect Tax for Beginners by Dr. V K Jain - 20 copies

3. You are a bulk supplier of electronic items – washing machines and refrigerators. You have received an order from a dealer of these items in a neighbouring town. Write a letter stating the reason(s) as to why the order cannot be executed.
4. Acknowledge an order for notebooks and registers received from an upcountry stationery mart, stating that the order would be fulfilled in 15-30 days, but in any case before the start of the academic session.
5. Write a letter that is to be dispatched alongside a consignment of tractors to a dealer in Bilaspur.
6. Place an order for readymade garments (specifying the items) with Lee Garments, asking for delivery 15 days before Dashehra.
7. Modify an order placed with Rohit Metal Works for nuts and bolts, saying that they should be of brass, not aluminium, as stated earlier.
8. Place an order in tabular form for ball-pens, refills and pencils, giving the reference numbers from the seller's catalogue.
9. Your buyer has cancelled an order for custom-made steel furniture. But you have already procured raw material for executing the order. Ask him to suggest an alternative customer or pay a 5% compensation for cancellation.

■■■

CHAPTER

8

Complaints (Claims) and Adjustments

What should you know?

8.1 Complaint (Claim) Letters
8.2 Adjustment Letters

8.1 COMPLAINT (CLAIM) LETTERS

8.1.1 Introduction

Sometimes the goods/services that you buy are delayed or not upto the mark and you have to lodge a complaint with the seller so as to get an **adjustment** (i.e. redressal of complaint).

A complaint letter is to be written as the receiver would like to receive it. It should not be an angry or emotional outburst. Hence, it is to be written calmly, with the assumption that the complaint is going to be corrected. It should be written tactfully, with due consideration for the feelings of the receiving party. We must also bear in mind the possibility that the party which receives the complaint letter may be different from the one responsible for the complaint.

Thus, we need to **avoid** expressions like –

I regret to report that……
We're quite surprised to find that…
It appears that enough care was not taken…

We should also be open to the possibility that the complaint may not be warranted but the result of some misunderstanding on our (the complainant's) part.

8.1.2 Guidelines for Writing Complaints (Claims)

An effective complaint letter is well grounded in facts and is worded firmly but courteously. Here are some tips for writing it:

(i) Write a complaint letter immediately. If time is lost, the party at the other end may have difficulty in investigating.

(ii) Do not assume that the supplier was to blame. The true cause of the complaint may be elsewhere.

(iii) Make a thorough enquiry and investigation at your end and make sure you have a valid ground for complaint. Also, when writing to the supplier, give all necessary details like date, invoice no., item or items, and the exact nature of complaint.

(iv) Ask for a specific remedy or adjustment to solve the complaint.

(v) Avoid being rude or sarcastic.

(vi) Address the complaint to the department designated for the purpose, e.g. Customer Relations Department.

(*vii*) If the first complaint does not receive proper attention at the other end, then of course you may take a harder approach.

Various causes for complaints on the part of customers

Some of the major causes for complaints in ordinary business are:

(i) Wrong goods have been supplied.
(ii) The service received is not up to the mark or as agreed.
(iii) The quality of goods is not satisfactory.
(iv) The goods are received in a damaged condition.
(v) Higher prices are charged.
(vi) There is a delay in supply.

8.1.3 Useful Expressions in Writing Complaint Letters

Openings

- *Our order no. T-125 dated.... has not been delivered yet.*
- *We have to inform that our order dated.... is already seven days overdue.*
- *We have to advise that your parcel dated... against our order no. GB-445 was received in a damaged state.*
- *Upon examination of the consignment sent by you on... we find that the goods are short by 10 pieces.*

Closing phrases

- *We hope you will examine the matter immediately and inform us when the goods are likely to reach us.*
- *Would you please explore how the damage occurred and make good the loss?*
- *Please examine the matter with your despatch section and let us know at once.*
- *We hope that you will make a suitable adjustment in this case.*

8.1.4 Specimen Complaints

1. Complaint concerning goods: In case the goods are not what you ordered, they may be returned at the supplier's expense or he may arrange to collect them.

Dear Sir/Madam

Subject: Wrong goods supplied.

On 3rd March 2011, I ordered one dozen triple edge shavers of your company under my order no. A-113. On opening the parcel it was found that I had received double edge shavers. They will not serve my purpose, hence I have to ask for a replacement or refund.

Please advise how the goods may be sent back to you and a replacement obtained.

Yours faithfully

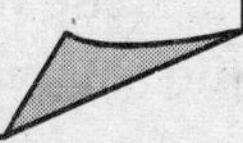

2. Complaint concerning quality: If the quality of the goods received is not upto the promise of the supplier, you may justly reject the goods or the unsold part of the goods and seek redressal.

Dear Sir/Madam

Subject: Quality difference in supplying our order no. G-45

We have to inform that in your consignment no. Mum/899 dated 5th June 2011, the diamond rings supplied are causing serious concern to our customers who are buying them. The diamond is loosely fitted and tends to come out of the ring. After receiving two complaints from our first two sales, we have stopped selling these rings.

By a separate insured parcel we are returning the rings to you for replacement with properly quality-tested rings. You will surely agree that these rings are symbolic of a lasting relationship and need adequate care in making.

Please let us know at the earliest the steps you are taking to grant us an adjustment.

Yours faithfully

3. Complaint concerning damaged goods: The complaint writer here finds that the damage to the goods is due to faulty packing, but tactfully writes to the suppliers without rubbing in the fault. The complaint stands on the merit of the facts.

Dear Sir/Madam

Subject: Our order dated 20th December 2011 for 100 tubes

This is to bring it to your notice that your consignment dated 3rd January 2011 contains 20 tubes that were punctured at the time of receiving them.

The parcel was accepted by us in the routine course. But upon opening it we discovered the fault and are unable to say how this could have occurred. You may, however, check up with your packing section.

The faulty tubes are kept aside and your representative may personally verify what we found with them. We hope you will replace them at the earliest.

We hope to hear from your soon.

Yours faithfully

8.2 ADJUSTMENT LETTERS (REPLIES TO COMPLAINTS)

8.2.1 Introduction

An adjustment letter is written in response to a complaint. It explains how the complaint will be remedied. The first step towards solving a complaint is to investigate the causes of the complaint and to assess your responsibility in the matter. Thereafter you may either grant an adjustment or refuse it.

8.2.2 Guidelines for Writing Adjustment Letters

From the supplier's point of view, to solve the complaint, the following rules may be kept in mind:

(i) A customer is satisfied when the seller takes the stand that the customer is always right. Whether this is true or not, it is good to start an enquiry into the complaint assuming that he is right.

(ii) Acknowledge the complaint promptly. State that it is being investigated. Ask for details that may be necessary to check out the facts, including documentary evidence.

(iii) If the complaint is not valid, point this out without causing offence to the party. Appeal to his sense of reason.

(iv) If you notice an error on your part, acknowledge it and set the correction in motion. Inform the customer of this, with due apologies. This will placate the receiver's feelings.

(v) Explain the circumstances in which things went wrong, and state the company policy in such cases. This will define your role in solving the complaint.

(vi) Do not name the person who is responsible for the wrong. It is your internal matter. Accept the error on behalf of the company.

(vii) Thank the customer for bringing the error to your notice.

In letters granting adjustment, mention what adjustment you are going to give and whether it is partial or full. Conclude the letter with words of goodwill and assure the customer that you will be careful that such a thing will not recur.

In letters refusing an adjustment, you need more tact. This is done with an indirect approach. Before you convey your refusal to grant an adjustment, create an atmosphere of goodwill. Explain why an adjustment is not admissible. Say this in firm and clear words. Seek a continued good business relationship.

8.2.3 Useful Expressions in Writing Adjustment Letters

Openings

- *We note with concern that the goods shipped to you on... have not reached you yet.*
- *Please accept out sincere apologies for the delay in the despatch of your order no.... dated...*
- *We regret that the goods under invoice no... dated... are short in quantity.*
- *We thank you for your letter dated... pointing out the unfortunate error of our despatch section in regard to your order dated...*

Closing phrases

- *We are taking steps to remove the delay in supply of the goods and request you to bear with us.*
- *We apologise once again for the error and assure you of our best services at all times.*
- *We trust this compensation will be satisfactory and hope to receive your continued goodwill and business.*
- *We deeply regret the inconvenience caused to you.*

8.2.4 Specimen Adjustment Letters

1. Reply to specimen complaint no. 1

Dear Mr. Aloney

We are sorry to learn from your letter that a mistake has occurred in despatching goods to you. Our despatch section is under heavy pressure due to an unprecedented demand for our goods. All the same, we request you to get in touch with M/s Krishna Medical Stores, Favvara Chowk, Indore and obtain your replacement locally. For the inconvenience to you, please accept an extra shaver as a gift.

We thank you for bringing this to our notice and assure you of our closer attention to your orders in the future.

Yours sincerely

2. Reply to specimen complaint no. 2 (admitting fault)

Dear Sir

Subject : Your complaint about rings.

Thanks for your letter dated 20th June informing us about the imperfection in the design of our rings. We have since tested these rings and agree that some if not all have a problem in manufacturing.

We would like to add, though, that this is quite an exceptional circumstance that has arisen in a newly opened section. Fortunately, now the staff and machinery in all our sections are ready to deliver the same reputed quality that we are justly known for.

We are sending you a replacement and a compensation for the postal expenses for returning the earlier goods.

We trust these goods will satisfy you and your customers fully and, in fact, positively delight them. We assure you of our best attention at all times.

Yours faithfully

3. Alternative reply to specimen complaint no. (rejecting the complaint)

Dear Sir/Madam

Subject : Your complaint about rings

We have at hand your letter dated 20th June expressing dissatisfaction with our VIRTUE rings. We have since tested each of the rings and find that the craftsmanship is perfect. As for the two rings that you have specially pointed out, we have to inform that they appear to have been tampered with, hence the problem you have stated.

In the circumstances, you will surely agree that there is no reason to reject the consignment altogether. In view of our longstanding relationship, we have repaired the two rings that had developed a fault and are sending you all your rings by courier at our cost.

Please rest assured about the time-honoured quality of VIRTUE rings.

Yours faithfully

4. Reply to specimen complaint no. 3 : The supplier understands the fault, and in the interest of his business, shows his keenness to give better service

Dear Sir/Madam

Subject: Your order no. G-105 dated 20th December

We regret to learn from your letter of 20th January 2011 that some of the tubes supplied by us reached you in a damaged state.

We are enclosing a replacement for the number stated by you, with your subsequent order dated 5th January. You may keep aside the damaged tubes for collection by our agent early in February.

He will also inform you in detail of the steps we have taken and are taking to transform the working of our supply section. We thank you for bringing the problem to our notice and bearing with us. Be assured of our superior service in the future.

Yours faithfully

A. Questions based on critical understanding. Comment in about 30 words.

1. A stiffly worded complaint is best to get attention and remedy at once.

Ans. Normally, in business a complaint is made courteously, though firmly, almost like a request or application. Because, if it turns out that the complaint is unjust and based on the writer's ignorance, the writer should be still able to look the other party in the eye. "Keep your words soft and sweet / You don't know when you may have to eat them."

2. A thorough investigation is a must for writing a complaint.

Ans. To complain and make a claim on the other party is to show his fault. Business tact requires that one should be entirely sure of the grounds of a complaint. Corporate offices are full of baseless and unresearched complaints, whereby the complainants lose face.

3. The customer is always right, especially in regard to complaints.

Ans. Nobody is always right, so why single out customers? Yet the buyer ego is a patronising ego, and a customer does not want to be told that he/she is wrong. So a complaint may be solved in the spirit that the customer is always right whether this is true or not.

4. A complaint can be so solved as to form a better business bond than before.

Ans. That is a managerial challenge. If a complaint is true and the seller accepts his mistake, and takes this as an opportunity to make his business better than before, the complaint may even lead to a better business bond. We all know that "to err is human," but few are the people who take their errors as stepping stones to higher success.

B. Questions for revision

1. Enumerate the steps is writing a complaint about being overcharged.
2. What tact is necessary in refusing to grant adjustment against a complaint?
3. What are the things in an adjustment that would really placate a buyer who has complained of supply of low quality goods? State with an example.
4. What should a manager do when his subordinate has sent to a business associate a stiffly worded but improperly investigated complaint? (Hint: Take back the complaint and apologise without blaming the employee.)
5. If a consignment of mangos is rejected because (a) 10% of the fruits were overripe and (b) the lorry carrying them reached late due to a "Rasta Roko," what would be your strategy as supplier in each case?

C. Drafting exercises

1. Your import parcel of shirts from China reveals that they are buttoned on the left flap (as against the right flap in India). Write a letter to the supplier refusing the goods.
2. A customer of a superstore has complained in writing that the sugar packet she bought was underweight. But there is no cash memo. As manager, respond to the complaint (a) granting adjustment (b) refusing adjustment.
3. As general manager of Candid Bank you receive a customer complaint about delays in ABC

branch. The complaint should have gone to the regional manager. Write to the R.M., endorsing a copy to the customer.

4. Your readymade dress retailer received your school uniforms late in the academic session and wants to reject the entire lot. Persuade him to accept a smaller consignment instead of refusing the whole lot.
5. Point out to the buyer that his complaint about being overcharged is invalid. The rates in your offer were expressed in sterling pounds and he took them for US dollars (whose exchange value in lower).
6. As branch manager of a courier service, you receive – with evidence - a complaint of delayed delivery of a parcel. The sender wants the charges back and a compensation of Rs. 5000 for the loss sustained. Write a letter granting partial adjustment under your rules.
7. Write to the branch manager of Candid Bank, pointing out the error in calculation of interest. You had complained orally, without avail.
8. Your younger brother's school collects donations every few days for vague causes. Write to the director to stop this practice.
9. The clock you purchased for your building's clock tower got out of order in its guarantee period. Complain and explain why replacement would be best.
10. Your cellphone postpaid bill shows overbilling. Complain, showing evidence, and seek a temporary as well as a permanent solution.

■■■

CHAPTER

9

Circular and Sales Letters

What should you know?

9.1 CIRCULAR LETTERS

9.1.1 Introduction

When the same information is to be sent to a number of people, circular letters are used. The occasion for sending them can be a development or instruction which is of potential interest to each receiver.

While the body of the letter remains the same in each letter, it can be personalised by insertion of the name of the recipient, his address and use of appropriate salutation. Various computer programmes make this especially easy these days. Mail merge is such a programme.

9.1.2 Guidelines for Drafting a Circular Letter

You must keep in mind the topmost common interest of all the recipients and highlight it so that each recipient feels well interested in it and finds in it a personal message. You need to follow these rules:

1. It should be to the point.
2. The main idea behind the circular letter on which you desire action should be presented in an appealing manner.
3. Making the circular letter read as if it is written personally, is another trick for success. A letter need not be addressed as *Dear Reader, Dear Customer, Dear Dealer*, etc. It can be made more effective by using the name, e.g. *Dear Mr. Chopra.*
4. Add force by using the You attitude. Circular letters are generally unsolicited letters, and to draw the reader's interest to them, the frequent use of *you* and focus on the reader's self-interest is necessary. Hence, you can avoid terms like *our customers, all customers, our clients, everyone*, etc. by rephrasing sentences.

9.1.3 Occasions for Writing Circular Letters

Some of the more common occasions for writing circular letters are:

1. Expansion of existing business, as when starting a new line of activity
2. Establishment of a new branch or reorganisation of departments within a company
3. Introduction of a new product or service
4. Change of address, phone number, etc.
5. Retirement/appointment of a partner or new appointment to major posts like general manager, managing director, etc.
6. Seasonal discounts or schemes for add-on
7. Conversion of a partnership firm into a limited company
8. Revision of prices
9. Delay in supply

9.1.4 Specimen Circular Letters

1. When moving to a new establishment

Dear Mr. Sanjay Sinha

WE ARE AT LOKHANDWALA ESTATE ALSO NOW!

......

We are glad to announce that to serve you better, we are moving to larger and more hospitable premises in the upcoming market of Lokhandwala Estate from 15th March. Our new address will be:

25, Dhanashree
Lokhandwala Estate
Nagpur – 440 027.
Tel. 0712- XXXXXXX, XXXXXXX

You will find the new location more easy to reach, with better parking facilities. There are handsome innovations in the office as well. We appreciate your valued patronage which has made this growth possible.

We look forward to meeting you at our new address and developing an even better business relationship with you.

Yours sincerely

2. Establishment of a Branch

Dear Shri Shrivastava

Meet us at our Hyderabad branch

We are pleased to inform that the recent expansion of our business in Andhra Pradesh has led to the logical development of opening a branch at Hyderabad for your greater convenience. Our senior and versatile manager Mr. N. G. Reddy will be in charge here.

This branch will enable us to handle the business in the area more promptly and efficiently and develop a closer bond with you.

The branch will start functioning from 7th December 2011 and will have the address:

111, F. A. Ali Road
Himayatnagar
Hyderabad.
Tel. XXXXXX

We trust this will provide you an incentive to direct your business in this region to our Hyderabad branch. We assure you of refined standards of service at all times.

Yours sincerely

3. A circular letter announcing discounts

Dear Mrs Pasari

A fabulous now-or-never discount on SHINEX jewellery

Now SHINEX American Diamond Jewellery is yours at discounts ranging from 40 to 60%. A necklace whose regular price is Rs. 800 is yours for Rs. 400. Bracelets whose regular price is Rs. 550 are yours for Rs. 250. And 80 other items to choose from.

This unbelievable offer is possible due to cancellation of an export order. It is open only upto 31st August 2011. For the best choice, we suggest you hurry up as our estimates show a large demand for this offer.

Our store timings have been extended, and are now 8 am to 9 pm to accommodate you better.

So, look rich without being rich. Come soon to make the most of this now-or-never offer.

Yours sincerely

9.2 SALES LETTERS

9.2.1 Introduction

A sales letter is a type of personalised advertising right into the customer's house. Unlike general media such as newspapers and public posters, it is sent to some select prospective customers whose list is prepared on the basis of their higher potential as customers. The purpose of a sales letter is to make the reader feel the need for an item and make him buy it. You take something desirable and convert it into a necessity; or you take a necessity and arouse a desire for it.

9.2.2 Guidelines for Drafting a Sales Letter

A sales letter, being a form of advertising, is framed on the principles of buyer psychology. It aims to grab the reader's attention and eventually make him buy your product.

The time-honoured formulas for a sales pitch are coded as AIDA or IDCA:

A – Attention
I – Interest
D – Desire
A – Action

Or

I – Interest
D – Desire
C – Conviction
A – Action

(i) It must get the reader's attention by an effective appeal to his needs and desires.

(ii) It must reveal the benefit of your goods or services to the reader.

(iii) It should sound convincing. This is done by facts and figures, naming satisfied users, revealing the kind of technology used, the years of experience you have, the accreditations you have, free trials, etc.

(iv) It must make the reader act and make it easy for him to do so. He may use the phone or email to get in touch, or read your website, or visit your showroom or mail a postal order coupon. The buying should be facilitated and the letter must tell how this is done.

9.2.3 Drafting a Sales Letter on the Principles of AIDA

1. Attracting attention: A catchy and novel phrase that goes directly into the reader's interests and desires is required to get his attention. In many cases this is the only sentence that is read. Hence, in minimum words the letter writer has to hook the customer to his sales talk.

Tips

- Begin with the customer and know what he wants.
- Stress value addition.
- There is little room for going off the subject.
- Draft letters according to the different customer categories.
- Make things easy to understand.

Some attention-getters are:

(a) By asking a question -
  - *Do you reach home tired?*
  - *Interested in making Rs. 50,000 a month?*

(b) By offering bargains -
  - *Benefits worth Rs. 7,000 on a brand new Savio car*

- *Knock off 5 kilograms in 7 days.*

(c) By quoting figures -

- *10,00,000 Jag motorbikes sold in 13 months*
- *No. 1 TV in 7 European countries is in India now.*

(d) By the use of "If" -

- *If you wish to chill out this summer in Simla*
- *If you wish to boost your children's IQ*

(e) By using proverbs/quotations -

- *Rome was not built in a day, nor was Sterling Tower*
- *Necessity is the mother of invention, also of Aquafresh mineral water*

(f) By using split beginnings -

- *Children's studies... husband's worries... You need a magazine to tell you all that a housewife should know.*
- *Climb up the Eiffel Tower... salute the Statue of Liberty... for as little as Rs. 99,999.*

The You attitude has to be used from the word go. You should read your own sales letter by putting yourself in the reader's shoes. You attitude will be easier to get.

2. Arouse interest: After you have hooked the reader's attention, you have to keep the letter interesting for him to go on. You have to stay close to his mind and heart, or the letter will fall flat and go unread. For this part of the letter you can begin with a question, an instruction or a quote.

(a) Appeal to his self-esteem

- *You would surely like your child to study in a prestigious school, whose very name makes the listener listen with respect.*

(b) An appeal to economy

- *Triad solar water heaters give you free hot water all the year round.*

(c) An appeal to health

- *Do your teeth shine like pearls and are tough as diamonds?*

(d) An appeal to fear

- *A cat has nine lives, but you have only one. Do you drive carefully?*

3. Create desire: What makes a product or service desirable to the prospective customer? It benefits his lifestyle in some way. If the product is something new in the market, you must describe what it does and how it can help the customer. Bring out how it is a thing which he/she misses in all existing alternatives.

Suppose you are introducing a tape recorder with two decks, one of which plays a cassette and the other records it. Begin:

> 'Now you need not go to a music shop or a studio to dub your favourite song or speech on your own cassette. ULTRA double-decker tape recorder has an in-built mechanism by which you can carry the recording from one cassette to another with over 99.5% fidelity.'

The appropriate class of reader will certainly find that there is not only a new product but also one that gives great quality.

Carry conviction: What convinces a reader about your claims on behalf of your product or service? Is the name in itself a guarantee? Are there testimonies from people whom the readers revere and trust, like great public figures? What is the experience of users elsewhere? How many numbers have been sold? What about the reputation of the technology used? Is there a warranty to back up the product and the assurance of after-sales service? Can you give a demonstration or a free trial offer? Can you give a money-back guarantee? What is the standing of other products from your company? If you are no. 1 in suitings, your readymade shirts may naturally carry the benefit of that reputation. Who are the satisfied users? E.g.,

"Our list of satisfied and repeat-order clients includes major government corporations like... and importers from Malaysia, Brazil, Afghanistan, Japan and Italy."

Such a standing will surely put the customer at ease and he can rely on the experience of reputed names.

However, in a sales letter it is against law to make false or exaggerated claims, and the words used for promotion must be backed up by performance.

4. Induce action: The closing note of a sales letter is an appeal for action and that too without delay, before the effect of the sales pitch wears off. Or before the opportunity to buy is over. You can use phrases like this:

- *So send for a free prospectus now. Write or ring...*
- *If you avail of this offer before 30th June, you can get the benefit of our special 10% discount.*
- *The free music system on our car is only till the stocks last. So hurry up.*
- *Fill in this order coupon and post it today with a DD for Rs. 1000.*
- *To subscribe, all you have to do is, fill up the reply-paid postcard and pay the postman on delivery.*

9.2.4 Specimen Sales Letters

As we go to write sales letters, we must remember that the reader is looking for his benefit and the reason why. This has to form the meat of your letter.

1. A sales letter promoting a magazine

Dear Mr. Kushwaha

The world-on-a-plate magazine

No other magazine delivers the world to you in 120 pages month after month as STORICA does..

To be well-informed today, you need to know about the important people, places and events that concern you and influence your life in a hundred ways.

Come, be a part of the global family and read about the future of the planet, the new emperors of entertainment, the scientific feats that are transforming lives, the habits you need to worry about, how to enjoy deeper marital bliss, where are the best workplaces for your talents...and a lot more.

Our expert editors choose for you from their wide experience. The inaugural issue of STORICA had a record sale of 1,14,000 copies off the counters.

This amazing magazine is offered to you at Rs. 600 per year (individual issue Rs. 75) with no risk to you. If at any point you are dissatisfied with the reading you get, you can cancel the subscription and get refund for the undelivered issues.

All you have to do is fill in the attached subscription coupon and mail it to us in the accompanying postage paid cover. You can pay the postman on delivery of the first issue.

One thing more. **If your subscription reaches here before 31-10-2011**, you will have a free gift of a PERSIST alarm clock. You also stand a one-in-50 chance to win a pair of ULTRONIC sunglasses.

Yours sincerely

2. A sales letter offering a new type of product

Dear Shri Sunil Saxena

Alarm clock that will ring on till you wake up

There are times when all of us shut down the wake-up alarm and go back to sleep – and miss the train.

Fortunately, this need not happen to you now. The new PERSIST alarm clock has a mechanism by which it gives a repeat alarm every five minutes for one hour. What is more, its sound is so soft and musical that you wake up from sweet dreams to a sweet day.

In the rushed modern life, in which stress slows you down and time limits push you fast, PERSIST comes as a blessing to keep you ticking right on time. It uses advanced Swiss technology from the home of great watches, and melodies from musical maestros. It runs on one inexpensive pencil cell for about six months of normal use and is greatly shock-proof.

This revolutionary time-teller is a must for every house, a faithful companion in travel, and comes in 60 handsome designs.

We enclose a list of dealers in PERSIST and you will find one right in your town at a convenient location. Be among the first to get there and race ahead of time.

Very truly yours

Padma Khetan
Marketing Counsellor

3. Sales letter for a luxury product

Dear Mr. Srikkant

ULTRONIC : Hot goggles for cool eyes

You have a fine eye for the good things of life, and we have the finest sunglasses for your eyes.

We call ULTRONIC sunglasses the hottest goggles in the land, but the truth is that they keep your eyes cool and protected during drives, on beach holidays, at blazing construction sites or while enjoying your favourite game or sport. The only problem with them is that others will be looking at you and not at the match, but that problem is theirs, not yours.

ULTRONIC designs are contoured to fit your eyes to perfection and protect them from all angles. The lenses are highly transparent in one direction, giving you a clear bright view even while your eyes stay covered. They are scratch-resistant and guaranteed for one year. The frames don't go loose as with ordinary goggles, which slip due to sweat or constant wear. Your success and demanding nature has deserved this invention.

These ULTRONIC sunglasses are riding a success wave in America and Europe and their reputation is travelling at the speed of light. This introductory offer, for your eyes only, will give you the famed lenses at 10 per cent discount if you mail this order coupon (postpaid or prepaid as you choose) within 15 days.

We enclose a list of endorsements from celebrities who found ULTRONIC sunglasses incredibly precious. But finally, seeing is believing. Or rather, seeing through them is believing.

Yours sincerely

Angela Coutinho
Area Sales Chief

4. Sales letter offering a discount on goods

Dear Mrs Tejasvini Mohta

PARIDHAAN saris at a fabulous festival discount

This Diwali season comes to you wrapped in a beautiful offer. A discount of 10 to 25% is offered on PARIDHAAN saris, famed for their designing and export breakthroughs. A new array of computer designed saris is at hand to reflect your festive mood in a variety of ways. They are expressive without being expensive now.

Further, you will be entitled to a charming decoration item as a gift on purchase of five saris. You will simply love these saris for your own use and as gifts to your dear ones. We are expecting a large rush, so pick up your time right now.

Have a great choice at a great price.

Yours sincerely

Sadhana Sreshtha
Vama Emporium

5. Sales letter offering a news magazine

INDIA

TODAY

Making sense of India today

Dear Friend

Over 13.8 million readers rely on one source, for a stimulating and scrupulously accurate picture of India, week after week – INDIA TODAY.

INDIA TODAY delivers wholesome content in a crisp, contemporary style. From sharp news-notes to in-depth stories to a lively back-of-the-book section, covering every aspect of life from politics to personalities, leisure to life-style, society to showbiz, science to sports, books to business, the arts, travel, health, InfoTech and beyond.

INDIA TODAY not only brings you a ringside view of events as they happen but also refreshing human interest stories from the varied world around us: stories like —

"Kerala : Destination 2001"
"Ayurveda: The Age-Old Science of Life"
"Survey of the Top 10 Colleges of India"
And of course our regular section "Offtract"

I have great pleasure in presenting the INDIA TODAY **Twin Bonanza Offer** that guarantees to bring you understanding, a taste for the finer things in life, and great gifts.

The **Twin Bonanza Offer** gives you the additional facility of subscribing to INDIA TODAY PLUS, the country's premier lifestyle magazine and avail of amazing discounts and gifts. You can of course subscribe to only INDIA TODAY if you so choose.

This offer is available only for new/renewal subscriptions received by us till March 15, 2002.

Use the enclosed subscription form and Reply Paid Envelope to send in your order today.

I look forward to welcoming you to the INDIA TODAY family of discerning readers.

Let's make sense of India, together.

Warm regards.

Sanjay Malik
Associate Publisher

Adapted

6. Voluntary offer of a loan to a depositor with a bank

ICICI Bank

July 1, 2011

Dear Mr Rajeev Chhabra,

Ask for your pre-approved "CASH-IN" loan of Rs.35,000

Now whenever you need cash, you need not look beyond your ICICI Bank Credit Card. By virtue of our relationship, a pre-approved loan of Rs.35,000 has been reserved for you and can be delivered to you as soon as you demand it.

CASH-IN has a number of compelling benefits:

- **Quick to get:** Avail of direct transfer to your ICICI Bank account, or ask for a demand draft to be delivered in 72 hours.
- **Pre-approved**: Just call 98904 78000 and dial 1122 to reach the CASH-IN desk or SMS 'CASHIN' to 676766. We will call you and confirm your request.
- **Free insurance cover**: You get free Personal Accident Insurance that is 5 times your loan amount. And, free Credit Shield equal to the loan amount.
- **No documentation**: No paperwork required! No post-dated cheques!
- **Easy repayment**: Equated monthly instalments (EMIs) billed to your Credit Card account.

Now, take a look at how convenient the EMIs work out. Here's an example.

Monthly instalment per Rs.1000 @13% flat interest p.a.

Tenure -->	12 months	18 months	24 months
EMI (including interest)	Rs.94.16	Rs.66.38	Rs.52.50

(A processing fee @ 1% is charged on the loan amount. Service tax @12.24% payable on the interest portion of the EMI.)

Hurry! This special offer is valid only till July 31, 2011. So, go on, make that call!

Don't hold back. Get CASH-in for anything you wish. For renovation or purchases. Or just to fulfil the desires of your near and dear ones.

Sincerely,

Anup Saha
Business Head – Retail Payment Solutions

Adapted

7.

Talwalkars

73 years of fitness experience

Dear Sir

Fitness solutions – first time in Nagpur

It is with great joy that we enter your wonderful city of Nagpur. This feeling increases manifold when we get an opportunity to meet fitness lovers like you, who have not only achieved great success in life but also know how to enjoy life in its true sense.

We have a 73-year-old tradition of providing the very best in fitness through our 33 centres spread over the country. Our newly opened Nagpur Centre offers you world-class equipment from Precor, Hammer Strength, Life Fitness and Icarian along with a few indigenously manufactured ones for cardio and strength training.

More than the equipment, however, it is the deep commitment of our fitness trainers, counsellors, doctors and dieticians who will help you look good, feel great and perform even better. Our superbly effective programmes for weight loss, weight gain and weight management are designed to give you faster and better results. They go a long way in helping you lead healthier, more enjoyable lives.

As a successful person, you will agree that everyone has to find time to pursue his/her goals in life. In the area of physical fitness, may I assure you that 45–60 minutes, 3 days a week is adequate to build a fitter body and enjoy the fruits of life in a more joyful manner.

Fitness, like success, is not automatic. Each of us has to **work out** for it. Talwalkars have invested a lot of talent in creating this excellent opportunity for Nagpurians to keep fit with tried and tested systems and world-class equipment. I can assure you that your fitness schedule will be easy to follow and enjoyable to perform. You, your entire family and friends of any age, can see striking difference in just 3 to 6 months.

We have a very interesting **early bird offer**. Drop in before 10th June 2005 and you will know more about it.

Thank you.

Yours in fitness,

Madhukar Talwalkar

Talwalkars Prime Fitness
401/404, Milestone, Ramadas Peth, Nagpur 440 010. Ph: (0712) 5618 397 / 5618 380

Adapted

A. Questions based on critical understanding. Comment in about 30 words.

1. **Circular letters are unsolicited letters.**

Ans. Circular letters are sent to a large member of customers aiming at conveying information like introducing a new product, change of address, seasonal discounts, increase in prices, etc. Thus such letters are unsolicited and mass produced.

2. **Circular letters differ from letters of quotation.**

Ans. Circular letters are unsolicited and mass-produced to convey some information. A letter of quotation is a specific offer of goods or services made in response to an enquiry and includes details such as price, mode of payment, conditions of delivery etc.

3. **Sales letters are persuasive in nature.**

Ans. Sales letters are intended to persuade the receiver to buy the sender's product or service. They have, therefore, to be in adequate detail, be imaginatively worded and appealing. They may be accompanied by a well-illustrated pamphlet or literature highlighting special features.

4. **Circular letters differ from letters of quotation.**

Ans. Circular letters are unsolicited and mass produced to convey some information. A letter of quotation is a specific offer of goods or services made in response to an enquiry and includes details as price, mode of payment, conditions of delivery etc.

5. **AIDA is a guide for drafting an effective sales letter.**

Ans. AIDA stands for Attention, Interest, Desire and Action. As sales letters are addressed to customers, they should generate all of the above states in order to be effective.

6. **You can appeal to reader's self-esteem or sense of economy to arouse his interest in a sales letter.**

Ans. A sales letter is unsolicited, and the seller has to talk about the consumers' various benefits. Everybody is interested in a better image in society and in saving money. Hence these appeals work, only they must be smartly and innovatively worded.

7. **A sales letter has to make buying easy to get action from the reader.**

Ans. This is the bottomline of a sales letter — does the buyer fill in the coupon, or lift the telephone or do that particular thing by which he commits himself to buying. The easier it is to place an order or go for shopping, the more the sales.

8. **A desire for a product is a stronger response than interest in the product.**

Ans. Interest refers to wanting to *know*. Desire refers to wanting to *have*. What does anyone go and get – something that one is missing or begins to miss from the time of reading the sales letter. Something that will bring the person fulfilment of some kind. And since desires are complex, the methods for arousing them are varied.

9. **To buy a product, the audience must believe the seller.**

Ans. Everyone thinks before spending in a competitive market. Given two equally desirable products, one goes for the product which carries greater conviction. It may be in the form of testimony of satisfied users, of famous and popular personalities, or proven technology, or ISO certification etc **B. Questions for revision**

1. Discuss the characteristics of a sales letter.
2. Illustrate the use of AIDA strategy in the drafting of a sales letter. Identify and describe the basic components of such communication.
3. What do you understand by sales letters? What are the objectives of preparing sales letters? What precautions should be taken while writing a sales letter?
4. What do you understand by a circular letter? Under what conditions is it written? What precaution should be taken while writing it?

C. Drafting exercises

1. As a manager of Bank of Baroda write a sales letter to your customers to promote the credit cards introduced by your bank.
2. You have started a computer centre. Write a sales letter to business houses in your city, offering to train their staff in using computers.
3. You have got a franchise of the reputed teaching institute Central Academy of Professional Studies for preparing students for the CA exam. Draft a sales letter to be sent to potential students of your city.
4. Write a sales letter to promote the sales of the following: a. Inverter b. Digital camera c. Latest books according to new syllabus d. Vacuum cleaners e. Basic computer course.
5. Write a letter to your dealers offering attractive incentive schemes for achieving higher sales.
6. Write a letter to the consumers of your company's products about a revision in the prices, giving reasons.
7. A sudden strike has been called by the transport operators. As a result, there is a likelihood of delay in despatch of goods to the dealers. Draft a suitable circular letter addressed to them.
8. Write a circular letter to your dealers about launching of a new consumer product.
9. You have published some new books on Commerce. Write a suitable letter (circular letter) to give information to different booksellers and teachers.

■■■

CHAPTER

10

Collection Letters

What should you know?

10.1 INTRODUCTION

Collection letters are written when you have to recover/collect your dues from a customer, for the goods or services given on credit. If the customer has not paid in time, it becomes necessary to remind him. This is a delicate situation, because on the one hand you want to retain the business relationship and on the other you want your money in time. Hence, tact of language is necessary to impress upon the customer (who may himself be in financial difficulties) to pay your dues anyway. In some cases, it is a reality of business that you have to accept part payment also.

10.2 GUIDELINES FOR WRITING COLLECTION LETTERS

1. **Tact and restraint:** To remind someone that he has failed to meet his financial commitment is a sensitive matter. Hence you have to use a language of tact and restraint. Moreover, you have to provide for two circumstances: that the payment is already sent/received but not within your knowledge, or that the goods/services are unsatisfactory. The buyer may be facing difficulties in realising value out of your supplies. At the same time, some customers are habitually late or negligent. Therefore each case will have to be taken on merits.
2. **Polite tone:** A good businessman has his future business angle in mind and uses polite language in a collection letter. He avoids hurting the reader. Even if it is the last collection letter threatening legal action, good business requires that you be polite and use words like "with regret."
3. **Show understanding of the customer's problems:** If the customer is caught up in a difficult financial situation himself, has no ready money and has been unable to realise cash out of your goods, he may have good reasons for not paying or not being able to pay. As a collector of dues, you may have to get involved to some extent in his problems and find a common solution to get value for your goods. This sensitivity needs to be shown in your letter and overall approach to the collection.
4. **Progressive steps in writing a series of collection letters:** It may happen that one collection

call is not enough to get your dues. The customer may wilfully or otherwise default on payment. The stages in writing collection letters in a series are:

(i) Formal reminder, assuming he will pay, in a mild tone.

(ii) A firmer and persuasive reminder stressing the necessity to pay here and now.

(iii) "Last resort" letter, which states that the customer must pay, otherwise legal action will follow.

10.3 FIRST STAGE COLLECTION LETTERS

At this stage the letter is a formal one. Even a printed form letter can be used. It is presumed that the customer just forgot to pay and will act upon the reminder at once.

Useful starters for first collection letters

- *We notice that your account, which was due for payment on... is outstanding in our books.*
- *We have to invite your attention to our invoice no... for Rs...*
- *We have to remind you that we have not yet received the balance shown against your name in our statement dated... amounting to Rs... which is now more than a month overdue.*

Closers

- *We hope you will settle the bill by return.*
- *We look forward to your remittance within the next few days.*
- *In case you have sent the payment in the meantime, you may ignore this notice.*

Specimen formal reminder

Dear Sir/Madam

Subject: Outstandings under our invoice no... dated...

This is to call your attention to our above invoice, the payment for which was due on 30th January 2011. A copy of it is enclosed for your ready reference.

We may remind you that you already have our best price on this deal and that you had agreed to settle the bill promptly.

It is possible that there may be some oversight in your accounts department, and now we have to request you to speed up the payment.

Yours faithfully

10.4 PERSUASIVE/ FIRM REMINDER

If the first collection letter does not bring in the payment after a due wait, a second letter is sent in about 15-20 days. In this letter the language is firmer but the tone is still polite. You are not to annoy the customer but rather seek his cooperation.

Some starters

- *We see from our records that our reminder to you for payment vide our invoice dated... is to this date unresponded.*

- *We refer to our letter dated... requesting you to settle your dues.*
- *We have to remind you again of your dues under our invoice no... dated... for Rs..., for which our first reminder dated... seems to be unresponded by you.*

Closers

- *We urge you once again to take this up on priority and settle the dues at once.*
- *We sincerely hope that this time you will take a serious note of the dues and clear them immediately.*
- *We trust that this impresses upon you the urgency of the matter and that you will act forthwith.*

Specimen collection letter stage II

> Dear Sir/Madam
>
> **Subject: Reminder for bill payment.**
>
> We refer to our letter of... requesting you to settle the dues under invoice no.... dated... and find that there is no reply yet. We hope you realise that this hampers our trade cycle and the money is required immediately. If, however, you have any special reason for not paying/ responding so far, you are welcome to have a clear dialogue with us.
>
> In view of your past good record, we await the payment within the next few days.
>
> Yours faithfully

10.5 LAST RESORT LETTER/ FINAL COLLECTION LETTER

If there is no response to the earlier collection letters, a final collection letter is sent according to the following plan:

(a) Record the past efforts for collection.
(b) Offer one more chance to pay.
(c) Mention the legal action that will be necessary if this request is also ignored.
(d) Set a deadline for payment.

Some starters

- *We wrote to you on... and again on... for recovery or our dues vide invoice no.... dated..., with still no action from you.*
- *We have to say that our earlier requests dated... and... for settlement of our bill dated... for... remain unhonoured by you.*
- *We note with surprise and disappointment that our two successive letters concerning the overdues from you in respect of our bill dated... are not answered.*

Closers

- *Now unless we receive our dues by... we shall have no option but to put the matter in the hands of our lawyers.*
- *Please treat this as our last request for payment in the matter before we resort to law. But we still hope you will act within a fortnight and pay up the dues.*
- *We still hope you will remit by... and save yourself the considerable cost and inconvenience of legal action.*

Specimen last resort letter/final collection letters

1.

23rd December 2010

Dear Sir/Madam

Subject: Final reminder to pay overdues

We refer to our communications to you dated… and… requesting you to pay your dues under invoice no… dated… We regret to find that the dues remain outstanding.

In the past we had regular payments from you, hence we chose to remind you and wait for these payments. The continued non-payment leaves us little option but to ask our lawyers to handle the matter.

However, as a matter of further concession, we now request you to settle the account by 10th January 2011 and conclude the matter satisfactorily.

Yours faithfully

2.

Dear Sir

Subject: Final request for payment of dues

We refer you to our invoice no. 104 dated 23rd March 2011 under which we shipped goods worth Rs. 56, 750 to you on 15 days' credit. Since the payment did not arrive in time, we wrote to you reminding thereof on 15th April and 2nd May, without results. We even gave you the option to make a partial payment, which was ignored by you.

Now if the payment does not materialise within 15 days of this letter, we shall have no choice but to seek a legal remedy. Hence, we now finally request you to remit the sum before 10th June 2011 and avoid the unpleasantness of legal action.

Yours faithfully

3.

Dear Sir

Despite repeated requests for settlement of your dues on account of our shipment dated... (invoice no...) the dues have still not been paid. Please pay Rs. 19,900 immediately by one of the methods described overleaf.

Failing immediate settlement, we shall have no alternative but to authorise legal action for recovery of the debt : the details will be passed on to our Collection Manager who will contact you.

Yours faithfully

P. K. Das
Accounts Department

QUESTION BANK

A. Questions based on critical understanding. Comment in about 30 words.

1. Chasing payments is a problem that has to be tackled with utmost care and cordiality.

Ans. In chasing payments, the supplier has to see that the defaulting buyer still remains a customer. So it begins with a courtesy phone call and then graduates to reminders. These are progressively stronger, but still you should keep a human face.

2. First reminders are generally short and sweet letters.

Ans. First collection letter is mild. The customer is just reminded about the payment which is due, in polite words. It is presumed the customer will pay and he has just forgotten the payment. This is often the case. Hence the insistence on politeness.

B. Questions for revision

1. "Correspondence with customers should be done with utmost courtesy and firmness." Comment. How can this be ensured in case of reminders and collection letters?

C. Drafting exercises

1. One of your customers had defaulted on payments and yet has placed a fresh order. Write a letter to him reminding of the payments due, and firmly letting him know that in terms of the trade practice of the company, fresh orders would be executed only after the previous dues are cleared.
2. Write an effective "last resort" letter to a client who has not replied to any of your five letters sent so far.
3. Maldar Industries have supplied goods on credit to Manmani Agencies. The payment is outstanding for the last three months. Write a persuasive collection letter.
4. Write a letter to one of your dealers who has, despite reminders, not paid the outstanding bills. Threaten legal action after setting a deadline for the final payment.
5. Write a final reminder to a major debtor who has failed to keep his commitment to make payment of monthly instalments.

■■■

CHAPTER

11

Status Enquiries and Credit Letters

What should you know?

11.1 INTRODUCTION

In business, the buyer sometimes desires credit, and then the seller has to estimate the buyer's creditworthiness. Although this is a routine matter, a credit decision is a critical one.

A businessman may expand his business by giving credit to the right parties, assured of payment in due course. The practice is to ask the buyer to give names of two of his suppliers or trade associates who may report on his credit standing, and the name of his bankers. A party's credit standing (status) depends on:

(a) **Capital:** His investment in business and the net worth of his business.

(b) **Capacity:** The potential of the party to generate profits and repay his dues. This depends, among other things, on his ability and opportunities.

(c) **Character:** The party should be basically honest in its dealings and have a will to pay up.

(d) **Circumstances:** Even a sound party that is willing to pay is subject to circumstances. The seller should know the state of affairs of the buyer's business at the time of giving credit. Environmental factors, the general trends in his business, political conditions and economic laws are the circumstances that may create ups and downs in a business.

Outline of the cycle of credit and status correspondence

From the time the buyer makes a request for credit till the grant/ refusal of credit, following are the situations for writing letters:

1. Buyer asking for credit from the seller

2. Seller asking for references – existing suppliers, banks, etc. – who may report on the buyer's creditworthiness. Trade organisations, merchants' chamber and agencies specialising in credit information may also be consulted.
3. Writing to references or bankers to know the buyer's status. A business house may seek the information through its own banker, and such information is freely exchanged between banks. However, a bank does not respond to a status query from a non-client.
4. Response to a status enquiry. The respondent may give a favourable report, unfavourable report or a neutral report.
5. Grant/partial grant/refusal of credit by the seller (issue of a credit letter).

Cycle of credit application, status enquiry and credit decision

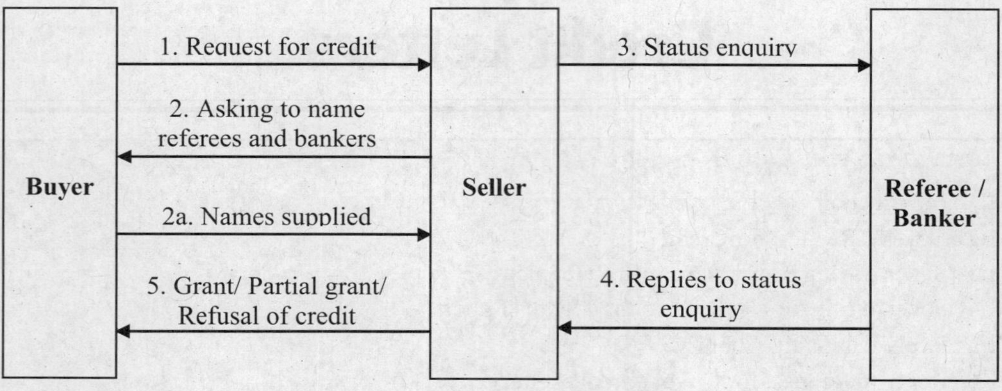

11.2 BUYER'S REQUEST FOR CREDIT

When a buyer makes a request for credit he should volunteer the references and banker's name with whom the seller may make enquiries. The credit asked for should be within his financial power to pay, and the seller should get a clear picture of this financial power.

Specimen letter

Dear Sir

Subject: Request for credit on purchases

We refer to your quotation dated 31st July and are willing to place orders for assorted plastic goods worth Rs. 50,000 with you. Since these are fairly slow-moving items and we have to stock a variety of goods to please varied customer tastes, we have to request you to grant us six months' credit on the purchase. To convince you of our creditworthiness, we furnish the names of two of our suppliers who are satisfied with our dealings and with whom you may enquire about us.

Further, our bankers are Canara Bank, Sadar Bazar, Nagpur (A/c no. CC S-125).

We trust this will help you decide the matter to your satisfaction.

Yours faithfully

Encl.

11.3 SELLER ASKING THE BUYER TO FURNISH REFERENCES

This letter is structured thus:

1. Thank the client for his order.
2. Explain why status enquiry is necessary. (This is a routine.)
3. Offer goods against cash payment in the meantime.

Specimen letter

Request to buyer to name referees (in case they are not already named)

Dear Sir

Subject: Your request for supplying steel furniture on credit

We thank you for your order dated 4th August. In this connection, since you have asked for credit on the supplies, we shall be happy if you furnish the names and addresses of two referees to whom we may write in the matter. We hope you will appreciate that this is a routine enquiry and we need to complete our records for credit sales.

You may please name your bankers also who can furnish financial information about you.

While this correspondence is under way, you may like to buy goods on c.o.d.* basis. We look forward to a good business relationship with you.

Yours faithfully

*cash on delivery

11.4 SELLER WRITING TO THE REFEREE FOR A STATUS REPORT

All status enquiries are delicate and confidential matters. Great tact is required in asking for and furnishing status information. A status enquiry is structured along the following lines:

(a) Name the prospective buyer and the amount and period of credit desired by him.

(b) Tell the referee that he has been named by your buyer.

(c) State clearly that you wish to know the referee's experience in credit dealings with the buyer. Enquire whether they are, at this time, good enough for the credit asked for by them.

(d) Offer similar information to them, should they need it.

(e) Assure that the information will be treated as confidential.

1. Specimen status enquiry to an existing supplier of the buyer

Dear Sir

Subject: Confidential enquiry about the credit status of M/s XYZ

We have to state that M/s XYZ have recently approached us for credit sales to the extent of Rs. 1,50,000. They are a new customer and have furnished your name as their referee in the matter. Would you please write to us about your experience with them as a creditor, especially as regards promptness in settling their dues. Please also let us know whether you consider them a fair credit proposition at present for the amount mentioned above, the period of credit being three months.

Please rest assured that the information given by you will be treated as confidential. We shall be most willing to provide similar information to you in case you require it.

Yours faithfully

2. Status enquiry with buyer's banker (written to your own banker)

Confidential

Dear Sir

Subject: Status enquiry about Ayurvedgram Health Centre, Lonavla

Ayurvedgram Health Centre, Lonavla have asked us to furnish medical supplies worth Rs. 4,00,000 on credit and have given the name of State Bank of India, Lonavla as their bankers. We request you to contact their bankers in the matter and let us know whether such a credit is a safe business proposition.

An early enquiry is requested to help us to execute the order promptly.

Yours faithfully

3. Specimen status enquiry from one banker to another

Canara Bank
Sion, Mumbai
Tel: xxxx xxxx Fax: xxxx xxxx

The Branch Manager
State Bank of India
Lonavla

Private and confidential

Dear Sir

Subject: Status enquiry about Ayurvedgram Health Centre, Lonavla

We understand that Ayurvedgram Health Centre, Lonavla are your clients. Our client Svadeshi Medicos have been approached by them for credit supplies of Rs. 4,00,000. Please let us know whether you consider the grant of such credit to Ayurvedgram Health Centre, Lonavla a safe business deal.

Your considered opinion will be much appreciated. May we request an early reply so that our client may process your client's order.

Thanks for your cooperation.

Yours faithfully

11.5 REPLY TO A STATUS ENQUIRY

When you sit as a judge on a party's credit rating, you have a large responsibility which you have to carry out with care and tact. In particular, if you are supposed to know certain relevant financial matters, and you do not inform the enquirer properly, you fail in your duty. If the credit goes bad, you cannot escape the blame in the matter. The following care may be taken when answering a status enquiry:

(*a*) Address it to the enquirer precisely and make it confidential.

(*b*) State the nature of connection you have had with the party under reference and the kind of dealings you have had.

(*c*) As a banker you may write the basic details like the constitution of the firm, date of establishment, etc.

(*d*) You may refer to the party's latest balance sheet and give concrete figures about its capital, net worth, etc. An audited statement may be consulted for replying to a status enquiry.

(*e*) Whether you have given them credit (as a supplier) or credit limits (as a banker).

(*f*) Your experience in getting your dues back.

(*g*) Your opinion about the party's creditworthiness for the amount in question.

(*h*) Request the enquirer to treat the information as confidential and use a standard clause about disowning responsibility in the matter (see specimen letters).

Specimen 1. Reply to a status enquiry as an existing supplier of credit (favourable reply)

STRICTLY CONFIDENTIAL

Dear Sir

Subject: Your status enquiry about M/s Indranil Builders

We refer to your enquiry dated 7th February about M/s Indranil Builders, New Delhi.

M/s IB have been dealing with us since 2001 and have enjoyed credit to the extent of Rs.15,00,000. They have always been timely in meeting their financial commitments to us and enjoy a good reputation in the trade.

We consider that their request to you for credit of Rs. 10,00,000 is within their means and a good business risk.

This of course is our personal opinion and you may use your own judgement in granting credit to them..

Your faithfully

2. Neutral (non-committal) reply to a status enquiry

Private and confidential

Dear Madam

Subject: Your status enquiry

We refer to your enquiry about the credit status of Jaykay Glass Works. We have to state that the firm has lately been reconstituted with the induction of a new partner. We have had little experience of the firm since its reconstitution and hence are unable to say authoritatively about their status now.

We regret our inability to help you in the matter.

Yours faithfully

3. Referee's unfavourable opinion on the buyer's status

CONFIDENTIAL

Dear Sir

Subject: Your status enquiry

We have known for three years the party about whom you have enquired in your letter dated 15th September.

We wish to advise that they had a credit line from us but have been repaying their dues with delays of 15 days to six months, usually with repeat requests. We are delisting them as our debtor.

You may therefore make your own assessment of the party and take a decision on your own.

This information is supplied in strict confidence.

Yours faithfully

4. A banker's reply to a status enquiry (from another banker)

Dear Sir

Subject: Your status enquiry

We have at hand your letter dated 6th March enquiring about Standard Medicare.

We enclose details about their constitution and creditworthiness on the attached sheet.
This is in strict confidence and without responsibility on our part.

Yours faithfully

Encl.

Enclosure

Status enquiry about: Standard Medicare, Bilaspur

Constitution: Constituted in 1999 as a partnership firm of
Shri A. K. Shah, age 59 years
Shri J. K. Shah, age 32 years
Shri A. J. Shah, age 27 years
Estimated net worth: Rs. 25.4 lakhs
Reputation: Good
Remarks: The firm enjoys a credit line with us and their account shows a healthy turnover.
Their term loan accounts are regular for the past three years.

5. Banker's reply to client about the status of a party obtained from the party's banker

Confidential

Dear Sir

Subject: Your enquiry about Arihant Tiles Ltd.

We refer to your letter of 24th August asking us to enquire about the status of Arihant Tiles Ltd. On the basis of the report obtained from their bankers, Bank of Baroda, Jamshedpur, we wish to state as under:

ATL have been dealing with this bank for 18 months. They enjoy a line of credit to the extent of Rs. 1.55 crores and maintain a satisfactory account. However, the period of dealing is rather limited, hence you may exercise due discretion in business expansion on credit with them.

This is without any responsibility on our part.

Yours faithfully

6. Banker's reply to a client reporting unsatisfactory credit record of the party

Private and confidential

Dear Sir

Subject: Your enquiry about Swapnalok Hotel

We refer to your letter no. SBI/88 dated 2nd January, asking us to make status enquiries with the bankers of Swapnalok Hotel. We have since received replies from ICICI Bank, Indore and Indore District Cooperative Bank Ltd. We must say that both the bankers report having large overdues from SH. Moreover, SH has serious police cases against it and the bankers are about to file suits for recovery of their dues. As such it is considered inadvisable to extend credit to them. You may use the information discreetly and attach no responsibility in the matter to us.

Yours faithfully.

11.6 REPLY TO REQUEST FOR CREDIT (CREDIT LETTER)

On the strength of status reports obtained from the referees named by the buyer and the reports from his bankers, the supplier decides to grant credit or refuse it. In either case, the letter has to be cautious, since credit is always a matter of chance. The reply to a request for credit may be structured along the following lines:

(*a*) Thank the buyer and refer to his request.
(*b*) If granting credit, state the limit, period of credit and other terms such as overdue interest.
(*c*) If refusing credit, it is better to avoid naming the exact source of information which makes you refuse credit and not assign a specific reason for your refusal. Mentioning names may involve other parties, who may not like to be quoted. Be frank, but be diplomatic. Try to retain business.
(*d*) In case of a refusal, offer to do business on c.o.d. (cash on delivery) basis.
(*e*) Express goodwill.

1. Partial grant of credit

Dear Sir

Subject: Your request for credit

We refer to your letter dated 8th March for opening a line of credit with us for supply of woollen blankets. We are pleased to state that a credit limit of Rs. 45,000 has been sanctioned to you. Though this is somewhat short of the figure you named, we hope you will understand that we are governed by market forces and have made our best offer to you. Normally, our credit is for 30 days, whereafter overdue interest @16% is chargeable.

We sincerely hope that you will find it profitable to start business with us. The matter may be reviewed after one year. For supplies in excess of the limit, you may pay cash on delivery.

We assure you of our best terms.

Yours faithfully

2. Refusing credit on account of an unfavourable report from bankers

Dear Sir

Subject: Your request for credit

We refer to your credit application dated 9th July and wish to state that we have given the matter our careful consideration. Given the position we are in, we are unable to extend credit to you. At the same time you may avail of our quality product on c.o.d. basis and take the benefit of the good reputation that our products enjoy in the market.

We hope to be of service to you.

Yours faithfully

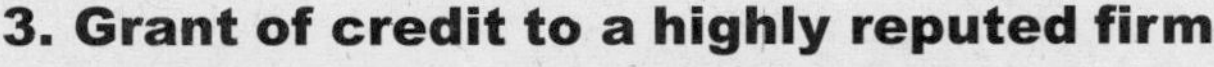

3. Grant of credit to a highly reputed firm

Dear Sir

Subject: Your request for credit

Thanks for your letter of 1st March requesting for a line of credit of Rs. 1.50 lakhs to you. We are happy to extend this facility to you with immediate effect. We enclose a charter of our standard terms of credit.

We look forward to an excellent business relationship with you.

Yours faithfully

4. Suspension of credit line due to unsatisfactory payment record

Dear Sir

Subject: Your credit line with us

We invite your attention to our correspondence about supplies on credit and recovery of dues.

You would note that you have enjoyed a large credit facility of Rs. 75,000 with us, but in the last three instances we have had to write two to three reminders, and send fax messages and our representative personally to secure our payments. In the circumstances, our own trade is affected, not to speak of the inconvenience of writing reminders, etc. As such the credit stands withdrawn from now on.

We may add that since you already have a market for our goods in your area, you may keep up the business relationship with cash purchases.

We assure you of our best services at all times.

Yours faithfully

A. Questions based on critical understanding. Comment in about 30 words.

1. If you receive a status enquiry about a defaulting buyer of yours, you need not reply to it.

Ans. That is not a good trade practice, since the trading community prospers by a fruitful exchange of information. To refuse to reply to a third party when you can caution him, is to miss an opportunity to earn his goodwill. Non-repliers may receive the same treatment in their hour of need.

2. Capital, capability and character sufficiently define a party's worth for credit.

Ans. This omits the fourth traditional aspect – circumstances. A capable, moneyed and honest party, too, may be subject to circumstances such as depression, glut in the market, tax laws, coming of new technology which makes old technology outdated, etc. The creditworthiness changes with circumstances, too.

3. You as a businessman can directly write to the buyer's bank to get a status report.

Ans. As a rule bankers **do not** respond to status queries from non-clients. You have to route the enquiry through your banker, since status information is freely exchanged between banks.

4. A status enquiry letter is sent by a customer seeking information about price, quality of goods, etc. to be purchased.

Ans. A status enquiry is a letter sent with the aim of finding out a customer's creditworthiness. Thus a status enquiry is a check on a customer's credit rating. It is a 'letter of enquiry' that seeks information about price, quality, etc.

B. Questions for revision

1. State the guidelines for getting a status report from the buyer's existing suppliers and bankers.
2. How will you respond to a status enquiry about (a) a new client of yours (b) an existing client whose management has changed?
3. What is a "neutral status report"? Can you take it as an unfavourable opinion?
4. Write notes (50 words each) on: (a) Moral responsibility in giving a status report (b) Legal responsibility in giving a status report (c) The 'disclaimer' in a status report.
5. What will you do if a new buyer has asked for goods on credit?

C. Drafting exercises

1. As manager of Candid Bank you receive an enquiry from a very prestigious business house (not your client) about the financial status of a client. How will you react?
2. You wish to buy goods on credit from Swatantra Udyog. Write, stating names of your referees and bankers.
3. Aditya Automobiles receives an order from an upcountry spare parts dealer asking for credit. Reply.
4. First National Bank of India receives status enquiries about three of its clients. Write (a) a favourable (b) an unfavourable, and (c) a neutral report in respect of the three clients.
5. On receiving (a) an unfavourable (b) a neutral report on two of your prospective buyers, write to them in response to their request for credit.
6. As a banker write a status report on an accountholder who has no credit limit from you but has deposited Rs. 10 lakhs in term deposits last month.
7. Write a status report on a client who has been dealing with you for five years with a regular turnover in his cash credit account.

■■■

CHAPTER

12

Export-Import Correspondence

What should you know?

12.1 THE NATURE OF EXPORT-IMPORT CORRESPONDENCE

When goods are shipped from one country to another, it creates an altogether different trading situation, with the parties often situated wide apart and working under different laws. Moreover, there are additional regulations imposed by customs and foreign exchange authorities which affect the trade. Goods are often sent by sea ships or air. With the increasing globalisation of our times, the volume of export and import has multiplied, making a study of this segment of trade far more important. While the broad pattern of letters remains the same, viz. enquiries, responses thereto, orders, replies thereto, complaints and adjustments, there come into play new terms like **shipping bill, bill of lading, letter of credit**, etc. The consular authorities of the countries involved and their certifications also play a part.

There are international trade laws, and authorities to supervise their implementation. International trade involves a lot of documentation, procedures, rules and regulations required by the two countries in the picture. The traders have to report matters to their governments, with factors like import licensing, export licencing, embargoes etc. coming into play.

12.2 EXPORT PROCEDURE

Export activity can be divided into six stages, viz.

(*i*) Preliminaries: Obtaining BIN (Business Identification Number) & IEC (Importer-Exporter Code) number, and registration with promotion councils

(*ii*) Offer of goods and receipt of confirmed orders

(*iii*) Production and clearance of the products for exports

(*iv*) Shipment

(v) Negotiation of documents and realisation of export proceeds, and
(vi) Obtaining various export incentives.

12.3 IMPORT PROCEDURE

Importing refers to the purchase of foreign products for consumption or sale in the home country.

Stages in import

(i) Preliminaries – to obtain licence if required and import-export number
(ii) Enquiring and placing the indent
(iii) Obtaining foreign exchange
(iv) Arranging for payment to seller – opening of letter of credit
(v) Payment of customs duties and taking delivery of goods.

12.4 TERMINOLOGY IN FOREIGN TRADE

Letter of credit (L/C): It is a guarantee on behalf of the buyer, made by the buyer's bank, to the supplier (through his bank) that his bills upto a specified amount will be honoured on submission of specified documents by the supplier to his bank. On the due date, the issuing bank is required to make the payment to the supplier for the purchases made under the letter of credit.

Importer's country	**Exporter's country**
Importer —Request to issue an L/C→ Banker (ABC)→	→ Foreign branch/ correspondent of ABC Bank → Exporter's bank ↓ L/C confirmed to the exporter

For example, DEF Ltd. of Nagpur intends to import goods worth Rs. 10 lakh from Robinson Inc., USA. It opens an L/C through SBI, Nagpur. SBI, Nagpur on opening the L/C, guarantees that if Robinson Inc., USA produces the documents as stipulated in the L/C, the bank would make payment to the exporter (called beneficiary), i.e Robinson Inc., USA. Importantly, bankers in an L/C transaction deal with documents, not goods. As long as the documents are in order, payments have to be made. If they are not, an objection is raised in writing refusing payment.

Thus, the L/C facility enables the customers to obtain credit from suppliers and it ensures to the suppliers that there is no risk of non-payment. The obligation of the importer under the contract is supplemented by a superior obligation of a bank to make payment. The exporter now looks to the bank which opened the letter of credit (the issuing bank) for payment instead of relying on the importer.

An L/C can be either **revocable** or **irrevocable**. A revocable L/C is one which can be cancelled or amended by the issuing bank at any time without prior consent of or notice to the beneficiary. An irrevocable letter of credit can neither be amended nor cancelled without consent of all parties concerned. In actual practice, a revocable L/C has little value. Most of the import-export transactions are with irrevocable L/Cs.

Some of the terms frequently used in L/C transactions

- **Bill of exchange (B/E)** or **draft:** A document containing an instruction, usually to a bank, to pay the stated sum of money at a specified future date or on demand
- **CIF (c.i.f.):** Cost, insurance and freight
- **C & F (c. & f.):** Cost and freight
- **FOB (f.o.b.):** Free on board

- **Ex-ship:** Used when all charges after the ship reaches the shore are to be paid by the importer
- **Bill of entry:** A form used by the importer to declare the information regarding the goods entering the port
- **Bill of lading:** A document of title to the goods that are shipped. It is also an acknowledgement from the shipping company for having received the goods on board the ship.
- **Insurance policy:** Policy of transit insurance which is insisted on in international trade
- **Invoice:** The document giving full details of goods shipped, their price etc., prepared by the exporter and sent to the importer
- **Certificate of origin:** A certificate in respect of the country of production/manufacture of the goods shipped
- **Shipping advice:** Exporter's letter to the importer advising him of the despatch of the goods and forwarding of the documents through the banker
- **Indent:** Order placed by an importer of goods from overseas
- **Indent house:** Agent or middleman in the importing of goods, generally having offices or branches in important foreign countries

12.5 SPECIMEN LETTERS

1. Letter of enquiry

PVS Engineering Works

Regd. Office: S-13, "SABURI", Bharatnagar, NAGPUR-440 001.
Tel. (O) XXX XXXX Fax. XXX XXXX

20 December 2011
Ref. ABCD/212

Park Industries
North way
London (UK)

Dear Sirs

Subject: Enquiry about your machines

We have been manufacturing insulated wires and cables of different varieties for the past several years. Now we plan to expand our production capacity by installing five additional machines. We have obtained import licences for such machines in the past as actual users.

Will you please send us an illustrated catalogue of your latest machines for use in the production of insulated wires and cables?

We shall appreciate an early reply.

Yours faithfully

R. Shaktiram
Purchase Manager

2. Direct enquiry with manufacturers

MYSORE PLASTICS LTD.

Regd. Office: Unity Building, J.C. Road, Bangalore
Tel. (O) XXXXXX, Fax. XXXXXX

5th January, 2011
Ref: IM/3

Messrs. Kogakusha & Co.
23 Central Street
Tokyo
Japan

Dear Sirs

Subject: Enquiry about your machines

We have been manufacturing a wide variety of plastic products for the last fifteen years. The use of plastic products in our country has been rapidly increasing in the recent past. Hence we plan to multiply our production capacity by installing five additional machines.

Your name was suggested to us by the Trade Commissioner of your country during his recent visit to Bangalore. Will you please send us an illustrated catalogue of your latest machines for use in the production of plastic goods of different types? May we look to a competitive quotation from you?

We shall appreciate an early reply.

Yours faithfully
For Mysore Plastics Ltd.

M. Suryanarayan
Director, Purchases

3. Reply to letter no.2.

KOGAKUSHA & COMPANY

Administrative Office: 27 Yodagava Complex, 23, Central Street, Tokyo
Tel. (O) XXXXXX Fax. XXXXXX

15th January, 2011
Ref no. K135

The Director (Purchases)
Mysore Plastics Ltd.
Unity Building, J.C. Road
Bangalore, India

Dear Sir

Subject: Your enquiry about our machines

Thanks for your inquiry about KOGAKUSHA machines. As requested by you, we enclose our latest illustrated catalogue and price list. You may please refer to the pictures, diagrams and functions given therein. All these machines are patented by us and hence unique. They are sure to put you ahead of the competition in your country. They are guaranteed for one year.

As the rate list informs, we give a 5% trade discount on them, valid upto 31 March 2011. The shipment is against an irrevocable letter of credit through our bankers Bank of Tokyo. You may state your documentary requirements. We would like to inform you that we sell these machines to 34 countries.

We look forward to the pleasure of doing business with you.

Yours faithfully
For KOGAKUSHA & Co.

Imura Tobo
Marketing Director (International)

4. Reply from the manufacturer

Dear Sir

We thank you for your letter dated 1st January 2011. We are glad to learn that you are interested in buying our machines. We are proud to say that we are leading manufacturers of wire and cable machinery and export 75% of our production to Asian countries.

As requested by you, we enclose our detailed catalogue giving technical information and photographs of our entire range of machines.

For export, we shall require a confirmed irrevocable letter of credit in our favour, to be opened by a reputed bank in your country. Our price is always on c.i.f. basis.

We look forward to your positive response.

Yours faithfully

Encl:

Correspondence relating to letters of credit

The following are the stages involved in the issue and confirmation of a letter of credit:

1. The importer requests his banker to open an irrevocable letter of credit.
2. The importer informs the exporter about having opened a letter of credit.
3. The importer's banker informs the exporter of an L/C having been opened in his favour through a branch or a correspondent bank.

Special: The documents are sent in two sets to meet the possibility of postal loss/delay.

5. Importer's request to banker to open an irrevocable L/C in favour of the exporter

The Chief Manager
State Bank of India
Parliament Street Branch
New Delhi

Dear Sir

Subject: Opening an L/C

You are requested to open an irrevocable letter of credit in favour of Sony Inc., 10 MTP Street, Hong Kong for US$ 1.25 million (US Dollars one million two hundred and fifty thousand only) for import of 6000 TV picture tubes.

The beneficiary should furnish the following documents along with the draft:

Bill of lading (2)
Commercial invoice (3) evidencing shipment of goods as specified in the enclosed sheet
Insurance policy (2)
Consular invoice (2)
Certificate of origin (2)

The credit is to be established through HSBC Bank, Hong Kong.

The credit is to be confirmed to: Head Office of HSBC Bank
Validity: 5 October 2011
Part shipment: Not allowed
Invoice: To be made c.i.f. Mumbai and to include bank commission also
Special instructions: Documents by air through yourselves

Yours faithfully

6. Letter from the importer informing the exporter of having opened an L/C

Dear Sirs

Thanks for your letter accepting our order. We have to inform that we have instructed State Bank of India, Ravi Nagar Branch, Pune to open an irrevocable credit for Rs. 11 lac in you favour, available in your local currency and valid upto 31st August, 2011.

The credit will be confirmed by SBI, Milk Street Branch, London. They will accept your draft on them at 30 days' sight.

Please attach the following documents to your draft, to be surrendered to us against our acceptance:

Bill of lading (2)
Commercial invoice (3)
Insurance policy (2)
Consular invoice (2)
Certificate of origin (2)

The invoice should be made to include price c.i.f. Mumbai and the bank commission.

Please advise us by fax immediately on despatch of the goods.

Yours faithfully

7. Importer's bank informs the exporter of the letter of credit favouring him

STATE BANK OF INDIA
(Head office: Mumbai (India))
Milk Street, London
Tel. (O) XXXXXX Fax. XXXXXX

2nd April 2011
Ref: SBI/MS/110

Jackson Industries
Port Street
London

Dear Sirs

Subject: Advising the opening of an L/C

We enclose a letter of credit for £125,000 opened by our Mumbai Main Branch in your favour, valid upto 30 August 2011.

According to the terms of the L/C, you may draw at 30 d/s. Upon shipment of the goods to M/s Babubhai Shah & Co. (clients of SBI, Mumbai Main Branch) you may please submit the following documents to us:

1. Bill of exchange (2)
2. Bill of lading (2)
3. Insurance policy (2)
4. Consular invoice(2)
5. Certificate of origin(2)

Please note that your B/E is to include all charges to Mumbai and our commission at 1%.

Yours faithfully

QUESTION BANK

QUESTIONS

A. Questions based on critical understanding. Comment in about 30 words.

1. **Export-Import is a different trading situation compared to domestic buying and selling.**

Ans. In export and import, the parties are often far away from each other and under different national laws. As such, this sector of trade in governed by international laws and the documentation is more elaborate. Much more expertise and caution is required in handling impex transactions.

2. **A letter of credit assures the exporter of payment.**

Ans. Import-export business frequently uses L/Cs. The buyer asks his bank to open an L/C in favour of the seller. Now the seller has to ship the goods and just submit the stipulated documents to his bank to get the payment. The buyer's obligation to pay is backed by the superior obligation of the bank to pay.

3. **While paying under an L/C, a banker has to gurantee to the buyer that the seller has shipped the correct goods.**

Ans. A banker deals in documents, not goods. As long as the seller's documents are in order (as required by the L/C), the banker has to pay. If, however, the documents are flawed, he has to raise an objection in writing and refuse payment.

4. **A revocable letter of credit is a perfect guarantee to the exporter.**

Ans. Not true. An L/C which can be revoked (i.e. cancelled) at any time without the seller's permission is as good as no guarantee. A revocable L/C is only notional and has little place in the bulk of import-export business.

C. Drafting exercises

1. On behalf of Messrs. Salgaonkar Bros., Goa, write a letter to a foreign supplier asking for a quotation for the import of some machinery required by you.
2. Respond to an enquiry from Khadim Brothers, Abu Dhabi seeking information about your readymade garments.
3. Make an enquiry with Hoechst Corporation, Frankfurt about supply of sports medicines.
4. As a manufacturer of transmission towers, respond to an enquiry from KJ Company, Ghana for supply of 30 towers.
5. Request your banker to open a letter of credit for French Francs 400,000 in favour of Marcel Chemicals, Paris for supply of glycerine. The draft should be at 30 days' sight and the exporter should submit insurance policy, bill of lading, invoice, consular invoice and certificate of origin.
6. Write to your foreign supplier having opened an irrevocable L/C in his favour for U.S.$55,000 for supply of printing ink. Mention the validity, the bank through which opened and the documents required.
7. As a banker situated in Los Angeles, CA (USA), inform a local exporter of an L/C opened in his favour by Reliance Infocomm for US Dollars 15,000 for supply of industrial plastic goods.

■■■

CHAPTER

13

Correspondence with Banks

What should you know?

13.1 INTRODUCTION: GENERAL INSTRUCTIONS FOR WRITING BANKING LETTERS.

Broadly, banking letters are similar to other business letters, but they require special care on the following points:

1. You should provide unerring financial facts and figures to banks. Also, you should verify the dates involved, the names of parties etc.
2. You have to fulfil the requirements under law and at the same time guard your company's interests.
3. The letter should, like any business letter, be clear about its objectives and in content.
4. You need to write with courtesy and tact to the bank officials.
5. Secrecy needs to be maintained in presenting important inside information about yourself and the names of other parties. You have to make sure that the letter goes into correct hands.

A bank's letters to customers:

For a banker, there are his own do's and don'ts.

1. Courtesy and tact need to be shown.
2. The bank should make its own position quite clear, giving good reasons therefor. The banker must keep his banking secrets intact.
3. To be customer-friendly in your use of language, you have to avoid legal and commercial terms whenever possible. The reader who may not be familiar with them should understand your letter.
4. Every letter should make an effort to bring the customer closer to the bank and do more business with it. To write a letter is an opportunity to advertise yourself. A satisfied customer becomes a walking and talking advertisement for your bank.
5. In dealing with customer complaints, you have to assure the customer that his letter is receiving serious attention. Even if the complaint is not on valid grounds, you should

remember that the customer comes with the feeling that "The customer is always right." Hence he needs to be tackled from his point of view.

6. Services offered by banks include deposits, loans, transfer of money and handling of trade documents. Recent additions to these are the credit card and the ATM (Automatic Teller Machine) card. Banks also offer inter-branch connectivity, phone banking and internet banking. With a credit card (plastic money) you can do your shopping in different parts of the world without carrying currency with you.

13.2 SPECIMEN LETTERS

1. Request to a bank for opening an account

Nagpur Industries Limited

111, Siddipet, Chennai
Tel.: xxx xxxx Fax: xxx xxxx

Ref: NI/2002/156
13th January, 2011

The Senior Manager
Bank of Baroda
Shankar Nagar
Chennai

Sir

Sub. : Opening of a current account

We shall be grateful if you open a current account in the company's name at your branch. We are enclosing the following documents along with the application form duly filled in:

1. Certificate of Incorporation
2. Certificate of Commencement of Business
3. Copy of the Memorandum and Articles of Asociation of the company
4. Certified copy of resolution of the Board of Directors to open a current account duly signed by the Chairman
5. Specimen signatures of the directors who are authorised to operate the account
6. Photocopies of their PAN cards
7. A pay-in slip duly filled in, along with Rs. 10,000 in cash as our initial deposit.

Please open a current account in our company's name and send us (i) a cheque book, (ii) a pass book and (ii) a pay-in slip book to operate the account.

We look forward to a pleasant banking relationship with you.

Yours faithfully

Sd/-
Finance Manager

Encl: as above

2. Letter to a bank asking it to stop payment of a cheque

Ref. No. BC-105

25th September, 2011

The Manager
State Bank of India
WHC Road
Raipur

Sub: Stop payment - Current account no. 1465

Dear Sir

This is to inform you that a crossed cheque for Rs. 10,000/- dated 23rd September 2011, bearing the no. RES. 32486 and drawn in favour of Mr. Rajesh Verma, has been misplaced at our end.

You are requested to take immediate steps to stop payment of this cheque.

Yours faithfully

Sd/-

Finance Manager

3. Letter from customer requesting an overdraft facility

Dear Sir

Subject: Request for an overdraft facility

We have been banking with you for the last four years and believe our transactions have been quite satisfactory to you. We have given you, at times, fixed deposits of Rs.10,00,000.

Now our expanding business and the need to extend credit to our customers has put us in a fund shortage. We enclose our financial statements of sales, profit and loss account, and balance sheet for the last two years and projected statements for the current and next year.

Our sales have grown by 200% in the past two years and are expected to go up another 140% in the coming 18 months. Hence, to be able to stock goods adequately and give credit to retailers, we need an overdraft of Rs.10,00,000. You will note that our net worth is Rs. 5,00,000 as of now, and the credit sought is quite reasonable. The facility is needed for six months. We are willing to give you personal guarantees of the partners for the overdraft, whose personal worth fully covers the amount. Copies of their income tax and wealth tax returns are also enclosed.

We hope you will grant this facility to boost our commerce and bring more business to you.

Please let us know at the earliest.

Yours faithfully

4. Letter from the bank sanctioning an overdraft

Jaipur Urban Bank Ltd.
3, Main Street
Jaipur
Tel.: xxx xxxx Fax: xxx xxxx

5th July 2011
Ref. MB-3

Mr. Manmohan Bang
43, Vijaya Nagar
Jaipur

Dear Sir

Subject: Sanction of overdraft

We refer to your application dated 20th June, and are pleased to advise that our Head Office has sanctioned to you an overdraft limit of Rs. 10,00,000 on the enclosed terms and conditions. It will carry interest @10.5% p.a. subject to change without notice, depending on RBI lending rates. The advance will have to be secured by the personal guarantee of yourself and Shri Jagjivan Bhai Bang. It should be used for genuine trading purpose only in your line of activity. The facility is extended for a period of 6 months.

If you are agreeable to this, please return a copy of this letter signed by yourself, and meet the undersigned for execution of documents.

We wish you all the best.

Yours faithfully

5. Another request for an overdraft

Jagjit Surgicals

123, Main Street, Agra
Tel.: xxx xxxx Fax: xxx xxxx

15th September 2011
Ref. Corp-3

The Branch Manager
Corporation Bank
Belan Ganj
Agra

Dear Sir

Subject: Request for overdraft

We have maintained a current account with you for the last five years and have a spotless record of dealing with your bank.

Now, since the opening of two medical colleges in the city and the establishment of a superspeciality hospital, our business is on the rise. In fact, as one of the oldest and most trusted dealers in surgicals, we are experiencing a heavy demand for our goods. This makes it necessary for us to arrange for immediate finance to extend credit to the corporate buyers, renovate our shop, purchase latest medical equipment and start our own repacking unit.

As such, we request you to grant us an overdraft of Rs. 5,00,000 (Rupees five lacs only) for business expansion as above. We shall need this facility for 3 months as a stop-gap arrangement. We offer government securities worth Rs. 6 lakhs as a collateral for the advance.

We are confident of liquidating the advance within the term and then we shall perhaps approach you afresh for a regular cash credit facility for working capital.

We await your early and positive decision.

Thank you.

Yours faithfully

A. Questions based on critical understanding. Comment in about 30 words.

1. **In giving a loan, a bank is your financial partner in business and has the right to know all about your company.**

Ans. In giving a loan, a bank incurs a financial risk since any loan can potentially turn bad (unless it is against cash or cash-equivalent deposits). The banker therefore has to secure his interest by knowing the financial affairs of your company. This he may do by examining your accounts or in a crunch situation, even by appointing auditors.

2. **When you introduce a depositor to the bank, you have to know his/her identity perfectly.**

Ans. Even a deposit account can be used for fraud if the account is opened in somebody else's name as the name-holder's cheques etc. can be cashed through the account. It is not enough that you know a person as "A.K.Parate" since "Anil K. Parate" and "Ashok K. Parate" have the same initials. You should to know the person's identity thoroughly well, or else the bank can hold you accountable for misleading it.

3. **You have to guard your business secrets from the bank.**

Ans. The banker has a right to your financial information when he is a sufficient stakeholder. But the business secrets unrelated to the banking transactions have to be fully guarded. Your secrets must not travel to places where they may hurt you.

B. Questions for revision

1. Mention the guidelines you would follow in handling correspondence with a bank.
2. What care would you take as a banker when writing to customers?

C. Drafting exercises

1. Write to your bank to increase the quantum of your gold loan in view of a 30% rise in the prices of gold since the loan was granted.
2. Inform the bank about the loss of your cheque book and passbook. Ask for stopping unsigned cheques and get duplicate books issued.
3. You wish to start practice as a lawyer. Ask the bank where you have maintained a deposit account, about its schemes for loans to professionals.
4. A bank has advertised about grant of loans without security or a guarantor. Seek the details for a loan to pay a security deposit of Rs. 10000 to your prospective employer.

■■■

CHAPTER

14

Correspondence with Insurance Companies

What should you know?

14.1 Principles of Insurance

14.2 Drafting Insurance Letters

14.3 Specimen Insurance Letters

14.1 PRINCIPLES OF INSURANCE

Meaning of Insurance: Insurance is a contract between two parties under which one party (the insurance company) agrees to indemnify the other (the insured), i.e. agrees to pay a certain amount of money as compensation for loss or damage to his life or property. Of course, in the case of a death claim under life insurance, it is the nominee that gets the claim money.

The following are the principles of insurance:

1. **Utmost good faith:** Insurance must be taken not from the point of view of making any profit, but to cover the risk. Insurance is generally based on the principle of good faith, which means that both the parties (the insurer and the insured) to the contract must give all the facts relating to the subject-matter of insurance.
2. **Insurable interest:** The party insuring the life of a person or goods must have an insurable interest while taking out an insurance policy. Under this principle, the insured party stands to gain if it is insured or stands to lose if it is not insured.
3. **Indemnity:** Under this principle, the insured party is not allowed to earn any profit. If there is loss by theft or by fire, he will be compensated for the loss insured. He stands to get neither more nor less than the actual loss he suffered.
4. **Subrogation:** Under this principle, a special right is given to the insurance company to take possession of the property if it has paid the full amount as claim for the damage. The owner of the property will have thereafter no right to his property. It is the insurance company that becomes the owner of that property.

14.2 DRAFTING INSURANCE LETTERS

The general rules for letter writing are applicable to correspondence with insurance companies. At the same time, the writer is expected to know the formalities of insurance transactions. The letter should be complete as to the information and the documents needed by the insurance company.

Insurance is classified as: a) Life insurance; b) General insurance, i.e. non-life insurance, covering fire, marine, theft, accident insurance, etc. A person who wants to take out a general insurance policy is required to make a proposal in a printed proposal form. If the proposal is accepted by the insurance company, a cover note is issued indicating the grant of protection for the period from the date of acceptance till the policy is issued. A cover note is usually valid for 30 days. Request for insurance, enquiry about premium rate, etc. may be made by letter. In fixing the rate of premium, the insurer takes into account the physical hazards of the risk.

When property covered by a fire policy is damaged or destroyed by fire, the insurer must be informed within 24 hours of the event. A claim on the prescribed claim form is to be made within 15 days, and must be supported by documents to prove the loss and the values stated in the form.

The insurance company sends its representative or a surveyor to estimate and investigate the loss and negotiate with the client to arrive at a settlement; he submits a **survey report** to the insurance company. The company examines the report and settles the claim according to it.

The insurer may accept, dispute, reduce or refuse the claim after making various enquiries as to the cause and extent of the damage, and taking into account the terms of the contract.

In case of marine insurance the insurance company requires particulars about 1) the client 2) the ship (or conveyance) 3) the voyage 4) the goods and mode of packing 5) the risks required to be covered and 6) the value of the goods for the purpose of insurance.

14.3 SPECIMEN INSURANCE LETTERS

1. Letter to an insurance company inquiring about the terms and conditions for fire insurance

RELIABLE INDUSTRIES LIMITED
Regd. Office: 2, Kanpur House, Gandhi Street
MUMBAI – 400 001

Ref. No. AS-102
19th August 2011

The Manager
ABC Insurance Company
24 Nariman Point
MUMBAI

Dear Sir
Our company intends to take out a fire insurance policy to insure goods worth Rs. 70,00,000. We request you to send us the relative proposal form along with your terms and conditions.

Yours faithfully

P. K. Patil
General Manager

2. Fire insurance proposal

October 10, 2011

Worldwide Insurance Company
Nariman Point
Mumbai

Dear Sir

Re : Fire insurance proposal

Our company has a heavy engineering workshop at M.I.D.C., Vidya Vihar and intends to insure the factory building, stock and other goods under a standard fire and special perils policy. The approximate value will be around Rs. 70 lakh. We request you to let us have your proposal form along with terms and conditions and the amount of premium payable.

Yours faithfully

3. Godown insurance

October 10, 2011

The Manager
Oriental Insurance Company Limited
WHC Road
Raipur

Dear Sir

Re : Insurance covering our godowns at Wadi

We wish to inform you that our company deals in electrical and electronic goods and we store them in a godown situated on Nagpur Road, Raipur.

We have hypothecated the stock to Bank of India, Raipur and wish to cover our stock under a Compehensive Fire Insurance Policy for an amount of Rs. 80 lacs.

We request you to send us your proposal form along with computation of the premium and your terms and conditions for accepting the above risk.

We hope you will quote your most competitive premium rates.

Yours faithfully

4. Letter to an insurance company regarding loss through damage by fire

Howrah Industries Limited

Regd. Office: 82, Vivekanand Marg
NAGPUR – 440 018

October 10, 2011
Ref: H/332

The Manager
United India Insurance Company Limited
Nagpur

Dear Sir

Re : Intimation of loss due to fire to our factory covered under policy no.333400/11/02/008

We have to inform that a fire broke out in our factory during night hours on 8.10.2011. The cause of the fire may be a short circuit. The fire resulted in extensive damage to the factory building and the stocks and stock-in-process that were placed in the factory building and godown. Our factory and godowns are insured with you under your comprehensive fire insurance policy mentioned above. The estimated loss is Rupees thirty lakhs.

We have reported the fire accident to Wadi Police Station. The fire brigade was summoned to extinguish the fire. We request you to send us your claim form for claiming the compensation under the above policy. Please also depute your surveyor for assessment of loss at the earliest so that we may resume work soon.

Yours faithfully

5. Letter of settlement of claim from insurance company

United General Insurance Company Ltd.

13, Bose Street, Nagpur
Tel.: xxx xxxx Fax: xxx xxxx

October 10, 2011
Ref: F/3/11452

ABC Industries Ltd.
MIDC Industrial Area
Wadi, Nagpur

Dear Sir

Re : Fire claim no. 99993333
Date of loss: 8.10.2011
Our policy no. 3333444/11/02/777

With reference to your above fire claim, we have received the Surveyor's assessment report as to the fire loss to your factory building and godown. The surveyor has assessed the loss at Rs. 15,70,000.

We have to inform you that we have obtained approval from the competent authority to settle the above claim for Rs. 15,70,000 according to the details given below:

Description	Rs.
Damage to factory building	10,80,000
Value of stock destroyed in fire	6,00,000
	16,80,000
Less: Under-insurance	Nil
Less: Salvage value of damaged stock	1,00,000
Less: Excess clause	10,000
Net payable	15,70,000

We enclose herewith our payment voucher for Rs. 15,70,000/- (Rupees fifteen lacs seventy thousand only) with a request to return it duly discharged by you and your bankers to enable us to issue the claim cheque.

Since the above fire policy was issued on reinstatement basis, you have to pay a premium of Rs. 19,300 to reinstate your policy from the date of loss till expiry. We therefore request you to let us have your cheque for Rs. 19,300/- for doing the needful.

We assure you of our best services at all times.

Yours faithfully

Sr. Divisional Manager

6. Letter intimating a claim in respect of marine loss

October 10, 2011

The Manager
Marine Tech. Dept.
The New India Assurance Company Limited
Head Office, M.G.Road, Fort
Mumbai

Dear Sir

Re : Claim under marine insurance o/a accident to Vessel S. S. Virat
Date of accident : 10th September 2011
Voyage : Mumbai to Singapore via Chennai
Marine policy no. 160200/21/04/136

We regret to inform you that the ship S. S. Virat carrying our goods over the board met with an accident near Chennai Port on 10th September 2003 during evening hours. The ship was on its way from Mumbai to Singapore via Chennai.

The goods were insured under your above Marine policy. The estimated loss is Rs.1,00,000. We request you to depute your surveyor for assessment of loss. Please also let us have your claim form to enable us to lodge a claim for the loss suffered.

Yours faithfully

7. Letter regarding insurance rates

Oriental Fire and General Insurance Company
Indraprastha Marg, New Delhi

Ref. No. GI/535
October 25, 2011

Modern Furnishing Co.
Okhla Industrial Area
Phase I
Delhi

Dear Sırs

Subject: Insurance rates

We thank you for your letter dated 19th October and have pleasure in enclosing our rate card.

The yearly premium payable on your stock and assets is Rs. 15,000 only.

We hope to receive your insurance proposal along with the premium soon.

Yours faithfully

Manager

QUESTION BANK

A. Questions based on critical understanding. Comment in about 30 words.

1. Marine insurance is generally effected through an insurance broker.

Ans. The statement is correct. A businessman who wants to have marine risks covered writes to a broker giving details of the risk. The insurance company decides the acceptability of the risk, quotes the rate and issues the policy after considering the details of the risk.

2. A person who wants to insure his property against fire makes a proposal to the insurer on a printed proposal form.

Ans. There is a standard proposal form which the insured party gives to the insurance company. This form requires the proposer to give all information about the property to be insured. If the insurance company accepts the proposal, a cover note is issued indicating the grant of protection for the period from the date of acceptance till the policy is issued.

3. The insured is not allowed to make a profit out of fire insurance.

Ans. Fire insurance contract is a contract of indemnity. The insured is to be put in the same financial position as he held before the occurrence of the fire; he is not allowed to make profit from the insurance. The insurer may make good the loss either by receiving cash payment or by replacement of his property.

4. If your car has been replaced under insurance, the insurer can take possession of your old car.

Ans. The insurance company generally does take possession of your old can after replacing it. The insured cannot retain the replacement as well as the original. This is the principle of subrogation.

5. The surveyor has a key role in assessing the value of the damage.

Ans. The insurer appoints an expert surveyor to assess the extent of loss sustained in a damage to the insured property. The insurance company has to be informed at once (within 24 hours at the most) of the loss, and evidence has to be preserved for the surveyor to make his valuation.

B. Questions for revision

1. What are the principles of insurance? (150 words)
2. What care would you take in writing insurance letters?

C. Drafting exercises

1. Write to an insurance company enquiring about its scheme for animal insurance and their norms for making good the loss in case of an epidemic.
2. A gas godown has been set up near your house. Ask the insurance company how this may affect the terms of your house insurance.
3. Your valuables have been stolen from the bank locker, which you noticed upon operating it after six months. Inform the insurance company.
4. A lorry containing mangoes was detained on its way due to a "Rasta Roko" stir for three days. You had taken out an insurance. Inform the insurance company of the loss to the quality of mangoes and their reduced market price, stating your desire to lodge a proper claim.
5. Write a letter to a general insurance company enquiring about insurance rates for your furniture company and a reply from the insurance company.
6. Write a letter to Oriental Fire & General Insurance Company, Nagpur Branch, requesting it to settle your claim in respect of your godown that has been destroyed in fire.
7. Write a letter to your client in Q.6 informing of the settlement of insurance claim.
8. Notify your insurance company of the losses in your premises on account of an earthquake, requesting them to arrange for an early inspection for assessment of the loss and settlement of claim.

■■■

CHAPTER

15

Job-related Letters, Group Discussions and Interviews

What should you know?

15.1 JOB APPLICATIONS AND CV (BIODATA, RÉSUMÉ)

Your job application may be the most important business letter that you write in your lifetime. Employers inform that nine out of 10 applications they receive are not even properly written. Hence you need to learn to present your case for a job. A job application is a sales letter at its best; through it, you offer to sell your services. You should be familiar with the modern practices in this regard and be aware of what kind of application the employer will appreciate. This differs from company to company. There are styles ranging from the traditional to the computer age presentation.

An application may be **solicited** (against employer's ad) or **unsolicited** (on your own).

You may divide your application into two parts: (a) the covering letter and (b) the bare details of your background, variously called **CV** (curriculum vitae), which is a Latin phrase, a **biodata** (which is mainly an American usage and quite popular in India), or **résumé** (read, RAY-ZYOO-MAY), which is a French word. They broadly amount to the same thing – your name, address, age, date of birth, educational qualifications, other achievements, job experience, interests, strengths, references etc. A CV gives this information pointwise, mostly in phrases rather than in complete sentences.

15.1.1 Tips for Writing an Application Letter

While applying for a job, you may compose a brief covering letter making a formal request for being considered for the post and stating that the biodata is enclosed. While writing the job application letter, keep this in mind:

1. Make it neat and attractive, using good quality paper and neat, clear typing (computer printout if possible).
2. Address it to the correct authority – Personnel Manager/Managing Director/ Principal/ Director, etc.

3. If responding to an advertisement, study the ad. and suit your application to the wording of the ad. You may even be required to apply in the form provided by the advertiser.
4. Keep the letter short. You may say that the biodata is enclosed, and recapitulate the highlights of it in the covering letter for immediate impact.
5. Do not presume that you will get the job or that you will find it suitable for you until you have known the employer well enough. Show keenness but keep an open mind.
6. Make sure that you have all the necessary qualifications for the job. Otherwise it is a futile exercise.
7. Ask for an interview. Express your sincerity to make a good job of the work.
8. Enclose all testimonials that are required to make up your case. Do not submit the originals. They can be shown at the time of interview or even later, as required.
9. If there is an application fee, enclose it in the form required, e.g. draft, postal order, etc.
10. Some don'ts:
    (a) Don't beg for a job.
    (b) Don't boast.
    (c) Don't exaggerate or make false claims.
    (d) Don't write on both sides of paper.
    (e) Don't blame your existing employer, nor show your weaknesses.
    (f) Don't ask for a job on account of financial need but on merits.

Remember to keep a copy of your submission to the employer, as he may interview you on the basis of what you have stated. You need your copy for reference when going for an interview.

Specimen letters:

1. Job application (solicited) covering letter

Rakesh Saxena
40, Friends Colony
Hyderabad 500024
Tel xxxxxxxx

16th August 2011

The General Manager
JVS Motors
Central Towers
Hyderabad 500 001

Respected Sir

I refer to your advertisement in today's *Deccan Chronicle* and wish to apply for the post of Customer Care Officer. As you can see from my attached CV, I am well qualified for the post, with a first class at graduation and two years' vigorous experience in sales.

I hope you will grant me the opportunity of an interview where you may know me better. I trust I can do proper justice to the job in case I am selected.

Yours faithfully

Sd/-

Rakesh Saxena

Encl: CV

2. Unsolicited job application

Ms. Shalini Gupta
125, Old Agra Road
Nashik
Tel xxxxxxx
Email: sgupta 125@hotmail.com

10th August, 2011

The Director
Shraddha Computer Institute
Station Road
Nashik

Madam

Subject : Application for the post of Instructor

I understand that you have openings for trainers and I offer myself as a candidate for the post of an Instructor in your Institute. I possess the necessary qualifications, viz. an MS (Computer) and a fair degree of fluency in English, Hindi and Marathi. Other particulars of my background are detailed in the enclosed biodata.

Would you please call me for an interview where you may judge my personality and knowledge for the post? I may add that I love teaching and would do my best in the position applied for.

Thanks.

Yours truly
Sd/-

(Shalini Gupta)

Encl: Biodata

15.1.2 Writing Your CV (Biodata, Résumé)

Your CV (curriculum vitae) is a summary of the course of your life, your autobiography in a nutshell from the employer's point of view (in this case).

Tips for writing an effective CV

The main thing in your CV is that it should contain all your details that are of interest to the employer. You may NOT use the same presentation of your biodata when applying for the post of a sports coach and a typist. You have to select your credentials that are relevant to the job and highlight them.

To draft a good CV, remember this:

1. Make it traditional or modern depending on how the employer may like it. (You have specimens of both in this chapter.)
2. Mention your latest educational qualification first and go backward in time. In detailing your job experience, start with the current job. During your interview you may have to explain gaps in employment, if any.
3. List out your scholarships, awards, titles, etc.
4. Mention your interests and strengths.
5. Give all information under suitable headings.
6. You have various options as to what information to give at the top. You may follow one of the three practices given here:
   I. As traditional résumés do, give your date of birth, marital status, educational qualifications, job experience, medals, trophies, interests, references etc. in that order.
   II. State your OBJECTIVE as the first item after your name and address. This is a recent practice. The objective may be stated thus: "To utilise my skills and experience as a Programme Analyst to grow with the organisation."
   III. Write a profile of your main qualifications and qualities in several bullet points. E.g., "PROFILE:
      - A consistent first class in education, showing hard work and intelligence
      - Two years' very good hands-on experience of documentation with a reputed export firm
      - Sociable nature, organising skill
      - Several extra-curricular interests and a bank of general knowledge"
7. If you have held various kinds of jobs, you may state the responsibilities you carried out and the qualities you acquired.
8. References (names of respectable persons who may give the employer their useful opinion about your suitability for the post) may be added at the end of the CV or may be offered "upon request." In any case, your reference should not be a close relative and you should seek his permission before giving his name.
9. Make the biodata sheet attractive and balance its layout. Keep sufficient open spaces.
10. Avoid handwritten additions to a typed sheet. You may store your biodata in a computer or a floppy, C.D. etc. and reorganise it as the job requirements suggest. You can make additions to it on the computer.
11. To present yourself with full force, you may have to use more sheets than one.
12. All qualitative comments about yourself should be backed by the information present in the biodata sheet or may have to be substantiated at the interview.

Specimens: Biodata (traditional)

Biodata

Name: Ms. Kavita Sharma

Address: 604 Jupiter Towers
Cuffe Parade
Mumbai 400005
Tel: xxxx xxxx
Email: kavitasharma@graphics.com

Date of birth: 4th July, 1986
Age: 26 years
Marital status: Unmarried

Educational qualifications:
M.Com. from Mumbai University in 2008 with 60.0% marks
B.Com. from Delhi University in 2006 with 65.5% marks
HSSC from Maharashtra Board in 2003 in the science stream with 78% marks

Other qualifications:
MS Office in 2006 from Apex Computers, Mumbai, a reputed institute
Yoga Teachers Training in 1998 from Yoga Niketan, Mumbai

Work experience:

2010-Present	Senior DTP Operator with Compugraphics, Mumbai handling complex job works and routine correspondence independently
2009-10	Cashier with ICICI Bank
2008-09	Accountant with Sandip Exports with additional charge of handling Customs transactions

Prizes:
Won the intercollegiate Table Tennis championship as a graduate student
Won singing contest organised by Zee TV, 2007

Interests:
Penfriendship, reading classics, music, IT

Languages known:
English(fluent), Hindi, Punjabi

References:
1. Prof. R.K.Mehrotra
Reader, Department of English
NM College, New Delhi 110064
Tel. xxxx xxxx
2. Dr. P.C. Gangwani
Department of Ophthalmology
Getwell Hospital
Mumbai 400064

2. CV (modern)

CV

Anand Shrivastava
C/VI/24 Railway Colony
Jabalpur
Tel. xxxx xxx

Email: anandshrivastava244@hotmail.com

OBJECTIVE

To employ my proven skills as a sales driver to be an asset to a progressive company's marketing department and achieve career satisfaction. To develop strong bonds with colleagues and clients.

EDUCATION

1. Post-graduate Diploma in Marketing from BVM Institute of Management Sciences, Chandigarh, 2008
2. B.Com. from Kurukshetra University, 2006 with a first class
3. HSSC from CBSE, 1998 with 62.5% marks

ADDITIONAL QUALIFICATIONS

1. Certificate in Public Speaking from British Academy, Meerut
2. Diploma in Computer Programming from Advance Computer School, New Delhi, a 9-months full-time course giving a good grounding in handling computer for general purposes
3. Received training in swimming from a national coach at Andaman

SCHOLARSHIPS/AWARDS

1. Was given the best student award at Jain International School, New Delhi successively for two years
2. Spitz Sports Scholarship at school for outstanding performance as a swimmer

INTERESTS

Organising events and charity drives, current affairs, swimming, sports, music

STRENGTHS

Balanced group behaviour with leadership qualities, a sound health, a sense of humour

REFERENCES

Will be gladly furnished upon request

3. Modern style of giving one's résumé

Résumé

Sachin K. Singh
B/4/125, MIG Colony
Indore 432001
Tel.xxx xxxx
Email: sachinksingh@rediff.com

OBJECTIVE

To deploy my talent in sales promotion for my employer's benefit and achieve an executive position. My recent training and work experience, as also my extrovert nature, qualify me very well for the objective.

EDUCATIONAL QUALIFICATIONS

- B.Com. from Mumbai University in 2009 with 61.1% marks and distinction in Economics
- Diploma in Marketing from Scholars Academy, Indore in 2008 with a second rank in the Institute
- HSSC from CBSE, 2006 commerce in the stream with 70.5% marks

WORK EXPERIENCE

- 2009-present, sales canvasser with Bhrigu Investments, Indore. Job involves extensive field work and communication in a competitive environment.
- We have an agency of solar water heaters at home where I assist in marketing.

EXTRA-CURRICULAR ACHIEVEMENTS

- Represented my college (P.D. Lions College, Malad) in volleyball for two years
- Sing for an orchestra group Swar Sadhna and play drums
- Help to organise Ganesh festival in my locality

PERSONAL DETAILS

Date of birth : 8th August 1985
Marital status: Unmarried

STRENGTHS

Persuasive speaker in English and Hindi, devotion to work

REFERENCES

Prof. R.D. Saxena
Head, Department of Economics
P.D. Lions College
Malad (W)
Mumbai 400064

Adv. Rasool Khan
14, Ganeshnagar
Indore 432001

15.2 WRITING REFERENCES AND TESTIMONIALS

In the present context, a reference is a report by a respectable person on a candidate's character and capabilities, useful to a prospective employer in deciding the candidate's appointment. The employer feels reassured when a man of responsibility affirms what qualities a person has.

A referee (or reference) is usually a teacher from the college where the candidate has studied, his previous/ current employer, or any person of authority. He must have known the candidates personally long enough to make a judgment about him. Normally, a reference from a close relative is not acceptable.

A candidate should take permission from the person whose name he proposes as a referee. Even more importantly, the candidate should be sure that the referee thinks really well of him.

Some referees ask the candidate himself to draft the reference letter! The candidate, in such a case, should be able to make an objective evaluation of his strengths. For the referee, the points to remember when giving a reference are:

- He should mention in what capacity and how long he has known the candidate.
- He should write of the candidate's character, professionally useful qualities, and specific achievements that have impressed him.
- He should wish the candidate success.
- If he has reason to give a negative reference, he should do so in clear language and state the reasons why he thinks the candidate unsuitable. Such a letter is normally brief and it should be sent with extra care as to its secrecy.

A testimonial is letter about a person's abilities and qualities. It is usually addressed "To whom it may concern." and is given in the hands of the candidate. Some people, however, make no difference between a reference and a testimonial.

1. Specimen reference letters recommending a candidate for an executive post

Dear Mr. ________

I have great pleasure in commenting on the abilities of Mr. Sumeet Chatterjee, an erstwhile student of MBA in this institution.

Sumeet is an ace communicator both in writing and speech and he won several debating and essay contests while a student here. He has clarity of thought, a lofty vision and a vast fund of knowledge. He is respectful to his superiors and is gregarious by nature, hence suitable for teamwork. As he matures in life, he may shape into a business leader of some standing. His moral character is good.

I wish him success.

Sincerely

2. Testimonial to a candidate for a sales job

TO WHOM IT MAY CONCERN

This is to certify that I have known Ms. Vaishali Shilledar for two years when she was a salesgirl in our department store (Param Superbazar, Mysore). Vaishali is a patient and soft-spoken lady with a knack for understanding customer problems and taking initiative in solving them. She speaks English, Hindi and Kannada with reasonable fluency and revels in converting a prospect into a sale. She thrives on challenges and is set to go far. I recommend her heartily for an executive position in sales.
I wish her very good luck in her profession and life.

15.3 GROUP DISCUSSION (GD)

Nowadays more and more business houses require a job applicant to appear for a group discussion as also an interview. A GD is to test his performance as a member of a team to arrive at a constructive conclusion on the given theme or to solve a problem.

The use of group discussion as a tool of the selection process is only logical. In a work situation a person, especially an executive, is required to interact with a number of people – colleagues or outsiders – share views and arrive at a consensus. If, for example, some banks have formed a consortium to finance a company, the representatives of the banks have to take a group decision about the quantum and allocation of finance. There are innumerable occasions for group decisions.

Purpose of group discussion in the selection process

An applicant's contribution to and behaviour in a group discussion help the expert observer to judge the candidate in so many ways.

1. It helps to know how much initiative he has to lead the group of assorted participants. Does he control the proceedings of the group discussion and set up the modalities of the discussion?
2. It helps to judge the quality of his ideas. Does he have a reasonable approach to the problem?
3. It shows the candidate's originality and creativity. How new and individual are his ideas? How does he handle unexpected situations in the group? For example, out of eight group members, only two may talk. Or someone may get angry or blunt in the course of discussion. How does he react to this?
4. It shows how dominating or self-effacing the person is. Both these extremes reveal faulty group dynamics.
5. The GD reveals whether he is equitable to his group partners.
6. It tests his sensitivity to non-verbal communication. If his thoughts or language are too difficult to grasp and the group members look bored, is he able to correct himself?
7. The GD brings out the candidate's attention to finer details of the issues. It tests how fine his vision can go. Does he, for example, distinguish between CPI (Communist Party of India) and CPI (M) (Communist Party of India(Marxist))?
8. In a GD, the candidate's voice and, to some extent, public speaking ability are tested.
9. The topic for group discussion may be a current problem facing the business house, and it may anticipate the candidate's utility to the company.

Tips for effective participation in a group discussion for job selection

While personal interview may be the more important technique for deciding the merits of a candidate, group discussion carries its own weight. You can make your GD performance better by using these tips.

1. The employer is looking for a natural leader who is also a balanced thinker. Leadership is by helping each team member achieve his full potential in solving the problem at hand. So, try to lead.
2. Observe the personality types present in the group. Greet the group cheerfully and decide the method you would like to follow to ensure equitable participation by all members. For example, you may have 20 minutes' time and seven members in the group. You may suggest that in the first round everyone should speak for two minutes and then throw the topic open for cross opinions. You may suggest that the speaker should not be interrupted during his talk; the members should make their notes and express disagreement in their proper turn. To say so much requires a good deal of confidence, which is best attained through practice.
3. Always maintain a calm temper. If unjustly opposed, use polite expressions to restate your position.

4. If there are private mini-discussions between two or three members, suggest that the whole group should get the benefit of their views.
5. Generally, job selection GDs are impromptu (the topic is given on the spot). If so, quickly plan an *ex tempore* speech to fill the time that you may fairly be allotted by the group. Practice in *ex tempore* stage speaking helps in GD.
6. Be a good listener. (Refer to the chapter "Listening as a Tool of Communication.") Do not talk when some other member is addressing the group, nor indulge in minor entertainment (e.g. fiddling with a pin). Cheer, appreciate, nod and in other ways be an active, dynamic listener.
7. See that the group arrives at a conclusion in the allotted time. Help the group to complete the task in time by active timekeeping.
8. If an idea superior to your idea is expressed by somebody with specialised knowledge, be ready to adopt it. Lee Iacocca, as American trade unions said, was one of the few adult Americans who could change their mind. However, take care to maintain your standing in the group in spite of conceding some ground to another.
9. If you find someone else emerging as a leader, you still can brighten your chances of selection by your healthy cooperation to the leader.
10. Part with the group as you started, with a cheerful smile. Make a proper farewell.

15.4 PERSONAL INTERVIEW

15.4.1 Types of Interview

Following types of interviews of an employee/prospective employee are held by employers:

(*i*) Job interview (to decide a candidate's suitability for a job)
(*ii*) Exit interview (when an employee resigns from a job)
(*iii*) Problem interview (when an employee states his problem)
(*iv*) Appraisal/evaluation interview (for periodic assessment of an employee)

Here we are mainly concerned with the job interview.

15.4.2 Job Interview

This is a formal meeting between the candidate and his prospective employers wherein the employer seeks to find out the candidate's suitability for a post through questions and answers. This kind of interview is usually held against an application by the candidate, and the time and place are fixed by the employer, sometimes in consultation with the candidate.

Nowadays, to save time, there is an increasing tendency to hold **walk-in interviews**. The employer announces the date, time and place of the walk-in interviews, and all interested can appear directly.

The same type of interview is held for a new job and for promotion within the organisation. For best performance at a job interview, the candidate has to know how to conduct himself at three stages:

i) Before interview (psychological, intellectual and physical preparation)
ii) Actual interview (how to face various situations and various types of questions)
iii) After interview

Let us consider these stages in detail.

I. Before interview

Contrary to the common notion, the pre-interview buildup has to start not after receiving the interview call but from the time you decide to apply for a certain job. If you are appearing for a competitive examination, say the IAS, or for a managerial post, you can and should find out what kind of interviews are conducted for it.

1. **Build a positive mindset:** As you prepare for the questions that may be asked, put yourself in a positive mental frame about the interview and, even more, for accepting and excelling in the job. Manage your mood.
2. **Meet successful candidates:** This helps you to know what qualities successful candidates have. You may consciously try to imbibe them.
3. **Confidence through mock interviews:** Appear for mock interviews and go through the interview experience as many times as you can. Then the actual interview would appear a familiar experience.
4. **Study your résumé:** Be prepared to face questions on your background and to explain gaps, if any, in your educational career and employment. Revise your subject knowledge, especially when this knowledge is relevant to the post applied for.
5. **Find out about the company:** Try to learn about the company where you are appearing for an interview – its products, reputation, working conditions, policies, recent advances, main position-holders, etc.
6. **Details about your existing organisation:** Study afresh the organisation where you are working. If you are appearing for a promotion interview, this is all the more necessary. For some reason, you are expected to know about departments other than your own.
7. **Brush up your general knowledge:** General knowledge is a common subject during an interview. Revise it. Study the news headlines and editorials regularly as the interview gets nearer, especially of the day or afternoon of the interview.
8. **Find out the interview location:** If you are in a new town for the interview, it is good to know the place of interview, the means for reaching there, etc. You should take care to reach the place well in time and be without any time pressure on you at the time of interview.
9. **Prepare your dress etc.:** You have to plan what dress you will wear for your interview. Your appearance may be judged from top to toes – your haircut, shaving, make-up down to shoes or sandals.
10. **Go blessed:** Most people find it helpful to seek God's and elders' blessings for an interview.
11. **Keep your testimonials ready:** Carry your originals (if required) in a presentable file. If you have developed any new credential since the application, e.g. a publication, you may take it with you. Your interview letter and other necessary documents should be with you for the meet with prospective employers.

In short, there is a great deal to do before the interview. Well prepared is half won.

II. During interview

The interview day is the acid test, or, as some put it, the D-Day (i.e. the Doom's Day or the Day of Judgement). All your build-up should be for making yourself as presentable as possible for the interview. During the interview, keep this in mind:

1. **You are judged first by your non-verbal communication:** As you enter the interview room, your standing personality, your dress, the way you walk, carry your file, your smile – all this make the first impression. Walk in halfway like a job-holder. Smile as you smile to helpful friends.
2. **Greeting cheerfully:** In most cases, even the interviewers are a little bit nervous when facing a new candidate. You can seize the lead by greeting in a cheerful, confident manner, looking the interviewers in the eye.
3. **Await permission to sit down:** In most cases, the interviewers offer a chair within a few seconds of your entry. Wait for the offer. Otherwise you may ask, "May I take a seat please?"
4. **Sit at ease but be alert:** Sit in an easy, relaxed manner, keeping your posture smart. Be ready to listen and take in the non-verbal communications coming from the interview board.

5. **Answer briefly and to the point:** Use few words to answer questions. Stick to what is necessary. Take a reasonable time to think up answers.
6. **Get the question clarified:** If you have not been able to get the question right, request the interviewer to repeat it. A short form (e.g. PIL = Public Interest Litigation) or a technical word (e.g. Ozone Hole) may pose a difficulty to you. Get the precise clarification you need.
7. **Avoid nervous movements:** Keep your hands in your lap and don't lean on the table. Don't joggle your toes, fiddle with your tie or cover your face with your hands. Don't shift in your seat.
8. **Be truthful:** Avoid bluffing to your interview board. Tell what you know for sure. Sometimes you may be encouraged to guess, but guess on the safe side. If you do not know the answer, don't beat about the bush. If your memory doesn't help you, you can say, "At the moment I can't recall."
9. **Keep your temper in check:** Avoid overanxiety and getting upset with the interviewer. In case an opinion contrary to your views is expressed, do not show a vehement opposition.
10. **Stay positive in all conditions:** Whether the interview is a long one or a short one, you have to hold your positive mental frame throughout. An interview can be a psychologically draining experience. Your mental stamina is tested. Keep your hope alive and go on.
11. **Use pen and paper where necessary:** To explain certain things, you may need pen and paper. Use them with skill and steady hands. This is where you are teacher and the interviewers are learners.
12. **Take up a You attitude for the company :** Your answer should reflect that you wish to grow with the organisation and not use the organisation for your profit, experience and growth. Take on the role of an employee who is devoted to duty and assured of rewards when duty is done.
13. **Keep your questions ready:** You may have your own questions about the working conditions, salary etc. to visualise your position as an employee. Keep these questions ready and ask them when the opportunity presents itself. However, do not presume you are selected.
14. **Make a graceful exit:** Whatever the kind of interview you have had, your exit is one more chance to impress the board. Thank the board members from your heart and exit as you came, measuring every step of the way with dignity.

III. After interview

In some cases, there may be a follow-up after the interview. In case you have promised to send something to the interview board, send it in due course, e.g. a copy of your project report, your summing-up of the interview, etc. Till the time it is received and read, a decision on your selection may be held in suspension. Reconstruct the interview mentally or with a well-wisher and evaluate yourself. This can help you in future interviews and, in fact, in life in general. A job interview can be a major learning experience.

15.4.3 Role of Interviewer

Just as a candidate prepares for his interview, the interviewer also has to get ready for the meet.

A. Preparing to conduct interviews

Here are some tips for good conduct of interviews:

1. Screen the applications and shortlist the applicants who are, on the face of it, fit for interview.
2. Make sure your interview call reaches them in time and gives all necessary instructions.
3. Make the interview room friendly and fit for a useful exchange of information. This is like preparing a stadium for a match.
4. Keep the interview time free from interruptions from visitors and cell phone calls.

5. Make a list of general questions you would like to ask. If you are a member of a panel, allocate roles between yourselves in mutual consultation. One of you may be a subject expert, another a psychology expert and so on. Get prior information via informal channels to know the candidate in his natural hesitation.
6. Circulate copies of application to all board members and make markings on applications in case you have specific questions for a candidate. Pre-planning of questions will help you to get the best candidate.
7. Make good arrangements for reception, recording the candidates' presence and payment of TA/DA etc .
8. Your interview style is an image-builder for your company. Use this opportunity to impress the candidate so that he speaks well of you.

B. During interview

An interviewee who is put at ease is likely to reveal himself better than one who has been put under pressure and made nervous. Everything about the interview board should reflect a friendly reception. Here are some general tips on the conduct of interviews:

1. Let each interview board member have a file on the candidate and paper for making notings.
2. Receive the candidate with a warm, cautious welcome. Respond to his greetings and offer him a chair. Use courtesies like "please," "thank you," etc. Treat him halfway as a colleague.
3. Let the first few questions be calculated to put the candidate at his ease. The real test can begin after that.
4. Avoid cross-talk among board members.
5. Listen well. Take in the non-verbal communications, too.
6. Avoid a sarcastic tone or making comments about his linguistic group, religion, etc. Keep yourself free from prejudice about simple or glamorous appearances. Judge what he/she is, but even more, visualise what he/she may become in reasonable time with your training and inputs.
7. If the candidate is at a loss for words, help him to give a full answer. You may ask sub-questions to the main question.
8. Don't show your positive or negative perceptions about the candidate.
9. Keep the interview of an optimal length, neither too short nor overly long. The chairman of the interview board has a major say in the time-planning of the interview.
10. Avoid asking the same questions to every candidate.
11. You may have to finish a given number of interviews in given time. Accommodate the number of interviews as planned.
12. Respect the candidate for the questions he/she asks to clarify your questions or to know about the organisation.
13. If the candidate is talkative, use your veto to get on to the next question.
14. At the end, thank the candidate. Don't reveal the outcome by word or gesture during the interview.

15.4.4 Some Useful Questions for Job Interviews

Here we list some questions for job interviews:

1. Tell us about yourself.
2. What are your strengths and weaknesses?
3. What subject do you like best?
4. What are your interests/hobbies?

5. Why is there a break in your education/employment here?
6. What were your extra-curricular activities and achievements? Tell us the details.
7. Why have you chosen to apply for this job?
8. Do you like to work in a team or alone?
9. Tell us about some circumstance where you took initiative?
10. What qualities are required to succeed in the job you have applied for?
11. What was the main news today morning? What do you think of it?
12. Who is your role model and why?
13. Tell us about your present job and boss.
14. Are you willing to accept a posting out of town?
15. Are you willing to work late hours?
16. Would you like to acquire any more professional skills? What are they?
17. Why did you leave your last job?
18. What is your parents' contribution towards making you what you are?
19. Which school/college has contributed most to your growth? How?
20. What do you do to keep healthy?
21. How do you spend your holidays and Sundays?
22. What do you do to keep yourself up-to-date in your specialisation?
23. Do you think you have been rewarded well for your talents? Explain.
24. How would your best friend describe you?
25. How would your enemy describe you? Your comment on it.
26. What have you enjoyed most in life?
27. What is your most important achievement in life?
28. Have you ever been seriously ill?
29. What are the major problems facing this industry?
30. How can you make the world a better place to live in?

15.5 APPOINTMENT AND DISCHARGE LETTERS

15.5.1 Appointment Letters

When you appoint a candidate to a post, your letter to him should go as good news, as a welcome, and set out the terms and conditions of service. It is a letter which has a bearing till the retirement of the employee/resignation and even after.

An appointment letter should contain the following details:

1. The appointing authority's name
2. The rules to which the appointment is subject, i.e. service rules
3. The exact name of the post to which the candidate is appointed
4. Date from which the appointment is effective. Last date for joining
5. Conditions the selectee must fulfil to accept the appointment, e.g. produce a health certificate from the civil surgeon or security deposit, etc.
6. The salary , increments and, if possible, about promotions
7. Whether the appointment is temporary or permanent. If on probation, the terms of confirmation
8. The allowances payable, and pension, provident fund etc.
9. The terms of resignation, e.g. the notice period or the salary payable in lieu of notice (on either side)
10. A clause about termination of service by employer.

Specimen appointment letters

Appointment letter 1

Dear Mr________

We refer to your application dated 22nd July 20__ and are pleased to inform you that the Selection Board of the Company offers you an appointment as a Trainee Manager.

The appointment is subject to the following terms and conditions:

1) There will be a training period of one year from the date of your joining . On successful completion of training, you will be placed in one of the divisions of the Company.
2) Your stipend during training period will be Rs. 6,000 p.m. On confirmation you will be placed in the scale of Rs. 10,000-1000-16,000.
3) You will be paid dearness allowance and city compensatory allowance according to the Service Rules of the Company, a copy of which can be had from the Personnel Manager.
4) You will be eligible for provident fund, pension etc. according to the government regulations in force in this regard.
5) You should report to the Chief Training Officer at the Company's head office to convey your acceptance of the post before 1st August, 20—. You should report for training on 1st August, 20—to the same officer.
6) The appointment can be terminated on either side by giving one month's notice or equivalent salary in place of it.
7) In case you do not report to the Chief Training Officer within the date given above, it will be understood that you are not interested in the offer and the appointment will be automatically cancelled.

Please acknowledge and convey your acceptance at the earliest.

Yours faithfully

Appointment letter 2

Dear Ms.________

We are very happy to inform you that in response to your application dated... and interview, you have been selected as a Trainer in the Institute. The appointment is on probation for six months and would be confirmed upon satisfactory performance during probation.

During probation you will be paid a stipend of Rs. 3500 p.m. On confirmation you will be placed in the scale of Rs. 5500-500-8500 with 15% DA and CCA @ Rs. 1500 for a posting in Nashik and Rs. 2500 in Pune.

Contributory provident fund will become applicable upon your confirmation in the post. The appointment can be terminated on either side by giving one month's notice in writing or equivalent salary.

Please return the duplicate of this letter duly signed by you to convey your acceptance of the post and please report for duty on or before 15th July.

We wish you the best.

Yours faithfully

15.5.2 Discharge Letters

These are the letters that set out the terms of an employee's discharge from service. A discharge may be honourable (i.e. with a good record of the employee) or dishonourable (i.e. on account of proven malpractices by employee).

The discharge letter gives:

1. The reason the service is terminated, e.g. resignation or retirement
2. Date when the employee will be relieved of his duties
3. Benefits payable to employee, e.g. provident fund, pension, etc.

> Dear Sir
>
> In terms of your resignation dated 23rd April and acceptance of it by the Company, you are hereby relieved of your duties as Assistant Manager w.e.f. 22nd May 20__.
>
> You will be paid the balance in your provident fund account on 22nd May 20__ by the Accounts Department.
>
> We hereby certify that the last salary drawn by you in the Company was Rs.25,000 p.m.
>
> Yours faithfully

A. Questions based on critical understanding. Comment in about 30 words.

1. **You must use the same résumé for applying to a company for the post of a salesman and a computer operator.**

Ans. The job requirements of the two posts are quite different. One is a public contact job while the other a technical one. Different qualities are required for success in them. You should highlight in each application such items of your biodata as would attract the department head.

2. **In writing an unsolicited application, you have to research the employer.**

Ans. Making an application involves expenditure of time and effort. You have to make sure that the company where you wish to submit an unsolicited application has an opening for someone with your qualifications and qualities, and that the company suits you.

3. **One can always speak spontaneously in a group discussion.**

Ans. A group discussion mirrors your group decision-making ability. In these competitive times, positively oriented persons with leadership skills and with practice in extempore speaking succeed in a GD. GD is a specialist activity and one must prepare and hone one's ability for it.

4. **A group discussion is for testing, mainly, how forcefully you can assert yourself among group members.**

Ans. Assertiveness, though on indicator of personal power, is not the only thing in a GD. Leadership is a subtler matter. In a GD there must be a healthy give and take of views to arrive at a useful collective decision. Others may know at least some things better than you, and you cannot afford to assert yourself all the time.

5. **One can steer a personal interview into one's strong areas.**

Ans. Oh, that is a great art. If you know what the interviewer is looking for, you can drop a hint about your past performance wherein he may find the quality/experience he wants. "At least that's how I managed when I lost my air ticket in a bus accident." Such a statement may attract the interviewer to the details of the episode where you managed without an essential of travel.

6. **An appointment letter is a very important document for employer and employee.**

Ans. In India, jobs are difficult to get and it is often difficult for the employer to remove an employee. The employer should state the terms of appointment very carefully, leaving no essentials out. The joining deadline, termination clause etc. carry much weight. For the employee, it is a second birth chart. He can judge his company from the way an appointment letter is drafted, printed and delivered, and this helps him to decide about joining.

B. Questions for revision

1. How would you make your job application a clincher? (200 words)
2. How can one adapt one's CV to the liking of the employer?
3. What are the differences between the traditional and recent practices in writing biodata?
4. Who can give a reference? What care must the referee exercise in giving it?
5. What would be your approach to preparing for a job interview? (200 words)
6. How can you improve your performance in a job interview? (200 words)
7. As an employer, how would you conduct effective interviews?
8. Give some tips for a meritorious performance is a group discussion.
9. State the guidelines for writing an appointment letter.

C. Drafting Exercises

1. Write an application to the Station Superintendent for employment as a temporary ticket checker.
2. Respond to the ad : "Wanted a call centre operator. Graduate or undergraduate, with/without experience, fluent in English and Hindi/Gujarati, willing to work out of Ahmedabad and accept night duties. International standard training given. Apply in confidence to Box GK-1185, Time of India, Ahmedabad."
3. Draft a résumé as a commerce graduate which you may use for applying for the post of accounts assistance or clerk in a commercial organisation.
4. Write an unsolicited application to Param Superbazar for the post of a cashier/shopping assistant. Enclose your biodata to it.
5. Write a reference for a science graduate for appointment in a testing lab.
6. Write a reference for a widowed lady of 35 who has no experience but can teach in a kindergarten.
7. Draft an appointment letter for XYZ's appointment to the post of watchman in the cooperative housing society's complex. What would be your stand about a security deposit and references (which have not been furnished yet)?
8. Inform Ms. Surendra Mohan of her appoitnement as a sub-editor in your house journal. Make her confirmation subject to her acquiring a diploma in MS-Office within six months of joining.
9. Draft a discharge letter for Prof. M. S. Galgali on his retirement from college.
10. Write a reference for Akshay Kumar, international athlete, for appointment as an officer in Reserve Bank of India.

CHAPTER

16

Correspondence with Public Authorities

What should you know?

16.1 INTRODUCTION

On behalf of a business house or in individual capacity, an educated person of today has a lot of occasions to write to the government or public authorities. We live under a rule of law, and in many cases we can get justice merely by writing letters and making a personal approach.

Good letters reduce the occasions for litigation. More and more government departments and corporations are trying to become public-friendly by making their procedures simple and issuing guidelines to the public to get good service and get their problems solved. Moreover, citizens have certain rights to information from the government.

Earlier, one tended to go to political leaders to get one's matters sorted out with the government or public authorities. But with the spread of information, a citizen can take the strings into his own hands and be his own leader, leaving the public figures to deal with public issues.

Occasions for writing to government or public authorities

One may write to the government etc. for:

(*i*) Information about schemes, procedures, addresses, etc.
(*ii*) Making suggestions for improvement of working
(*iii*) Complaints when there are delays or misservice
(*iv*) Appreciation of good work
(*v*) Warning about dangers that one knows of

Tips for writing effective letters to government and public authorities

1. "Respect" is the key word in dealing with those in authority. Address the post-holder with respect and chances are that he will reciprocate it. The government officer, on the other hand, has to deserve the respect given to his chair.

2. Write to the correct authority. If you are writing about faulty street lamps, you need not address the Circle Engineer (in charge of the state). The concerned junior engineer would be enough for the purpose.
3. When asking for justice, make sure of your position in law. Consult the rule books or those who know, and quote the rules and section where you can.
4. Write with an open mind, with the facts on your side.
5. Observe the eight C's of letter writing closely. In a nutshell, use good stationery, type or write clearly, be brief and cogent.
6. Write promptly but be prepared to wait a long time for the reply. Remind often enough and use oral communication to reinforce your writing. If the lower authority does not respond, go to a higher one.
7. Government officers are tired of stereotyped phrases. Bring freshness in your writing. It can do wonders.
8. It is said that we get the government we deserve. Naturally, we have to improve our deserving.

16.2 CORRESPONDENCE WITH GOVERNMENT DEPARTMENTS

As a businessman you may deal with many functionaries, departments and public bodies to ensure the smooth functioning of your business: the municipal corporation, the electricity board, the passport office, the tourism department, the directorate of small industries, the collector, the commissioner and the district information officer, to name but a few.

Specimen letters

1. Letter to the Electricity Department to issue prior notice of power-cuts

The Executive Engineer (Urban)
Maharashtra State Electricity Distribution Corporation Ltd.
Nagpur

Dear Sir

Subject : Request to inform about power-cuts well in advance

May we invite your attention to the fact that in the past 15 days there have been sudden power-cuts at different hours in Sadar Bazar area, where several workshops and industrial complexes are located. When a power-cut comes suddenly and stays for hours, it becomes very difficult to plan our work, and man-hours are lost. On the other hand, if the Corporation issues advance notification about the hours of area-wise power shutdown, the area's business houses can reorganise their working and save production.

We hope this will elicit an immediate positive response from you.

Thanks for your cooperation.

Yours faithfully

2. Letter to the Municipal Corporation to prevent waterlogging

The Executive Engineer
Public Works Department
Devpur Municipal Corporation
Devpur

Dear Sir

Subject: Request to prevent waterlogging in Shankar Nagar in the monsoon

We wish to invite your attention to the waterlogging that takes place on West High Court Road, Shankar Nagar during the monsoon every year.

Many office complexes are situated in this area, including some important government departments with public dealings. Owing to waterlogging after heavy rains, this area becomes impassable. Water floods the engines of two-wheelers that try to pass through it. Parking in the area becomes impossible. In short, the working of sensitive offices is severely affected for up to three days, until the water recedes on its own.

We trust you will agree that the problem deserves - and has - a solution. Now the monsoon is only two months away. May we request you to clean the drains well in time and ensure smooth traffic even if it rains heavily?

We take this opportunity to congratulate you on your efforts to beautify Devpur and make it green. We hope you will show the same care to solve the problem stated here.

Thanks.

Yours faithfully

3. To the District Industries Centre to conduct an Entrepreneurial Development Programme for capable youths

The District Industries Officer
Devpur

Dear Sir

Subject : Need for an Entrepreneurial Development Programme in Devpur

We are glad that the DIC is keen on taking a major initiative for the industrial development of the district, as reported in the press recently.

May we suggest that the DIC launch an Entrepreneurial Development Programme for the graduates of the district, training them in the basics of setting up an industrial unit? DIC may further assist them with know-how, securing of finance and step-by-step guidance till they start their factory. Such programmes have been conducted in the past by some nationalised banks in the backward regions of the country, with reasonable success. We take pride in the fact that Devpur has three good engineering colleges and several meritorious business schools. The graduates of these institutions would benefit greatly from an EDP.

We are prepared to participate in the conduct of such a programme in case the DIC, with its competent official machinery and its drive, takes the lead. We hope you will respond positively. Please let us know your perceptions about the proposal.

Yours faithfully
For Devpur Industries Association

Sd/-

Secretary

4. To the Chief Commercial Superintendent of railways about delay in getting refund

The Chief Commercial Superintendent
Central Railway
Nagpur

Dear Sir

Subject : Request to expedite refund on account of cancelled tickets

We enclose a copy of our application dated 2nd March 20__, requesting refund against six AC first class tickets for journey by Kerala Express from Nagpur to New Delhi on 28th February, cancelled at Itarsi. More than two months have passed since all the documents were duly lodged in your office, but there is no refund still. We earnestly request you to look into the matter personally and ensure a speedy refund.

As our trains are getting superfast, we trust that our services also will.

We thank you for your concern.

Yours faithfully

5. To the Regional Passport Officer, enquiring about procedure for changing the name on passport

Dear Sir

Subject: Enquiry about procedure to change the name on a passport

A senior executive of our company has recently changed his name and wishes the new name, published in the Punjab Gazzette, to be on his passport. As we are situated away from your centre and have no major travel agents here, may we request you to advise the procedure for this.

We enclose a self-addressed stamped envelope to help you reply.

Yours faithfully

16.3 CORRESPONDENCE WITH INCOME TAX AND SALES TAX AUTHORITIES

Most tax payers have some occasion or other to make enquiries with or complaints to the taxation authorities. I-T and S-T departments have crores of accounts. Given these numbers, tax payers's initiative is necessary to get prompt service. The broad rules for writing to government have already been outlined. As for income tax, the tax payers need to quote their Permanent Account Number (PAN). If you wish to enquire about the status of your refund, you have to give the particulars of submission of your return also.

Specimen letters

1. Issue of a duplicate PAN card

The Commissioner of Income Tax (PAN Cards)
Pune

Dear Sir

Subject: Issue of a duplicate PAN card

I lost my PAN card (No.______) during travel with no hope of finding it. I request you to inform how I can get a duplicate.

Thanks.

Yours faithfully

2. Request to expedite refund

The Income Tax Officer
Salary Ward 2 (3)
Devpur

Dear Sir

Subject: Request to expedite refund of income tax for A.Y. 2009-2010

I recall my recent visit to your office to enquire about my IT refund for the assessment year 2009-2010. I filed my return on 3rd July 2009 (acknowledgement no. 1245) and although nine months have passed and my colleagues have got their refunds, I am yet to get it. May I earnestly request you to enquire into the matter and speed up the substantial refund. You may also enquire if the ITRO* has been posted and lost in transit (as appears to be the case in one instance).

Thanks for your cooperation.

Yours faithfully

*ITRO = Income Tax Refund Order

3. Reply to proposed rectification by Assessing Officer under section 154

The Assessing Officer
Circle/Ward.............
....

Sir

Name of assessee......................
PAN/GIR No..............................
Asst. Year................

Sub : Application under section 154 for allowing set-off of brought forward losses

Please refer to the assessment order dated......in the case of my above client.
I have been instructed by my client named above to state as follows:

1. That my client has been assessed under section 143(3) on a total income of Rs... . But your honour has not considered the setting off of unabsorbed business loss of Assessment Year... After the said set-off, the correct assessed income of my client would be Rs... and not Rs... . as computed by your honour. Total tax payable in respect of said "correct assessed income" would be Rs.... . The assessee-firm has already paid Rs... on... and Rs... on__ respectively under section 210 as advance tax aggregating to Rs... . Besides a sum of Rs.... has been realised by your predecessors-in-office by way of payment in pursuance of regular assessment and a further sum of Rs.... had been collected by the Tax Recovery Officer... resulting in a total payment of Rs... by my said client (copy of relevant evidences are enclosed). As a result, the said assessee-firm is entitled to a refund of Rs...
2. In the premises aforesaid, it is respectfully submitted that your goodself may be pleased to consider the facts, circumstances and/or omissions mentioned above and be kind enough to issue a Refund Voucher for excess payment of tax to the tune of Rs...together with interest accrued thereon under section 244A of the Income-tax Act.1961 after making necessary rectification under section 154 of the Income-tax Act,1961.

Trust, this will be done at an early date with due intimation to my client. And for this act of your kindness my client shall remain grateful forever.

Thank you.

Yours faithfully
....
(Advocate/Chartered Accountant/A.R.)

Encl: As stated and Vakalatnama/Power of Attorney

c.c.to: Client for information.

4. Application seeking permission from Assessing Officer under section 281(1) regarding transfer or creation of charge on assets

The Assessing Officer
Circle/Ward...............
....

Sir

Name of the assessee..................
PAN/GIR No...............................

Sub: Permission under section 281 regarding charge of certain assets

We would like to inform your honour that our company has been sanctioned a loan of Rs. 5 crore by IDBI vide their letter dated......... (copy enclosed at Annex. A).

The said loan shall be granted by IDBI against charge on our factory premises at Mumbai and Surat.

Therefore, your honour is requested to grant us permission under section 281(1) for the same, so that we can enter into an agreement with IDBI in respect of the said loan.

We would like to clarify that no tax is outstanding from us.

Recently a general Income Tax Clearance Certificate had been obtained by us. We enclose a photocopy (Annex. B) of the same for your kind perusal.

Your early action for granting the permission is required.

Thank you.

Yours faithfully
....
Signature of the assessee

Encl: as stated.

CC to : Advocate/Chartered Accountant/A.R. for information and for follow-up

Note : The language of specimens 3 and 4 is legal and official in a very conventional way. This is a carryover of the British period and is given for the students' wider understanding of letter writing.

5. Application for amendment in sales tax registration certificate

ABC Corporation

7, MG Road, Nagpur 440001

17th August 2011

The Sales Tax Officer
Vikrikar Bhawan
Civil Lines
Nagpur

Subject: Application for amendment/addition in sales tax registration certificate

Dear Sir

We currently deal in hardware items and intend to diversify in the field of cement and steel. For this purpose we have to amend the sales tax registration certificate.

We request you to amend the registration certificate by adding the items cement and steel. The original certificate of registration is enclosed for necessary amendments.

Thank you.

Yours faithfully
For ABC Corporation

Finance Manager

6. Letter to Sales Tax Officer to change the name of proprietor

Mohan Sweets

Dharampeth, Nagpur

18th August 2011

The Sales Tax Officer
Vikrikar Bhawan
Civil Lines
Nagpur

Subject: Change in the name of the proprietor

Dear Sir

This is to inform you that Mrs. J. K. Ram was running a restaurant business in the capacity of proprietor of Mohan Sweets, located at Dharampeth, Nagpur and was registered with MVAT – 2002 having VAT no. 440012/V/0008 w.e.f. 1.4.2011.

Now w.e.f. 1.9.2011, Mr. Krishna Ram has taken over the running business along with assets and liabilities of Mohan Sweets and now he is the proprietor of the concern. The photocopy of the affidavit in respect of change in the name of the proprietor is enclosed for your reference.

Thank you.

Yours faithfully
For Mohan Sweets

(Krishna Ram)
Proprietor

16.4 CORRESPONDENCE WITH PROVIDENT FUND(PF) AUTHORITIES

Employees' Provident Fund Organisation is a vast body, bigger than many a nationalised bank. It has about 3 crore subscribers and deposits exceeding Rs. 1,50,000 crore. The administration of this fund has over the years been in the headlines. For a more efficient functioning of the EPFO and redressal of public grievances, Regional Provident Fund Commissioners are posted in major cities.

They issue a booklet for public guidance, distributed free of cost upon request. Recourse to the higher authorities should be had only after due effort at the office which maintains your account.

Specimen letters

1. Request to expedite final payment of EPF

The Regional Provident Fund Commissioner
Nagpur

Dear Sir

Subject: Final withdrawal of EPF (account no. DAG/NAG/4519)

I invite your attention to my application dated 13th September 2010 for closure of my EPF account no. DAG/NAG/4519 and payment of balance. Nearly 11 months have passed and I still have no information where my application stands. During this time, I have made regular oral and written enquiries with my employer (M/s Dave Industries, Nagpur) and the Provident Fund office, with no definite reply. The key functionaries are generally not in their chairs in the PF office. Further, the file is always stated to be with the one who is absent on the day of enquiry. Telephonic enquiries are not attended to properly, and sometimes out-and-out false information is given.

I hope you will appreciate that a retiring employee needs the balance of his PF account from day one to start a new life. As such, 11 months is quite the limit.

I hope you will take suitable steps to expedite my withdrawal. I enclose a set of copies of my earlier correspondence on the subject. I hope there will soon be occasion to thank you heartily for your cooperation.

Yours faithfully

Encl : As above

Based on a real-life case

2. Issue of statement of EPF

Dear Sir

Subject : Request to issue statement of account for the last two years

May I invite your attention to the fact that while EPF statements of account are due at the end of every financial year, I have not received them for the last two years. My employers M/s D. Krishna & Sons plead their helplessness in the matter as the statements are not received from your office.

May I request you to issue statements of my account (no. DKS/BHO/3455) at the earliest?

Yours faithfully

16.5 CORRESPONDENCE WITH POSTAL AUTHORITIES

India tops in the number of post offices, with postal access to remote and difficult terrains. With the low-cost machinery we have, and the postal motto of "We serve day and night," this service has always been under pressure. There is the Universal Postal Union with its headquarters in Geneva, Switzerland to help and coordinate various national postal services – and help postal customers globally.

In recent times, we have seen the growth of hundreds of private courier agencies for taking letters and parcels, but postal service is postal service . Its far-reaching and convenient presence and its sheer range is mind-boggling.

Post offices carry letters, parcels, make money transfers and keep money deposits. They function within the limits of government procedures. Hence the customer has to exercise patience and tact to get the best out of them. A recent development is the appointment of agents to canvass deposits for post offices. These agents act as buffers between the public and the government. Thanks to their departmental contacts, their services can be used suitably in almost all matters relating to post offices.

Specimen letters

1. Delay in the delivery of speed post money order

The Superintendent of Post Offices
Giripeth
Nagpur

Dear Sir

Subject: Abnormal delay in delivering speed post money order

On 10th September 2011 I booked a speed post money order for Rs. 1000/- favouring Mr. Ashok P. Ram, Rajguru Ashram, Haridwar. It was delivered to the beneficiary on 22nd September, i.e. after 12 days. This, too, was after several telephonic enquiries at both ends and my personal visits to the GPO*, Nagpur (issuing office).

When the address was clear and continual enquiries were being made both by me and the beneficiary, where did the speed post M.O. get lost?

The cost of inconvenience to the beneficiary stranded at a remote place is incalculable. The money was required for the beneficiary's return journey, which had to be put off by 12 days. It was a situation where he could have been reduced to starvation and beggary.

I request you to enquire thoroughly and hereby prefer by claim for a token compensation of Rs.1000.

A photocopy of the M.O. receipt is enclosed.

Please keep me posted.

Yours faithfully

Based on a real-life case

GPO = General Post Office

2. Request to make postal orders of various denominations available during the admission season

The Senior Post Master
General Post Office
Devpur

Dear Sir

Subject : Request to make available postal orders of Rs.50 and Rs. 100

June-July is the admission season when thousands of students send their request for prospectuses, for which they have to send postal orders. However, it is found that suburban post offices and even the GPO pleads that these *IPOs are exhausted halfway during the working hours. The applicants have to come again to find that the queue is several hours long.

May I request you to anticipate the demand for IPOs more realistically and make them available at all post offices in sufficient quantity in this season?

We shall thank you for your cooperation in the matter.

Yours faithfully

*IPO= Indian Postal Order

A. Questions based on critical understanding. Comment in about 30 words.

1. **A display of impatience in your letters can get quicker results from a government office.**

Ans. Government offices are bound by a host of rules and hierarchical functioning. As such, work there takes time in any country. Your display of impatience may hardly be heeded and may even be wasted at the wrong table. This may be doubly frustrating. However, your letter may be supported by personal visits, preferably with prior telephonic notice/enquiry.

2. **One may write to the government proactively, too, and improve one's standing.**

Ans. Yes, it is not necessary that your should write to the government only to complain or follow up matters. You may suggest, recommend and appreciate good work. The suggestions etc. should go to the proper authority, especially when there is a dynamic incumbent (post holder). You may be valued for your contribution of ideas and appreciative words.

3. **In government correspondence, proper channel in very important.**

Ans. Quite often, routine matters have to be routed through the proper channel – the prescribed chain of officials for upward movement of papers. A police commissioner requires that your complaint be routed though your area police station. And so on. Sudden appearance of a letter on a higher official's table would put him in a position where he has to get the details from lower officials and hence route the letter downwards.

4. Grievances to government departments and public authorities should be courteous and factual.

Ans. The general rule about courtesy and factual truth in complaints specially applies to government correspondence. The ability of a government official to function effectively depends on the importance given to his "chair." This must be kept up. The grievance has to be factual, well-documented and within the framework of rules.

5. People get the government they deserve.

Ans. The government is made of leaders elected by citizens, and officials are selected from people who are just like ourselves. The tendencies of the general population are reflected in the MPs, MLAs and IAS and other officers. Just consider what we would do in their position. This might explain why we get the kind of government we have. But, "Eternal vigilance is the price of democracy."

B. Questions for revision

1. What would be your thumb rules for writing to government and public bodies? How would you supplement your written communication?
2. How would you adapt the essentials of business letter writing to government correspondence?

C. Drafting exercises

1. Write to MSEDCL (Maharashtra State Electricity Distribution Corporation Ltd.) saying you feel that you have been grossly overbilled. Request suitable and urgent action.
2. Draft a group representation (in letter from) to MSEDCL, on behalf of Grahak Manch, to reduce power tariffs in the domestic sector for the low income group.
3. Write to the GMMC (Greater Mumbai Municipal Corporation) for regular removal of garbage from near your house.
4. Write to your city Municipality or Municipal Corporation to take action on stray cattle on busy roads.
5. The water supply in your locality (a newly developed one) is irregular. Ask the Water Supply Department to regularise it or provide tankers.
6. Write to the income tax officer dealing with your return to expedite the refund.
7. Write to the Post Master General of Devpur to shift Ramnagar Sub Post Office to larger premises with good parking facility.
8. While PPF withdrawals take 2 hours, EPF/GPF withdrawals are taking anything between one month and six months. Write to the Regional Provident Fund Commissioner to make EPF as efficient as GPF, endorsing a copy to the CAG (Comptroller and Accountant General, New Delhi). You may quote a news headline which appeared 18 months ago that EPF would be paid on the day of retirement.
9. Write to the Health Department of the Municipal Corporation to control the menace of stray dogs.

■ ■ ■

CHAPTER

17

Internal Communication

What should you know?

17.1 INTRODUCTION

In a small company, communication within itself is fairly easy. As the organisation grows in size and complexity, the communication becomes varied and multi-layer. In a small company, everyone interfaces (*i.e.* has face-to-face communication with) everyone else, and the modes of communication are also simple. We shall discuss here the communication patterns within a large organisation.

The departments or officers often communicate by means of a **memorandum** (plural, **memoranda**) or **memo** for short.

The management of a large company may instruct its employees or groups of employees through **office orders**. It may give general information by means of **office circulars**. Another means is **office notes.**

Memorandum (memo): In format, this is more informal than a proper letter, and is a quick and precise way of informing or getting things done. It may be used for conveying a warning to an employee, information about arrival of goods, resolution of complaints, etc.

Office order: An office order is, as the word signals, an order from a superior to his underlings. It is downward communication. It may be used for conveying instructions about maintaining punctuality or change in working hours.

Office circular: An office circular brings to the notice of certain employee departments any matters of importance. It may be used for conveying a new scheme of discounts, a facility to employees, etc.

Office note: These are exchanged between two departments and are an example of horizontal/ lateral communication.

17.2 MEMORANDUM

A memo is an important method of internal communication. It is used internally only. A memo may be from one officer to another or between juniors and seniors. Some organisations insist that even small events and requests be recorded in the form of memos. Its advantages are:

- It is a simplified form of communication.
- When things are in writing, they are quite clear and leave no room for doubt or ambiguity.
- It helps in fixing the accountability of the sender and receiver.
- With a written communication in hand, the receiver gets time and facility to think and act.

A memo is meant to inform or to persuade. It should clarify the writer's purpose and answer the receiver's needs. Otherwise it fails as a tool of communication.

How to write an effective memo: As in business letter writing (Chapter Five), there are three stages of memo drafting: pre-writing, writing, review.

Pre-writing: Answer the four key questions involved. What is the goal of this memo? Who will receive it? How many points should it cover and how? What action is desired from the receiver?

Write: Write down the memo in a systematic order. Attach any enclosures, photocopies, etc. that are necessary.

Review: Edit it for clarity, accuracy and brevity. Remove any errors of grammar, typing, facts, etc. Make sure it will go to all concerned.

1. Specimen memo from the managing director to the customer relations officer for not attending to a customer complaint

COMPEX CORPORATION

From the desk of: The Managing Director
To: The Customer Relations Officer
1 June 2011
Ref: MD-106

Subject: Complaint from Pyramid Megastores

The Chief Manager of Pyramid Megastores has just telephoned me that his written complaint dated 28 May about the colour printers in their store remains unattended. You must be aware that they are our valued customer and their work of promotions is hampered. When we are on a business drive, you will surely appreciate that good after-sales service and satisfied customers give a major boost to this drive. I trust you will resolve the complaint without further loss of time and keep me informed.

Sd/-

Managing Director

2. An office memorandum warning an employee against his habit of reading newspapers and magazines during office hours

ABC Limited

Office Memorandum

22nd January 2011

To Mr. P.K.Verma, Senior Clerk, Purchase Department
From General Manager

Ref 109/PD/2011

It has been reported that during office hours, you were often found reading daily newspapers and film magazines, in spite of clear direction against this practice by your immediate superior. Reading newspapers etc. during working hours in against Service Conduct Rules.

You are advised to desist from such activities and to follow strictly the directions given by the superiors. Any violation of these instructions in future would be viewed seriously.

Sd/-
General Manager

3. A memorandum warning an employee on account of being habitually late (different format)

Office Memorandum

NGPC Limited

22nd January 2011

To Mr. Alok Das, Steno, Sales Division
From Personnel Manager

Re 119/SD/2011

It is noticed that for the last four days you have been reporting very late on duty without permission. You are advised to attend office in time and maintain office punctuality. Failure to maintain office discipline would invite disciplinary action on you.

Sd/-
Personnel Manager

17.3 OFFICE ORDER

As the term denotes, it is an order containing directions or instructions, which are required to be complied with by the recipient. In case of non-compliance of office orders, disciplinary action may be initiated.

In an office, office order may be issued for transfer, extension of probation period of an employee, refusing leave to an employee, for sitting overtime to complete the work, distribution of work, termination (dismissal) of services of an employee, granting promotion to an employee, declaring benefits, or for other office work.

An office order should be drafted carefully, typed, and signed by the concerned authority. It has to be duly acknowledged by the person who has to comply with it.

This document is mostly used in government departments and public companies.

While drafting an office order, the following points should be kept in mind –

1. It should be correct, short and to the point.
2. It should draw the attention of the person/s who have to comply with it.
3. It must contain specific instructions or directions for compliance.
4. It must be authentic and duly signed by a competent authority.

1. An office order asking an employee to show cause why disciplinary action should not be taken against him for being disobedient to his superior

XYZ Limited

Delhi

Office Order

1st June 2011
Re: 108/PER/05

Shri S.K. Patel, Junior Assistant is hereby required to show cause in writing by June 15, 2011 as to why disciplinary action should not be taken against him for his persistent refusal to carry out faithfully the instructions issued by his section officer.

Shri Patel is hereby informed that on his failure to give satisfactory explanation about his conduct, disciplinary action will be taken as per Company's rules.

Sd/-
Personnel Manager

2. An office order banning smoking in the office premises, except the canteen

It has been decided that all the offices of the Company shall be made a non-smoking area with effect from 1st January, 2005 in view of their centralised air-conditioning. However, smoking within the canteen premises would not be prohibited. This decision has been taken to protect the general health of the employees and also members of the public visiting the Company's offices. All employees are requested to cooperate and adhere to the decision strictly.

Sd/-
Office Manager

17.4 OFFICE CIRCULAR

A circular is in the form of a letter addressed to all office branches or departments of a company and is drafted in such a way that the information is useful and understandable to all concerned.

The purpose of a circular is to circulate the information contained in it. Whenever the management has to inform anything to the entire organisation, or maybe a department, it uses office circulars. Further, a circular may be issued for various purposes ranging from invitation to the office staff for a party to information about the installation of a card punching machine in the office.

Office circular	Circular letter (see Chapter Nine)
It is a letter or memorandum addressed to a number of persons or intended for general circulation in the organisation.	It is a letter conveying some information from a businessman or organisation to a large number of customers and/or suppliers.
It is an intra-office communication which seeks to bring to notice important matters of the organisation.	It is an unsolicited communication sent to customers/suppliers.
It is usually brief and precise.	Being unsolicited, it is persuasive in approach with emphasis on You attitude and an appealing format.

- The circular must be made in simple language. Technical terms may make it difficult. It has to be clear, precise and complete.
- An office circular is in the form of a letter addressed by the office to all branches or to all departments.
- The purpose of a circular is to circulate some useful information. Whenever the management has to convey anything to the entire organisation or, sometimes, a department, it uses an office circular.
- Since there may be many occasions when a circular is issued by the management, and also since they pertain to different subjects, or emanate from different departments, circulars bear a reference number which is self-explanatory of the purpose/department for which it is issued. Note that in the example below, the reference number of the circular is HR/02/2005/5. The number itself shows that the circular is issued by Human Resource Department in the 2nd month of the year 2005, and that it is the 5th circular of the year.

1. Circular regarding a computer training programme

PQR Limited

New Delhi

February 1, 2011
Circular no. HR/02/2011/5

To all employees

A four-hour computer training programme has been arranged for all employees on Sunday, 5 February 2011, in the office premises. The programme will start at 10 A.M. All employees are required to attend the programme.

Sd/-

Rajesh Suri
Human Resource Manager

2. Office circular for contribution to Tsunami Relief Fund

PSG India Private Limited

New Delhi

March 23, 2011
Circular no. FD/03/2011/9

To all employees

A devastating tsunami has struck the southern coast of India leaving a vast trail of destruction, misery and suffering. We appeal to all employees to contribute generously to the Tsunami Relief Fund for rehabilitation of the affected people. Any contribution to this fund is entitled to 100% income tax deduction. The contributions may be handed to Mr. Salil Chaudhary, Finance Department from 4 pm to 6 pm, Monday to Friday.

Sd/-

Arvind Sahni
Finance Manager

17.5 OFFICE NOTE

Office notes are regarding a problem/project under consideration to facilitate its disposal. In fact, noting is the way by which an employee gives his suggestion or decision. This is widely used in public sector enterprises.

A note may consist of a summary of all relevant papers, a statement or an analysis. The characteristics of a good note are:

- The note should be concise and clear.
- It should be written in courteous language and be free from personal remarks.
- If information to be included in the note is lengthy, it should be incorporated in a separate statement forming an appendix.
- The note must be signed by its writer with his name and designation below it.
- It must be clearly marked to the concerned person or department for further action.

These are exchanged between two departments. Thus they are a typical example of horizontal or lateral communication.

1. For appointment of a temporary computer programmer

ABC Limited

Office Note

From Company Secretary, Secretarial Department
To Mr. Raju Kamat, Personnel Department

22nd July 2011

Ref 109/CS/2011

The Annual General Meeting of the Company is scheduled to be held on 25th September, 2011. In this meeting the accounts will be presented to the shareholders for their approval. Before the Annual General Meeting, two Board Meetings will be held. For the preparation of the papers and other documents for the above meetings, we shall need a computer operator for one month. Please make the necessary provision.

Sd/-

Prashant Sharma
Company Secretary

2. Informing about stock-taking

XYZ Pvt. Limited

Office Note

From Stores Department
To All Administrative Departments

22nd July 2011

Ref. 110/SD/2011

Subject : Stock-taking for the year ending 31.3.2011

The stock-taking for the closing of accounts for the year ending 31.3.2011 will begin on 1st March 2011. All departments are advised to draw their requirements latest by 28th February 2011. Also, there will be no supplies to customers from the stores on 30th and 31st March, 2011. I shall appreciate your cooperation.

Sd/-

Padmashree Gupta
Stores Officer

17.6 CORRESPONDENCE WITH BRANCH OFFICES

When your company's business grows, you set up branches within the city, in other cities or even abroad. Hence, branch office correspondence is a special area of business letter writing for intra-company communication. The letters may be from the head office/regional office to branches or the other way.

Following points need to be noted in such intra-company letter writing:

1. Writing from head office to branch office is downward communication, and from a branch to head office is upward communication.
2. The letters exchanged between branch offices and head office are mostly routine letters. You may or may not use the company letterhead.
3. Even though they are of a routine nature, you need to be polite and observe due courtesies, especially in upward communication. Familiarity should not reduce the respect.
4. These letters may be short or long, depending on the purpose.

1. Letter from a branch manager to head office recommending an employee's confirmation in service

Bhaskar Udyog

Balrampura
Bhopal

12 July, 2011

The Personnel Manager
Bhaskar Udyog
A-24 Connaught Circus
New Delhi

Dear Sir

Subject: Confirmation of Mr. Ramprasad Tiwari

I enclose the service record and confidential record of Mr. Ramprasad Tiwari, Trainee Sales Executive, for the last twelve months.

As you can see therefrom, he has been a punctual and disciplined worker, intelligent and hardworking, and capable of bringing good business to the company. His performance both in the office and on field duty has been quite satisfactory and his conduct to superiors and peers blameless.

In view of this, according to Company norms, he may be confirmed in service and put in the scale of Rs.20,000–2000–30,000.

Please instruct.

Yours faithfully

2. Letter from head office to branch office regarding an employee's training

Mr. Vinod Kumar, Management Trainee, is being sent to your Branch for fifteen days to do part of his three-month training course in various departments of the company.

You may please impart him suitable training in branch work and branch administration.

3. Letter from head office to a branch office pointing out delay in recovering dues

On examining the monthly return of debtors, we find the following amounts outstanding beyond the due date:

M/s R. G. Das & Co.	Rs. 25,007.50
M/s Sheel Sons	Rs. 35,005.45
Rockwell Furnishers	Rs. 30,900.00

Please advise whether the amounts have been realised by you since. If not, please let us know, at your earliest, the reasons for delay in recovering these amounts and the steps being taken now.

4. Letter from regional office to head office suggesting the opening of a branch office

At present we have three branch offices in the Northern Region - Agra, Chandigarh and Patna. The market for the company's products is growing in the states of Punjab and Haryana where we have only three sales representatives. Looking at the scope for business growth in Punjab and Haryana, we suggest that a branch office be opened at Chandigarh with the following staff:

Branch manager	1
Sales representatives	4
Peon	1

The cost of maintaining a branch, as worked out in the enclosed sheet, is Rs. 20 lakhs p.a.

We look forward to your early decision in the matter.

5. Letter from head office to branch office asking for stock statement

The stock statement for the fortnight ended 31 July has not yet been received in this office. Would you please expedite the despatch of the statement?

6. Letter from Branch Office to Head Office for celebrating silver jubilee

We are pleased to inform you that our branch has completed 25 years in March 2011. We would like to celebrate the silver jubilee in a befitting manner. We have planned to organise a grand function to celebrate this event in which the loyal customers of the company will be felicitated and also the employees who have completed 25 years of service. We request you to be the chief guest at the programme.

For this celebration, an amount of Rupees one lac is estimated to be spent. We request you to sanction the amount.

A. Questions based on critical understanding. Comment in about 30 words.

1. A memo is different from a letter.

Ans. The term *memorandum* is derived from the Latin word *memorare* which means to mention or tell. It is a short official note that is written to a person or to several people, especially those with whom one works. Though it is a piece of written communication, it is not a letter as it differs in format from a formal letter.

2. Office orders can be issued only by superiors.

Ans. Office orders are meant to communicate matters relating to certain rights, withdrawing rights, imposing restrictions, making postings/transfers etc. Thus office orders can be issued only by superiors and are binding on subordinates.

3. Office circulars and office notes mean the same thing.

Ans. There is, in fact, a difference between the two terms. Office circulars seek to bring to the notice of a certain audience important matters of the organisation. They are widely used to disseminate information like inviting applications from employees or promotion test/interview etc. On the other hand, office notes are exchanged between two departments. They are mostly an instance of horizontal or lateral communication.

4. Office orders indicate downward communication.

Ans. As the term 'office order' denotes, it is an order containing directions or instructions issued by a superior which are to be complied with by a subordinate receiving the order. Thus it indicates downward communication.

B. Questions for revision

1. Explain with examples the difference between office orders and office circulars.
2. What are circular letters? How are they different from office circulars? Explain briefly the main objectives of writing circular letters. (200 words) (Hint : Refer to Chapter Nine also.)
3. When does an office issue circulars? How are they drafted for economy, clarity and effect?
4. Enumerate the features of correspondence between a branch office and head office. What are the occasions for them to write to each other?

C. Drafting exercises

1. Draft a circular for employees insisting on the following (i) Punctuality (ii) Hygiene and cleanliness.
2. Write an office order transferring an employee from one department to another.
3. Write an office note as a Production Manager to the Managing Director of the Company for replacing the old machinery with new imported machinery from Japan.
4. Draft an office memorandum relating to warning an employee for his carelessness in work.
5. Write an office memorandum warning an employee for submitting fake medical bills.
6. Write an office memorandum warning an employee against his habit of reading newspapers and magazines during office hours.

7. Draft an office note announcing suspension of transactions for two days due to annual stock-taking.
8. Write an office note from the personnel manager to the departmental heads for ensuring punctuality in their respective departments.
9. Draft an office order requiring employees to sign attendance register at the specified time in both sessions.
10. Write an office order asking an employee to show cause why disciplinary action should not be taken against him for being disobedient to his superior.
11. Write an office circular informing the employees about a change in office timings.
12. Draft an office circular for reduction in the telephone expenditure.

■■■

CHAPTER

18

Précis and Summarising

What should you know?

18.1 WHAT IS A PRÉCIS

A précis is defined as a summary, traditionally in one-third the number of words of the original. The main ideas of the author are retained and the language is the précis writer's. The reduced passage is given a title that sums up its theme.

Précis is a French word (with *s* silent – PRAY-SEE). The plural is *précis* (PRAY-SEEZ). Précis writing is a valuable art. It enables you to convey the sense of a given passage in brief, saving the reader's time. It requires a high degree of comprehension power and editorial skill. For success in précis writing, one should start developing one's wordpower. One should also practise with short, easy passages. To write a précis is first a mental act of abstraction (reduction and grasping of main ideas). Once you get used to the art of précis writing, you can use it in oral communication as well. Thereby you can save your time in office, especially over the phone where every minute has to be paid for.

18.2 USES OF PRÉCIS

We use a précis or a summary when we have to give a lot of information in limited space and time. In official life there are always occasions to reduce incoming and outgoing messages to just a few words. Since a good précis retains the main ideas, avoids the repetition that may exist in the original and does away with examples and analogies, it serves the purpose of giving the gist of the original writing.

In term of academics, précis writing teaches you to use language with precision and economy. You substitute one word for two or more with similar meanings. For examples, if the original says "beauty, charm and elegance" the précis may say "grace." When students have to take out notes from what they read, they have to willy-nilly exercise the art of précis. If they don't, their thinking and analytical skill is not developed. Précis writing helps you to tell what is essential and what secondary.

18.3 HOW TO WRITE A PRÉCIS

Writing a précis normally amounts to taking out the leading ideas and rewriting them in one-third of the number of words. Précis writing, like all other important writing, can be divided into three stages:

I. Pre-writing

- Read the passage carefully and locate the main ideas.
- Make sure you understand what you read.
- Underline key phrases and take out rough summary notes.
- Pay attention to what the author has stressed.
- Note the more important details. Some details are vital, some are minor.
- You may ignore specific examples, figures of speech, quotations etc. used by the author.
- Re-read the passage to pick up any important ideas left out.

II. Actual writing

- You may write on alternate lines, five/six words per line. This makes it easy to insert words and count them.
- Arrange your notes in a logical order and start at a logical point. This may not be the author's order.
- Think of a heading and organise your précis around it.
- Make long sentences with two or more verbs to save on the word count.
- Use your own words.
- Do not use abbreviations unless they are used by the author. Names of organisation are counted as one word.
- Do not add ideas of your own.
- Do not criticise the author's ideas, nor add you own examples and explanations.
- Manage in the given length.

III. Post-writing, i.e. revision

- Go through what you have written. Make sure that all important ideas are there.
- Maintain continuity in your write-up.
- Correct any mistakes of grammer, spelling, punctuation, etc.
- Adjust within the word limit.

In short, your summary must give to a reader who has not read the original, a clear idea of what the passage contains.

Short practice passages for précis writing:

1. A precarious situation has arisen in the icy parts of Kashmir. The mercury has dipped below zero and many lakes including the Dal lake have frozen. Kashmir looks a landscape painted in white. While Kashmiris take an icy winter in their stride, this year the earthquake victims are especially hit, and are living in the open in makeshift housing. (59 words)

Précis: An Icier Winter in Kashmir

Kashmir's icy parts are facing sub-zero temperatures with the land snow-covered and lakes frozen. This makes life hard for earthquake victims. (21 words)

2. The assault of the developed economies of the world on the economies of the poorer and developing countries goes on at an accelerated pace. (24 words)

Précis: Developed countries are exploiting poorer countries even faster. (8 words)

3. I wish to apply for the post advertised in today's *Time of India*. I passed my S.S.C. from Nagpur Board in 2000 with 83.2% marks and H.S.S.C. from Pune Board in 2002 with 75.1% marks. I passed my B.Com. from Nagpur University in 2005 with 58.2% marks and this year I expect to score a first class at the M.Com. Part I examination.

I have secured a certificate for typing 40 w.p.m. and can handle a computer for DTP operations.

I have worked as a part–time office assistant with a senior chartered accountant. As such I feel that I qualify well for the post of personal secretary to your marketing manager.

Précis (This is written in third person): The writer applies for the post of personal secretary to the marketing manager. He is a B.Com. with a good academic record, can type 40 w.p.m. and knows DTP operations. He also has some good office experience.

4. If you stand up and think clearly and keep going for two or three minutes, that is all that will be expected of you during your first few talks. A topic, such as why you enrolled for this course, is very easy; that is obvious. If you will spend a little time selecting and arranging your material on that topic, you will be almost sure to remember it, for you will be speaking of your own observations, your own desires, your own experiences.

Précis: Initially, you have to speak clearly for about two minutes on a simple topic: why you have joined this course? You can speak well by organising your thoughts about yourself.

5. Yet I must say that you ought to spend time getting rich. You and I know there are some things more valuable than money; of course, we do. Ah, yes! By a heart made unspeakably sad by a grave on which autumn leaves now fall, I know there are some things higher and grander and sublimer than money. Well does the man know, who has suffered, that there are some things sweeter and holier and more sacred than gold. Nevertheless, the man of common sense also knows that there is not any one of these things that is not greatly enhanced by the use of money. Money is power.

Précis: Why Become Rich?

The author recommends becoming rich. He knows that there are things far more sublime than money. But through sad experience he also knows that all sublime causes are greatly helped by money power.

18.4 SOME SPECIMEN PRÉCIS

1. Child labour is not a recent phenomenon. It prevailed in India as far back as three centuries B.C., almost in the form of bonded labour. Kautilya's *Arthashastra* speaks in no uncertain terms of poor children kept as slaves in the houses of rich people. Despite efforts to control the evil of child labour, it still flourishes mostly in economically backward areas in our country.

The reasons for child labour in India are not far to seek. The prime reason for prevalence of child labour is poverty. Poverty-stricken parents, in order to supplement the meagre family income, do not feel reluctant in sending their small children for work. The children get the job involving manual work with comparative ease because they can be hired with low wages. Also, child labour is more prone to exlpoitation, because the child cannot raise any protest against employer on account of his weaker bodily strength. Besides, child labour cannot form a union and hence the absence of union is likely to be exploited. In certain cases, employees also force female workers to bring along with them their young children to be employed with them. Another important reason for the problem of child labour is lack of educational and cultural facilities for young children. In many far-flung areas in our country, schooling facilities are scarce and inaccessible. In many places schools are not fully equipped with proper library, playing fields and other educational infrastructure and hold little attraction for children. In many cases children are forced to stay back at homes, because their parents cannot afford educational expenses.

Children are mainly employed in the unorganised sectors like agriculture, small restaurants, construction work, carpet manufacturing, in houses as domestic servants, etc. The number of child workers in the organised sector is comparatively quite low except in match factories etc. The reason for employment of large number of children in match factories is that their small fingers are easy with match sticks and hence they work with good efficiency.

The available evidence shows that child labour in India is being exploited too much. He works for longer hours, in unhealthy conditions and for low wages. Agreed that physical work may not harm the health of child workers in all cases, but what is harmful is long and total, irrevocable subordination to their masters. What kind of men will they grow up to be as there is no place for sensitivity and love in their lives. The exploitation and ceaseless hatred for the society make these children unhappy and pessimistic about the society they live in. **(423 words)**

Précis:

The Evil of Child Labour
OR
The Soul-crushing Child Labour

In India's poor parts, child labour has been there for over 2000 years. This practice is especially widespread today. But child labour is an evil which destroys the sensitivity of youngsters. It is the result of poverty of some families and the upper hand of the upper classes. Low income families are forced to send their children to work. Lack of proper schooling facilities and their high cost add to the problem. Children are diverted to agriculture, help in small business or housework. Since children are unorganised, their wages are low and exploitation high. In fact children are used even in the organised sector of match factories because of their small hands and greater skill in work there. Poor mothers are required to bring their children to work. Victims of child labour grow up into dejected citizens, which is a serious concern. ***(140 words)***

2. The rash of strikes, gheraos, and alarming rates of absenteeism in our country is a symptom of despair of various classes of workers and employees in the face of extreme insensitivity on the part of managements and employers in both private and public sectors. Unfortunately, management, barring in a few cases, has a peculiar tendency to sleep over even the genuine demands of workers. Only when the normal life in the factories or in the organisations is completely or substantially disrupted by workers' strikes with consequent colossal loss of production that management wakes up from its deep slumber to take necessary remedial measures. In the wake of a spate of strikes by workers almost everywhere in the country, managers and researchers have been attempting an anatomy of the problem.

It is a pity that absenteeism – a major problem in the workforce today – continues to elude that attention of the Government, managements, trade unions, and researchers. And this despite the fact that the cost of absenteeism is quite high for the society, the affected organisations and individual employees. A high rate of absenteeism adversely affects the industrial growth. For a country like India which is on its way to rapid industrialisation, the cost of absenteeism is quite high. Absenteeism is also harmful for an organisation because of its costs and operating problems. It not only leads to decline in production and profits, but also in reduced productivity. In the case of frequent absenteeism, either casual or temporary workers, who are comparatively inexperienced, are appointed. Where the existing staff is asked to do extra work on overtime basis, it often results in accidents and other mishaps in factories.

The problem of absenteeism should be taken more seriously by all concerned – managements, trade unions and the Government. Managements should take specific steps to reduce absenteeism only after identifying the factors responsible for it. Complete elimination of absenteeism appears to be rather difficult, but it can be reduced substantially through some suitable measures. Before taking any action on the problem of absenteeism, a systematic study should be carried out in organisations/departments affected by absenteeism to find out its various aspects, such as the number of absentees in a particular period, the rate of absenteeism, the number and names of chronic absentees and part of the year in which most of absenteeism takes place. Such a study would facilitate a proper diagnosis of the problem and that in turn would help managements in taking specific remedial measures. **(412** words)

Précis:

Absenteeism – an Industrial Malady
OR
The Ignored Problem of Industrial Absenteeism

The high rate of strikes, gheraos and industrial absenteeism in India's private and public sector is a big malady. It causes loss of efficiency, production and profits, but is largely ignored. The government, managements and trade unions need to tackle it firmly. Absenteeism often reflects the management's unconcern for the workers' genuine demands. Only strikes resulting in large losses bring a remedy. For a developing country like India, absenteeism hampers industrial growth and hurts workers too. Operating problems arise when unskilled workers are employed during strikes or regular workers work overtime, sometimes causing accidents. The government, managements and trade unions need to study its causes and features like the number and identity of those absenting themselves. Once the problem is well understood, it can be controlled. For an aspiring economy like Indias, this is necessary to strengthen its industrial network, functioning and growth. **(143 words)**

3. Career development relates to the readiness for progression through a series of positions during an individual's working life. Career issues emerge as a result of increasing stress of the organisation on developing its human resources and growing expectations of the individuals about what they need to do to facilitate career growth as they become more educated.

Career development as a responsibility of the organisation necessitates collection and analysis of data, decision-making and their implementation. It must be realised that organisational objectives can be accomplished effectively by integrating individual needs and organisational goals. Usually, line supervisors and human resource managers are responsible for implementation of Career Development Programmes. The line supervisors are responsible for the assessment and development of their subordinates and for assisting them in attaining desired positions with the help of varied measures, especially counselling. Indeed, their day-to-day involvement in career development of subordinates stems largely from counselling. Although they need not be professional counsellors to accomplish effectiveness in career development, they must realise that it forms an integral part of managing, and varied skills and techniques are required to perform this role.

The human resource executive plays a significant role in promoting the development of career paths to satisfy the needs of people. They provide career planning assistance to employees, arrange training for supervisors in career development techniques and coordinate career development programmes. Indeed, a human resource department initiates varied career development programmes in the organisation. **(238 words)**

Précis:

Management of Career Development
OR
An Organisation's Role in Employees' Career Growth

Career development is what employees expect and an organisation needs. The term means an employee's rise in position for better satisfaction. To achieve career development for its employees, an organisation has to take data-based decisions. Line managers, whether specially trained in counselling or not, have to assist their subordinates to attain their targeted positions. This task requires skill. On the other hand, human resource managers have to implement Career Development Programmes and train supervisors and employees suitably for the purpose. **(80 words)**

4. Mr. Soni has recently joined as Managing Director of a Car Manufacturing Company, which at present is incurring heavy losses. Mr. Soni has been entrusted with the formidable task of rejuvenating the company. He faces many challenges to achieve the task such as controlling costs and expenses, increasing productivity and boosting morale of the employees so that they unhesitatingly cooperate to achieve the set standards of output.

Mr. Soni, who was Deputy Managing Director in his previous company, also a Car Manufacturing Company, had proved to be a proficient Manager and a talented leader, who had successfully inspired his employees to increase the productivity. He was commended for his maximum concern for both people and production and also for bringing about an integration and harmony between the needs of employees and of production.

In the new company also, Soni has continued his policies of participative management and his high concern for production and people. With a view to reviving the company back to health, he has effected some major changes. First of all, he has decentralised the organisation so that subordinates can exercise their discretion and initiative in decision-making and their imagination and creativity in performing other managerial functions. Furthermore he has empowered junior managers to sanction expenditure upto approved limits without seeking prior approval of the higher management. Communication system is also improved to facilitate free flow of upward and downward communication.

He has also adopted several measures to cut costs and wasteful expenditure. He has banned donations to charitable institutions, but increased the amount being spent on the welfare activities of employees.

Some employees are of the view that a lot of things are being done, but they might not be effective in the long run. The majority of employees disagree with them and say, okay, we will give it a try.

(303 words)

Précis:

A Strategy for Reviving a Company
OR
A Drive from Loss to Profit

Mr. Soni, a car manufacturing company's newly appointed managing director, is required to revive a loss-making company. This is a tough job. He has to take financial recovery measures, boost production and raise employee morale. In a similar position in another car company, Soni was a successful executive, reputed for care of his employees and generating profits. In his new position, Soni has included juniors in management processes, increased their sanctioning powers and improved internal communication. He has cut costs and wasteful expenditure and given more amounts for employee welfare. Most employees support the plan, only a few doubt it. **(100 words)**

5. Mr. M. K. Sinha was appointed as office assistant in V. K. Institute of Technology. The appointment letter stated that his appointment was on a temporary basis and his services could be terminated at any time with one-month notice or one-month salary in lieu of a notice. Assistant Registrar of his department observed that the performance of Mr. Sinha was not at all satisfactory. He was neither punctual nor regular in his office. He made many mistakes in his work and often argued with his colleagues. He was found to be indifferent, irresponsible and indisciplined. Therefore, he was orally warned a number of times by his Assistant Registrar to improve his work performance. But he was never issued any written memos or notice, and nothing was kept on record by way of adverse remarks against him.

According to the Institute's rule, temporary employees became permanent automatically after two years of service. So at the end of the one year and eleven months, the Assistant Registrar gave in writing to the Director that Mr. Sinha should be removed from his job, as he had not shown any improvement at the work-place and that he might be given one month's salary in lieu of one month's notice.

Mr. Sinha went to the court of law stating that natural justice was not given to him as there was no adverse record against him in writing. He remarked that if he could be tolerated for one year and eleven months, he could not be regarded as totally incompetent. Mr. Sinha further argued that the Institute did not offer enough guidance and support to him, as a result of which he could not perform very well and committed several mistakes at his work. The Lower Court and subsequently the High Court and the Supreme Court upheld his case and asked the Institute to reinstate the office assistant. The Institute had to do it.

The Chairperson of the Institute soon after this incident issued a confidential circular to all the Directors that in future every Director must keep detailed records of omissions and commissions made by every temporary employee and even a small error committed must be carefully recorded. **(363 words)**

Précis:

Lessons of Not Keeping a Written Record
OR
The Need to Maintain Written Records

Mr. Sinha was a temporary office assistant in V. K. Institute of Technology. His services could be terminated with one month's notice or payment of one month's salary. Sinha was lax and careless in work, but was warned only orally, not in writing. However, he failed to improve. Two years of service would make him automatically permanent, so one month before this, he was recommended for dismissal and an order was issued. Against this order, Sinha filed a case for reinstatement as his *written record* was good. He further argued that the Institute did not guide him properly and kept him undertrained. He won the case all the way to the Supreme Court. The Institute's chairperson issued instructions to record employee errors in writing. **(124 words)**

A. Questions based on critical understanding. Comment in about 30 words.

1. **A précis can be conveniently made by picking out the important sentences from the original and putting them together.**

Ans. That is a cut-and-paste job and out of favour with most examiners and authorities. The précis is expected to be in the summariser's language. Moreover, in picking up some few sentences outright, one may miss out what the other sentences contain, and it may not be possible to give continuity to the précis.

2. **Practice with short précis passages helps in writing précis of longer passages.**

Ans. Indeed, that is *the* way to go about the job. If you wish to break a bundle of sticks one day, start by breaking individuals sticks. "From easy to difficult" is a time-honoured principle of learning.

3. A précis specialist saves time and money.

Ans. A précis expert masters the art of abstraction, i.e. taking out important ideas of the original. This sharpens his mind and develops in him an eye for the essentials. Using this mental equipment, he can get to the heart of the matter anywhere, communicate in less time and space, and make savings.

4. Précis writing helps in academics too.

Ans. In your studies, there are occasions to take out notes for exams and future reference from the books your read. The précis art tells you to pick out the essentials. Moreover, by adopting your own language, you develop originality and freshness.

B. Questions for revision

1. Describe the steps in writing a précis.

C. Drafting Exercises

1. Reduce these short passages to one-third their length. Give your precis a title.

(*a*) What convinces a reader of your claims on behalf of your product or service? Is the name in itself a guarantee? Are their testimonies from people whom the readers revere and trust, like great public figures? What is the experience of users elsewhere? How many numbers have been sold? What about the reputation of the technology used? Is there a warranty to back up the product or an assurance of after-sales service? Can you give a demonstration or a free trial offer? Can you give a money-back guarantee? What is the standing of other products from your company? These are the questions to ask and answer in making your sales pitch. *(111 words)*

(*b*) A businessman may expand his business by giving credit to parties that can - and want to - repay. The creditworthiness of a party is not a constant but a variable. It depends on the party's capital, i.e. his net worth and investment in business. Then comes his capacity, his potential to generate profits. This depends, among other things, on his ability and opportunities. Cases are known when credit was given to a zero-capital buyer, merely on the strength of his ability to generate profits. The party's character is the third factor here. With all documents and all laws in your favour, you would still want to have your money without the hassles of a lawsuit. And last but not least, it is the circumstances. The market can go up and it can go down. The buyer may be overstocked, over-extended. He may be rich but also in the red. His sterling character and his capacity still leave the question, will he be able to pay in time? *(166 words)*

(*c*) Every effective speaker vouches for this, that he went deep and wide into his subject. A good speaker gathers more information than he may actually require, following the law of *overages* (from the medicine world). That is how he has a back-up, a reservoir of extra information that boosts his conviction and confidence. When you say, "The farmer in Vidarbha is pushed to the wall," you have at the back of your mind the figures of suicides daily reported in the newspapers, the circumstances of individual cases, the visits by dignitaries, the shallow schemes, and inclemency of weathergods and the sheer bafflement of their situation. A mastery of the subject requires that you see the subject from many angles including that of your opponents. *(124 words)*

(*d*) A conclusion normally aims that your audience should act in the way you want them to. You may want them to buy your product or service, or to speak well of your company, or to give up some habits or acquire new habits (e.g. punctuality or better proof-reading or greater courtesy). The conclusion has to emerge logically from the talk like the proof of a mathematical theorem. And yet, the speech is anchored more in an emotional appeal than an intellectual one. You have to make a good idea likable. *(90 words)*

e) A letter of credit is a guarantee from one bank, through another, to pay a seller upon submission of specified documents. An L/C enables a buyer to obtain credit and ensures payment to the supplier. The obligation of the importer under the purchase contract is supported by the superior obligation of his banker to make payment to the seller. A bank, however, deals in documents, not goods. As long as the documents are as specified in the L/C, the bank pays. However, if the bank comes to know (say, from news reports about forged documents being issued to exporters) that documents have been acquired without shipping the goods ,the banker must exercise more than normal caution and tact. In case the opener of the L/C challenges the payment made by the bank, the court may take the stand that although the documents were prima facie in order, the banker had reason to know that they were forged. Hence the payment made under the L/C against "correct" but forged documents may not be upheld. *(173 words)*

2. Practice passages for précis.

(*a*) IT WASN'T exactly music for their ears and quite a few may have been extremely uncomfortable, but you don't invite a tiger over for dinner and not expect to be slightly mauled either. The angry man of the Indian industry and the most vocal proponent of "swadeshi," Rahul Bajaj, after all, hasn't yet been criticized for not speaking his mind – detractors be damned.

The Chairman-cum-Managing Director of Bajaj Auto Limited is not wholly opposed to the debt recovery mechanism being adopted to clear mounting non-performing assets (NPAs) of public sector banks, believes electricity theft has to be curbed and if some innocent industrialist suffers or has to go to jail under the new regulation being contemplated it's just too bad, but living with power theft is even worse. Ouch? There's more.

No company was efficient in accordance with world standards pre–1990. There was no competition and because of this customers suffered. Should we go back to that time? Should we fear competition to such an extent? Or should we improve and capitalise on our core competencies, learn what competition teaches, become more efficient, reduce cost and better quality of products?

An open economy is better than a closed economy. I prefer it to the socialist pattern of economy we followed for over 30 years which was bad for the customer, encouraged corruption and offered more discretionary powers to politicians. An open economy means no controls but lots of regulations.

There are four major aspects that need to be addressed while running a company. The first is naturally improving the quality of management. If the quality of management is not improved upon we don't stand a chance in hell. Those that cannot improve get out of it. Allow your child to take the reins for it brings a sense of commitment to the business in addition to continuity, but only if he has the competence to add further value and create wealth. Not if he is going to sink it all.

Focus on the product development capability. Earlier, products could be brought from abroad. But joint ventures are a thing of the past. Bring technology and absorb it, but product development capability will have to be improved. Thirdly, you have to be in a listening mode. Unless you listen to what your customer, employee or the market is saying, you'll never understand what to do. Lastly, the organisation's interest should be above the family interest. *(404 words)* (*b*) CRM or Customer Relationship Management is a buzzword for a set of software tools designed to gather more information about the customer. It is the information technology wing of a business strategy that aligns the organisation around the customer, sharing information across all arms of business, and leveraging data from disparate sources to understand the customer and maximise profitability by anticipating his or her needs. CRM involves getting information about the customer from customer contact points. These contact points could be call centers, help-desks, e-mail or sale invoices.

This customer data is stored, retrieved and analysed for performance management. Information is extracted from the data by trying to discover patterns or trends connecting data. This information is used to extract intelligence for making business decisions. CRM can thus help create an appropriate marketing mix for each customer. By understanding the customer, an organisation can create a product that the customer wants, sell it at a price the customer can afford, design an interesting promotion strategy and distribute it in a manner that the customer finds convenient.

Often, changing business conditions compel organisations to implement CRM. Earlier steel demand was predictable. However, with manufacturing booming in China, demand fluctuates violently. So steel companies are planning to implement CRM to keep track of demand and prices, and route its production through the most profitable distribution channel.

CRM is important because understanding customers helps to get repeat business by changing organisational products and services in tune with the customers' needs and requirements. It's a philosophy born out of the understanding that it costs less to grow with an existing customer than to acquire a new one. One just needs to look at the revenues of Indian software companies to realise this. Seventy per cent or more of the revenues of Indian software companies come from existing customers. Moreover, the sales cycle in software is rather long – it takes six months to a year from the cold-call stage to closing the deal. Hence many software companies lay stress on account management of existing customers as much as efforts to acquire new ones. *(Approx 348 words)*

(*c*) Multinational corporations are large companies with assets in different countries. Their area of operations spans different nations. The size of multinational companies is staggering. General Motors, the biggest multinational in 1999, made US $ 161 billion in gross revenues – a sum larger than the Gross Domestic Product (GDP) of many nations including Ukraine, Israel and South Africa. Globalisation is linked to Multinational Corporations. Globalisation is the process by which these multinational companies work with an endeavour to turn the world into one unified market place. In a globalised world the idea of a product might come from the company headquarters in New York, be produced in factories in India and marketed to consumers of France. The internet and mass media which includes Hollywood Movies and American television shows, are also part of globalisation. Globalisation paves the way for merging the nations of the world into one global culture.

The impact of globalisation on human rights is a mixture of good and bad. On the one hand we move towards a world that is drawn closer together by trade. Globalisation promotes free trade and it is fairly clear that free trade produces more wealth. It also increases employment opportunities in different countries. Many observers, however, emphasise the negative aspect of globalisation by companies which often concentrate on making more profits. They are not so concerned about the well-being or human rights of their workers. Their aim is to be allowed to operate freely. If corrupt and oppressive regimes allow them to operate freely, they often support such regimes and hinder human rights.

Thus critics of globalisation usually agree that though globalisation has had some benefits, the driving force behind globalisation is the large multinational corporations that dominate the world economy, and these companies have no interest in human rights. The multinational corporations are unaware of or disregard the impact their activities could have on economic, social and cultural rights, whether at the collective level or at an individual level. Globalisation has tended to benefit rich nations more than the poor ones. The world's seven largest industrial economies make up less than 12% of the world's population but consume 43% of the world's fossil fuel production, 64% of world's paper and around 60% of all aluminium, copper, lead, nickel and tin. Translated, this means that the average person in these industrialised countries consumes and benefits from far more resources than the average citizens of the developing world. If a decent standard of living is a universal human right, globalisation may have only succeeded in granting that right to a small minority of the world's population. Globalisation has to be tackled with caution though it has done some good and is not inherently evil. It has the capacity to do great harm. *(460 words)*

(*d*) The assault of the developed economies of the world on the economies of the poorer and developing countries goes on at an accelerated pace. Even countries like India which show some concern for self-reliant growth have to suffer a great degree of exposure to this assault from abroad in very many ways. Foreign aid is, of course, the most potent means of this assault in that, in a tied-aid, the aid-giver obliges the recipient country to accept technologies and equipments of the former's choice which may not necessarily be in keeping with the requirements of the recipient countries. Recently, the industrial countries have found an argument against even conditional assistance for industrial development being given to the poor nations, since even such aid with strings adds to the economic capability of the recipient country.

The strategy is now to sell equipments which do not strengthen any buying country's economic capacity. This is done by promoting a theory of environment protectionism and anti-pollution endeavour. There is no doubt that environment is very important and pollution is a great threat to human welfare, but for most people in the developing countries these are rather distant threats, the most pressing ones being to get two morsels of food to survive the day and to get a job even in the most hazardous occupation and to find a place to be able to pass the night even if that place be the most foul and polluted one. Those living in our cities see this truth in the countless footpath and slum dwellers. "Environmental protection" and "pollution freedom" while increasing the cash flow of the foreign sellers of equipments do not promise to make a difference to the position of these hapless human beings even after a decade or a quarter of a century. Foreign cars built to international environmental specifications have undoubtedly added to the availability of cars – only there is no road to use them even after the pedestrian footpaths have been encroached upon to make roads wider, putting the man on foot at a greater jeopardy of his life and limbs.

The increasing dependence of the developing countries on the industrial countries seemingly gives rise to the need to be acquainted with the intellectual work done in the industrial countries relating to the economy and there is greater pressure on academicians and intellectuals to become members of international forums and organisations to counter the spread of such pernicious theories. When one considers that the agricultural practices of the state of Punjab cannot be adopted by the cultivators in the State of Maharashtra, the irrelevance of most so-called international 'economic studies' is seen in the true perspective. *(445 words)*

■■■

CHAPTER

19

Report and Proposal Writing

What should you know?

19.1 REPORTS?

According to the British Association for Commercial and Industrial Education, a report is a document in which a given problem is examined for the purpose of conveying information, stating the findings, putting forward ideas and sometimes making recommendations.

" Report is a communication from someone who has the information, to someone who wants to use that information." (C.A.Brown)

"A report is a document which describes an opinion, situation etc. through observation, enquiry, collection of data, etc."

Thus, a report is an oral/written communication in which the sender gives information to an office-bearer or an organisation as a matter of responsibility. It is the sender's assigned duty to submit the report.

A report differs from other forms of written communication in the following ways:

1. A report is objective and projects the facts of a situation. Unlike some other forms of communication, it has little room for subjectivity.
2. A report researches data from outside sources, analyses them, draws conclusions and makes recommendations. In this way, it forms a distinct mode of writing, which is essentially structured.
3. The language of a report is concise and concrete with a clearly defined outline.
4. A report, during its presentation of data, tends to use tables, charts, graphs and diagrams to make the matter vivid and easy to grasp and correlate.
5. Longer reports should give a summary so that the receiver may get the content in a nutshell.

19.1.1 Purpose of a Report

Usually, a report serves one or more of the following purposes:

- To inform about a department's, company's, or individual's progress
- To tell the facts of an event for future reference or management action
- To argue out a course of action
- To help to take a well-informed stand on a problem or controversy

An alternative presentation of the purpose is:

✓ Monitor business operations (e.g. operating reports, plans)

✓ Bring about new policies and procedures (e.g. internal reports, promotion policy reports)

✓ Comply with statutory requirements (e.g. directors' reports, corporate governance reports, auditors' reports)

✓ Help in decision making (e.g. performance reports, research reports)

✓ Helps in organisational control, and taking corrective action. (e.g. activity reports)

19.1.2 Types of Reports

(*a*) Oral
(*b*) Written
(*c*) Informal
(*d*) Formal
(*e*) Informational
(*f*) Interpretative
(*g*) Routine

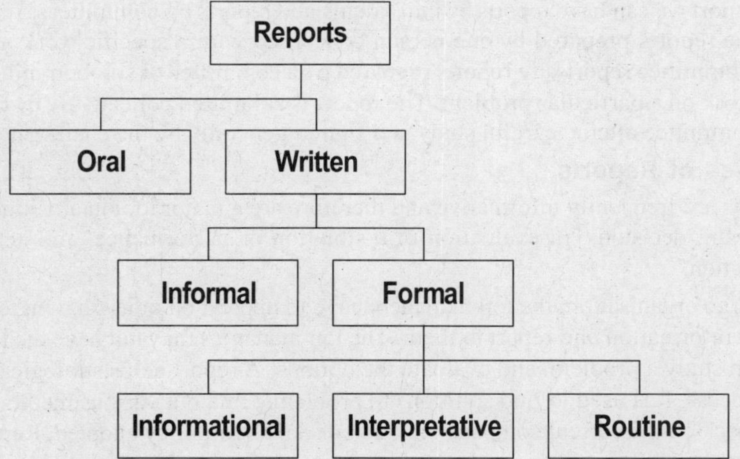

- Reports can be oral or written.
- Written reports may be formal or informal. Informal reports have a friendly way of transferring information from person to person within an organisation. They do not have a rigid format. They can be written in the letter form on a simple sheet of paper or in a prescribed format in the form of a memorandum. Formal reports are official reports. They are prepared in a prescribed form according to the official procedure and presented to the appropriate authorities. The language and structure is specific and pre-defined.
- **Routine reports and special reports**: On the basis of frequency of issue, reports may be routine or special.

  Routine reports: These are reports that are repeated over a period of time. They usually have a fixed format. They may be submitted annually, quarterly, monthly, weekly or even daily. Generally such reports contain statistical data or brief information without any opinion or recommendation. Branch reports, annual reports etc. are all examples of routine reports.

  As distinguished from routine reports, special reports deal with a certain specific issue or situation, like a report on labour strike.

- **Informative and analytical reports**: On the basis of functions a report can be informative and analytical.

  Informative reports: Informative reports are given when certain information has to be given to someone who needs it. They give a matter-of-fact representation of the situation. These generally pertain to meetings held, any incident, situation etc. Informative reports are given as a part of assigned duty or when asked for. Informative reports can use informal language and can include explanatory details that are relevant.

  Interpretive or analytical reports: These reports are written after a thorough investigation and analysis of a given problem or situation. They play a major role in the decision-making process as they influence the managerial decisions with their recommendations and suggestions. They are similar to informational reports, only with an addition of the writers' view. Interpretive reports are usually submitted for topics which require a far-seeing action to be taken. An interpretive report would always have suggestions or recommendations from the writer, which may or may not be accepted by the management. Reports for computerisation of activities, introduction of a new product, etc. could be classified under interpretive reports.

- **Individual and committee reports**: On the basis of people responsible for writing the report we can have reports by individuals and reports by committees. Individual reports are the reports prepared by one person concerned with a specific work area or department. Committee reports are reports prepared by a committee or sub-committee that is formed to work on a particular problem. The report is submitted collectively by the members of this committee after a careful study and signed generally by the chairman of the committee.

19.1.3 Uses of Reports

Reports are frequently informative and therefore are a major tool in any kind of business. They help in taking decisions, in evaluation of a situation or performance, and act as a basic tool of communication.

In a large organisation, the top managers have to depend on others having expertise to observe and collect information and report to them. The top managers may not have the time or the required expertise to study a problem, and evaluate the options. A report helps strategically in the decision-making process. It is used to find solutions to problems, find out various methods of improvement, get a feedback on the current company situation or on a new policy adopted. Reports come in handy mostly in large-scale organisations where it is not possible for the management to pay personal attention to all the aspects of the organisation in order to maintain smooth functioning.

19.1.4 Structure and Style of a Business Report

Elements of structure

The structure of a report depends, of course, on its purpose and scope. All the same it has to -

1. Arrange the facts in a logical manner
2. Analyse them with the help of the sender's experience and insight
3. Bring out the inferences
4. Recommend a course of action

A report has its **terms of reference**, that is, the areas which it is required to cover. For instance, an official may be assigned to report on absenteeism with the following terms of reference:

1. The extent of absenteeism
2. The causes of absenteeism
3. Any period or category of people with regard to which absenteeism is high
4. Suggesting remedies to contain it.

In any investigative report, it is necessary that the sender know his terms of reference. Only then can the report be to the point. In the absence of clarity about the terms of reference, the sender/investigator may go on a false track and waste his time and effort.

Elements of Style

Style is the way we couch our message in words. The style of a report is essentially objective and scientific, yet a person may leave the stamp of his personality on the style. Good style requires mastery of the language directed for a specific purpose. The same thing may be said in two different ways with stylistic differences:

1. **A** : The cyclone left the workshed in a disarray.

   B : The cyclone has put the workshed topsy turvy.

   While style A is direct and non-idiomatic, some writers may try to create an impact through colourful idioms (style B).
2. **A** : The result of the petrol price hike is – crowded buses, drop in the business of petrol outlets, adulteration at full go, explosive tempers.

   B : The steep rise in petrol prices has made millions of vehicle users abandon driving, crowd the public transport and protest violently. On the other hand, the sudden decline in the business of petrol pumps has led to losses to them, and then adulteration to cover up the losses.

Nowadays, masters of style bring relief to the reader in the form of a relaxed, personal, metaphorical or even humorous touch to the writing. An analogy is seen in the Union Budget which is governmental writing spiced up for easy and interesting listening even though the subject is grave and affects the bread and butter of the nation.

Here are the necessaries of good style in business report writing:

1. **Use of concrete and objective words**: A trim report goes like a mathematical theorem. The tone is third personally and avoids the use of *I* unless necessary. The style is specific. "New gadgets have been acquired" is general. "The company has acquired a fax machine and a photo copier" is specific.
2. **Time to be technical and time to be non-technical**: Some parts of a report may be meant for a general reader and hence need to be in non-technical language. At the same time, a survey of the technicalities of an issue can make it necessary to use technical terms.
3. **Use of active voice**: Active voice is direct and easier to follow. It is therefore generally preferred in report writing. At the same time, in certain parts of the reporting, we are more interested in the result than the agents causing them. For example, "trees are uprooted, electric poles are bent and telecommunication is disrupted." While revising a report, one may carefully judge which voice would be better and convert passive voice into active for easier reading.

   Passive: The workers have been organised by the ringleader.

   Active: The ringleader has organised the workers.

   Passive: Our financial matters are decided by the finance chief.

   Active: Our finance chief decides the financial maters.
4. **Making it readable:** A report has to use techniques that make it understandable, even racy. Readability is increased by using shorter sentences, less use of hard and long words, variation in the length of sentences and organising the word order for producing a good sound effect upon reading. Long sentences and difficult words make one's writing foggy. A collection of hard sounds makes it brittle.

   (a) Foggy: The orchestration of the contributory factors by devising suitable plans is now essential.

   Clearer: It is necessary to marshal the events by making proper plans.

(b) Brittle: Decidedly, it was tough to have to drag it.

Softer: It was surely hard to have to drag it.

Still softer: The need to drag it was surely painful.

5. **Precision:** Your report should reach the level of precision that is necessary for the occasion. To be precise, you have to give the details, the dimensions, the specifications.

   Level 1 : A quick accelerating bike.

   Level 2 : A bike with the quickest acceleration in its class.

   Level 3 : A bike that goes from 0 to 60 kmph in 5.5 seconds, which is the best acceleration in its class.

6. **Conciseness:** To be concise is to take a short-cut to meaning. It means economy in the use of words, restraint in descriptions.

   Wordy: We take guidance from the principles of panchsheel.

   Concise: The principles of panchsheel guide us.

   Wordy: Instead of going into the elaboration, make a brief presentation.

   Concise: Don't elaborate, present your report in brief.

7. **Plainness:** Sometimes one is tempted to create an "effect" by using heavy, polysyllabic words. This may even be due to lazy habits of thought.

Heavy word	**Plain alternative**
Demonstrate	show
Accordingly	so
Residence	house
Substantial	large
Terminate	end

8. **Avoiding jargon and foreign words:** Jargon is the specialised language of a profession; constant familiarity with it may prompt one to use it in a report meant for a non-professional reader. Similarly, a scholar may be accustomed to foreign words. But he has to simplify his writing for the non-scholarly reader.

   Jargon based: The property is hypothecated to the bank.

   Simpler: The bank has a charge on this property.

   Foreign usage: English is the lingua franca on this campus.

   Simpler: English is commonly used on this campus.

19.1.5 How to Write a Report

There are three stages in composing a report:

(*i*) Pre-writing
(*ii*) Actual writing
(*iii*) Revision and rewriting

The reader may refer to Chapter Five, item 5.5 on Tips for Clear Writing/Craft of Business Letter Writing.

19.1.6 Specimen Reports

1. A report after conducting a survey on absenteeism (in letter form)

The General Manager
ABC Co.
New Delhi

Dear Sir

Subject: Absenteeism in the Company - causes and remedies

As instructed by you in your letter no. GM-105, I have investigated the above matter and have to report as follows:

Whereas 105 workers are employed in our factory, the average attendance in the past six months is 79. It can be as low as 49 on some days in August and as high as 100 when things are normal.

On questioning the employees, their relatives and observing where the absent employees went, it was found that most of them feel underpaid. In the rainy season they find seasonal employment in agriculture, which is on daily wages basis but pays better. About 10-20 employees always feel physically unfit due to the stress of factory work. Many of these workers are willing to work regularly and even overtime if paid better.

Recommendations:
In view of the above, it is recommended that a commission be set up to review their pay structure, especially to match the ones that are implemented by our competitors. Impressionistically, one feels that a raise of 10-20% may motivate many workers to work regularly and enable them to keep fit. This would enhance our productivity and more than make up for the rise in the salary bill.

Yours faithfully

Personnel Manager

2. A report on the scope for marketing shoes in tribal Chhattisgarh (letter form)

The Chairman
Better Shoes Co.
Nagpur

Dear Sir

Subject: Marketability of our shoes in tribal Chhattisgarh

In terms of the Board resolution no. 12 dated 14 April 2006, a committee was set up to explore the scope for our shoes in four backward districts of Chhattisgarh. The committee members and Idea Marketing Group conducted a joint survey by visiting the district centres and other towns of the region.

It is found that the common people of the region mostly wear tyre-made chappals or sometimes rough-and-ready shoes made by cobblers. The chappals do not protect their feet enough during long walks, while the shoes have a short life-span. Hence, basically, a need exists for tough and comfortable shoes such as we make.

However, the paying capacity in the region is largely below average and the artisans, farmers etc. are willing to pay no more than Rs.150 for a pair of shoes. Even this amount is spent only when they are convinced of the merits of the product.

Recommendations:
The committee therefore recommends that a new line of low-cost shoes be made especially for these consumers, which should be long lasting if not glamorous. As for publicity, the periodic fairs and religious gatherings appear ideal to create an instant awareness about our product. We may even sponsor some religious functions. The committee estimates that within a year we may be able to sell 10,000 pairs of shoes per month in the four districts surveyed.

Yours faithfully

A. B. Shukla
Chairman, Marketing Survey Committee

3. Routine progress report on the production of tape recorders (memo form)

Jay Electronics

Lucknow

Periodic Progress Report

Month: July 2011
Unit : 6

Production figures:

Model	Estimated	Actual	Shortfall (–)/ Overachievement (+)
C-45	3000	2750	– 250 (8.1%)
C-46	800	550	– 250 (31.3%)
C-47	200	100	– 100 (50%)

Comments:

1. The production is below estimate in all three models.
2. The percentile shortfall is highest in the C-47 model, which is our most sophisticated product.

Reasons:

1. The factory was unable to function at full capacity owing to frequent power breakdowns during July.
2. Our senior technical advisor Mr. Malhotra resigned suddenly on 5th July, affecting the working of the hi-tech section.

Recommendations:

1. A prior notification may be sought from the Electricity Board about the powercuts, and the working hours may be rescheduled accordingly.
2. The post of senior technical advisor may be filled immediately or one of the supervisors may be trained for hi-tech jobs.

Sd/-
Production Manager

4. Report on the feasibility of opening a pure veg restaurant (letter form)

The Managing Director
Eatvel Chain of Food Outlets
New Delhi

Dear Sir

Subject : Feasibility of a pure veg restaurant

This writer was commissioned to explore the feasibility of opening a multi-cuisine vegetarian fast food restaurant in Main Market, Gwalior (through memo dated 4.4.2011).

Here are the findings of his investigation:

1. While there are three Class I restaurants in the Main Market which serve both veg and non-veg food, there is no pure veg restaurant in this category.
2. Nearly 20% residents of the city in the income group of Rs.20,000+ p.m. are vegetarians. Half of them never go to a restaurant that serves non-veg food alongside.
3. The affluent class in the town is on the rise owing to industrial growth and return of NRIs. Even people earning below Rs.10,000 p.m. welcome the prospect of eating in a tasteful vegetarian food joint once in a while. Outstation students also want to eat good vegetarian food on Sundays and holidays as a change from hostel food.

In short, we have an encouraging market for our kind of restaurant.

Recommendation:
A space of 2000 sq.ft. can be acquired in one of the upcoming shopping complexes that would be right for our multi-cuisine venture. A suitable franchisee may be identified through advertisements and personal approach to select hoteliers and caterers. A list of them is enclosed.

Yours faithfully

Development Manager

Encl:

5. Covering letter for a survey questionnaires to learn about consumer taste in classical and semi-classical music

Music Innovators
New Delhi

Dear Patron of Music:

We would love to listen **to you** this time.

You have enjoyed our music collections in popular and film categories in the past 20 years. Hi-fidelity recording and long cassette life benchmark our products.

It may be time to spice up your music library with some classical and semi-classical albums. We want to know from you about your taste and preference.

In the attached questionnaire, we list a number of instrumental and vocal musical offerings that are catching up with the audiences all over the world.

Most of the names are of maestros and celebrities in their line, be it the sitar, the santoor, the flute, the devotional, the ghazal or fusion.

You can do us a favour of taking time out to mark the items that interest you – and tell us what you would like to have from us and in what form. And mail the sheet in the postage prepaid envelope to us at your earliest. We assure you of the closest attention to your voice and hope to regale you in the coming month with the music of your new choice.

Love music.

Yours sincerely

Alarmel Seetha
Customer Care Secretary

P.S. : You will have a FREE melodious gift from us as soon as we receive your reply.

19.2 TRANSMITTAL LETTERS

A transmittal letter is the written equivalent of the oral message that might accompany the presentation of a report to a small readership. In other words, a relatively long report is generally topped by a transmittal letter, which introduces the report and prepares the reader for it. In the case of a broader report, meant for a large and widespread audience, the preface or foreword presents the report. A transmittal letter is, thus, also the equivalent of a preface or foreword.

Features:

1. It is more or less a personal message from the report writer/s to the reader, often written in the first person, to launch the reader into the report.
2. It tells how to read the report, understand it and use it.
3. It suggests follow-up studies to be made, limitations of the report and remarks on side issues.
4. It may be combined with an executive (action-oriented) summary of the report.
5. It opens right into the heart of the matter about which the report is.
6. It acknowledges the contributions of those who helped in writing the report.
7. It may request a feedback.

Specimen transmittal letter

The Chief General Manager
International Division
Great Bank of India
Central Office
Mumbai

Dear Sir

Subject: Submitting a study report on setting up a diamond trading centre in Mumbai with the Bank's participation

As instructed in Central Office letter no. ID/05 dated 5th January, I undertook a survey of the diamond exchanges (bourses) in Antwerp and enclose my report.

In the context of the recent and very rapid rise in India's diamond export, the first thing one notices is the disorganised state of Indian diamond market when compared with the age-old markets of Europe. I met some key functionaries of the diamond trade at Antwerp and had frank discussions with them. I have tried to incorporate the essence of what they said about the Indian diamond trade, and the viability of a diamond trading centre (or exchange) in India.

I don't wish to reveal the conclusion too soon. All the same, I would suggest another and a deeper study of the subject, maybe after two years.

I thank the Bank for the opportunity given me to undertake this study and hope my researches will be of some value to the Bank.

Yours faithfully

19.3 PROPOSALS

19.3.1 What Are Proposals?

A proposal can be defined as an offer document presented to undertake work affecting the future of an organisation. Usually a proposal is given for any additions or amendments to be incorporated within a business framework.

Proposals are also tools of communication but in a different sense. They do not just give the facts but also a probable solution to a particular problem or situation. They can be written to people within or outside an organisation.

19.3.2 Types of Proposals

Proposals concern the future and play a major role in bringing about changes in a setup. Proposals are classified into two types: **sales proposals** and **research proposals**.

Sales proposals are written with the aim of bringing gains for the proposing organisation. Such kind of proposals are also known as business proposals. Sales proposals need to be creative in order to make a mark on their target audience. **Research proposals** are of an academic nature.

Proposals can be further classified into two types, viz. **solicited** and **unsolicited.**

Solicited proposals are those which are asked for by the management or authorities. They can be internal or external, depending on their subject. These kind of proposals usually face a lot of competition.

Unsolicited proposals are given by individuals or companies on their own. These may be from internal or external sources. They form a major part of sales technique in various sectors.

19.3.3 Basics of Writing a Proposal

The proposal is similar to a report and therefore all the stages of writing a report apply here. The only difference is that since a proposal is result oriented, it has to achieve its purpose. Therefore it has to be written on the basis of the AIDA (Attention,Interest, Desire and Action) formula. The beginning of the proposal should attract the attention of the reader and retain it throughout.

It should start with a clear objective, stating the aim of the proposal.

You have to gather relevant information to put forward the idea in a well-defined and self-explanatory manner.

The arguments should be put forward effectively and convincingly.

The problem should be dealt with from the point of view of the audience.

The proposal should be worded in a way that initiates a positive action from the reader. It has to fulfil its basic purpose of achieving an end.

The rules to structure a proposal are very liberal and can be altered according to the writer's choice. It should be innovative, interesting and convincing. However, for the purpose of laying out a structure, it should be based on four P's

Position – This shows the current status.

Problem – This shows what are the negative aspects of the current position and highlights the need to change.

Possibilities – This gives the options for change to be brought about.

Proposal – This lists out the actual proposal, the plan for bringing about the changes and the requirements for implementing it.

The structure of a proposal can be divided into introduction, body and conclusion. Its major characteristics are:

- ✓ It is informal and has a personal approach to the problem and-way of expression.
- ✓ It is a creative form of business communication.
- ✓ It should be structured properly with an attractive presentation.
- ✓ It should keep in mind all the requirements of the audience.
- ✓ The language should be direct, simple and easy to understand.
- ✓ It should be practical.
- ✓ It should be concerned with the person or company it is meant for.

The structure of a proposal for general reference can be as –

Name of the company
To: From: **INTRODUCTION**: This should contain the aim and scope of the proposal. It can also contain a summary if the proposal is too long. **BODY**: **Problem**: The problem would be a briefing on the existing facilities, procedure or scheme of work and the difficulties faced due to it. **Background**: This would include previous experience and work done regarding the issue on hand. What has been the effect on performance till date. **Purpose and scope**: The purpose should be clearly stated and the scope properly defined giving the reader a complete idea of the proposed activity. The limitations, if any, should also be listed out to keep things transparent and in full knowledge of the audience. **Procedure**: The procedure would contain all the activities to be performed in order to bring about the desired changes. The time and effort required needs to be clearly stated. This would be the actual plan of action of the proposal. **Cost estimate**: The audience would require to be made aware of the costs involved in the implementation of the proposal. A cost estimate would therefore prove beneficial in getting the point across convincingly. **CONCLUSION**: This is the last part of the proposal which lets the audience know the exact proposal with all its implications.

19.3.4 Distinction between a Report and a Proposal

Report	Proposal
A report is nearly always solicited	A proposal can be either solicited or unsolicited.
It is an official means of giving information.	It is a sales device/or a tool for suggestion.
It concerns the past.	It concerns the future.
It is just a statement.	It is a request for action.
It need not be convincing.	It has to be convincing.
It does not need the AIDA formula.	It is based on the AIDA formula.
It does not await a decision.	Its success lies in a favourable decision.

19.3.5 Specimen Proposals

1. An unsolicited (voluntary) proposal for automation in a printing press

M/s Vijayant Printers
Cantonment Road
Nashik

Dear Sirs

Subject: Dust-proofing your printery

We have the pleasure of introducing ourselves was bringers of a mini-revolution in printing technology: automation and dust proofing of modern printeries.

Please have a look at the enclosed specimen four-colour car pictures, one using conventional technique and the other with automation and dust-proofing such as we do. You will surely notice the quantum leap in the art work that uses our technology.

Happily, you will find that this enhancer of quality (and sale) is not so expensive as you might think. Why not see the technology in action? At your nod, we will arrange for your visit to some printeries nearby which have installed our automation and are reaping the benefits.

Please call me on xxx xxxx. Also visit us on www.printautomation.com.

Yours faithfully

Jagjit Arora
Marketing Development Officer

2. Response to a request from Evolution Investment Corporation for training their manpower in computerised banking (solicited proposal)

The Chief Training Officer
Evolution Investment Corporation
New Delhi

Dear Sir

Subject: Advanced Computer Training in banking

We have pleasure in offering a knowledge bank of computer technology suitable for your financial operations. Two packages are on offer for updating your banking staff in the use of computers:

i) Junior level – executives with 1 – 5 years' experience
ii) Middle level – executives with 5 – 15 years' experience

Our training programme can be conducted in your training school or in a hotel as it suits you. It provides detailed manuals on computerised banking as it is practised in Japan, Hong Kong, Singapore, Shanghai, etc. It covers deposit servicing, money transfers, import and export.

One speciality of this package is the safety devices to maintain banker's secrecy of a higher degree. We have the hardware to give hands–on training to batches of 15 at a time. The programme duration is seven days and the cost can be discussed with you personally. It ranges from Rs.12,000 to Rs.18,000 per person.

We must add that we are impressed by your progress in the past three years, the enviable reputation you have earned, and the visionary goals you have set for yourselves.

We are confident of giving your staff the technological advantage that will put them ahead of the competition. Please call me on xxx xxxx any time to hammer out a final deal so that you get going to your cherished aims.

Yours faithfully

Dr. Anuj Marka
Director

3. Internal proposal for relocating the packing unit of Aurobindo Jewellers

The General Manager
Aurobindo Jewellers
Pondicherry

Dear Sir

Subject: Relocating the packing unit

This is to volunteer an idea about relocating the packing unit of our company which is now three streets away from the factory. The proposal has two sides:

i. Merging the packing unit with the factory
ii. Redesigning the factory shed

Currently, we manufacture our jewellery on St. Bernard Street and send it to Kurien Street for packing. This arrangement had become necessary due to a sudden rise in production. However, we have to transport valuables worth crores of rupees through busy lanes and the recent transit insurance claims have taken a lot of our precious time.

We can now bring back the packing unit to the factory shed and take some of the manufacture to a mezzanine floor to create room for packing. Such a mezzanine is now possible due to the use of new, smaller machines in ring-making. I hope this idea will meet with your approval. I am willing to supervise the relocation and reconstruction.

Yours faithfully

Works Manager

4. Proposal from workers to arrange for a grand farewell to a senior employee at his retirement

The Chairman
Wardhman Couriers
Mumbai

Dear Sir

Subject: Felicitation of Mr. R.K. Gopal Krishnan

The Staff Union feels that Mr. R. K. Gopalkrishnan's 35 years of devoted service to our organisation deserves a rousing felicitation as he retires on 1st July 2011.

Mr. Gopalkrishnan joined in 1976 as a delivery boy and through sheer dedication and sincerity, achieved success in jobs which most others would have given up as impossible.

Due to limited education he could not rise to a high post but was happy enough to work as an exemplary office-in-charge at Mulund for the last ten years.

Mr. Gopalkrishnan's personal qualities, viz. help to all who touched him, generosity to the poor, and organising skill, have impressed everyone.

Just as we will remember him for the rest of our lives, he deserves a farewell that he should remember always. We propose for him:

(i) A special cash award that should help him to buy a residence
(ii) A scroll describing his qualities and services
(iii) A dinner with a guest of the rank of a minister

We hope you will approve.

Yours faithfully

Ashim Bose
Secretary, Staff Union

5. Proposal to buy an in-house photocopier

To: The General Manager
From: The Manager (Administration)

Subject: Proposal to purchase of photocopier for office use

As you are aware, the business operations of our company have increased manifold and so also the photocopying work. At present we are getting the copying work through an outside agency. This is proving very costly and time-consuming. Moreover, we have to depute one person for this work.

According to our calculations, the cost of photocopying outside is Rs.3 per page. This includes the cost of fuel, salary paid to the peon and, of course, the photocopying charges.

Thus it makes a lot of sense to buy a photocopying machine and get the copying work done in-house. It will cost us less than 35 paise per page and we will be able to save a lot of time as well.

The initial investment in a good copier will be around Rs.1 lac and the maintenance cost will be 10 paise per copy. Thus we will be able to recover the investments in the first year itself. Hence, I strongly suggest the purchase of a photocopy machine.

Manager (Administration)

A. Questions based on critical understanding. Comment in about 30 words.

1. **A business report should avoid the use of technical words.**

Ans. Though broadly useful, the statement is too sweeping. The use of technical or non-technical language depends on the audience. If an automobile engineer is reporting to his production head about the failure of the self-start mechanism, he can be as technical as he wishes. That would save space and time and achieve exactness. But, for the general reader a business report should avoid technical terms.

2. **Reasoning is the backbone of a proposal.**

Ans. Proposals are persuasive, and they need to appeal to the intellect as well as the emotions of the receiver. The plan proposed should offer benefits by a logical chain, but the benefits should also be offered in a manner that satisfy the receiver emotionally.

3. **A transmittal letter stands in the place of a preface or foreword.**

Ans. Whereas a preface or foreword is used in presenting a report to a wide audience, a transmittal letter is used when the audience is limited. But the orientation of it is the same as that of a preface etc. – to prepare the reader for the report and to touch side issues.

4. **You cannot make a proposal unless asked to.**

Ans. A proposal can very well be unsolicited as well. Within an organisation, you may make a proposal to improve the working of your department. To external companies you may offer proposals to meet their needs that you assess.

5. **Terms of reference facilitate report writing.**

Ans. The terms of reference are the areas to investigate and points to report on. They define the report writer's work and help him to make a focussed effort.

B. Questions for revision

1. Distinguish between proposals and reports.
2. 'Report writing is an important activity.' List out the main points to be kept in mind while writing reports.
3. What is a proposal? What guidelines should be kept in mind while drafting a proposal? (Answer to be given in about 200 words)
4. What do you understand by the term 'Report'? Explain briefly the points which are considered while writing a report.
5. Describe the stages in writing a report. Comment on the style and structure of a good report.
6. How does one make a proposal effective?

C. Drafting Exercises

1. Write a report on the theft of students' mopeds from the college scooter stand.
2. Draft a letter from the Regional Sales Manager to the Area Sales Manager asking him to explain the drop in sales.
3. Draft a proposal to extend library hours during the exam season.
4. Draft a proposal from a Customers' Association to your bank to multiply the number of ATMs (automatic teller machines) in town.
5. Write a proposal as in-charge of College Debating Society, to conduct public speaking classes in the college.
6. Write a proposal from the Temple Management Committee to the Municipal Corporation to shift the meat shops near the temple.
7. Write a report on the frequency of rejection of computer printers from users, suggesting suitable remedies.
8. Report on the lightning strike by workers in your factory upon a coolie receiving an electric shock from an exposed wire.
9. Make a report suggesting ways to popularise two-wheeler covers.
10. Draw up a feasibility report on setting up a bank branch in a small town.
11. A committee was set up to look for a 10-acre plot of land for teak plantation. Recommend a plot, detailing its merits.
12. Offer an unsolicited proposal to a housing cooperative society for painting its buildings.
13. Make a voluntary offer to a private bus company to redesign its coaches and install sleepers.
14. Respond to an advertisement seeking entrepreneurs who can take up a franchise of a computer institute.

15. Write an internal proposal as sales manager of an agro-products unit to recruit more field staff and to provide them with mobile phones.
16. Draft a proposal from the personnel manager to reinstate an employee suspended for joining a political party, which was against service rules.
17. You are writing a report on the All India Sales of your latest product. Of the topics listed below, identify those that should and those that should not be included in your report. Please explain your choices.
    (*i*) Regional breakdown of sales across the country
    (*ii*) Sales figures from competitors selling similar products in other countries
    (*iii*) Impact of Chinese competitors selling similar products in the country
    (*iv*) An evaluation of your company selling this product internationally

■■■

CHAPTER

20

Corporate Communication

What should you know?

20.1 CORPORATE COMMUNICATION

Corporate communication is a wide term. It denotes, first, the communication channels – downward, upward, horizontal and crosswise – that are at work in an organisation. (See Chapter 2.) More importantly, it denotes the governance of an organisation's image-building communication within itself and with the outside world. Like production, marketing and finance, now communication is also taken as a specialised functional area. Hence, by corporate communication we also mean an organisation's conscious effort to make its managers better speakers, better writers and more polished personalities.

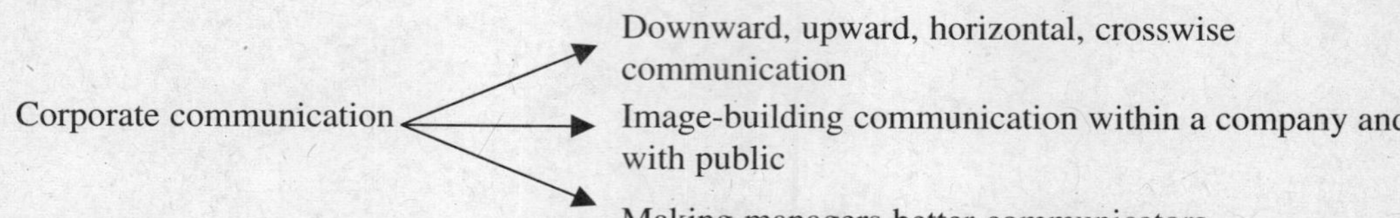

The need to nurture corporate communication skills has been especially felt after World War II, which ended in 1945, leading us into an Age of Information. People are more conscious of knowing about the company with which they deal as shareholders, customers, sellers, etc. To meet this situation, corporations are overhauling and fine-tuning their communications. Much of corporate communication is governed by the public relations (PR) and marketing wings of an organisation.

Here we shall not deal with the routine internal communication (letters, meetings, etc.) of a business house, since various earlier chapters cover it. We shall take up the other aspects of corporate communication.

Corporate communication takes many forms. Within the organisation, it works by means of a house journal and ongoing programmes to improve its managers' speaking, writing and personality calibre. With the outside world, an organisation communicates through corporate brochures, information booklets, press releases, press conferences, ads, etc. Larger companies have a public relations department which communicates two-way with the various publics of a company and helps foster a good image of itself.

Through effective management of corporate communication, a company earns a good name, attracts good workers as employees, keeps the existing staff satisfied and growing, gets prestigious business houses to deal with it, gets government recognition and, of course, creates a market for its products.

International communication is another aspect of corporate communication. This is a study of fruitful communication across international cultural differences.

20.1.1 Skills Developed in Managers

Nowadays it is customary to develop in the managers of a company various personality skills to project a good and uniform image of the company, reflecting the corporate culture.

Managers are taught –

- How to greet properly
- How to conduct themselves physically, how to work, sit or take a stand on the stage
- How to dress
- How to listen proactively
- How manners differ in different regions and countries
- How to show special regard for senior citizens, ladies and poorly communicating clients

Communication abilities required in a manager:

A manager of a modern corporation is often required to spend the largest part of his time listening, speaking, writing or reading as part of his duties. Specifically, he has to –

- Receive and react to communications from other departments
- Send appropriate information to his colleagues
- Transmit new ideas to his higher-ups
- Brief his subordinates to get things done the required way
- Keep his communications free from bias

20.2 HOUSE JOURNALS, CORPORATE BROCHURES, INFORMATION BOOKLETS

20.2.1 Nature and Functions of a House Journal

A house journal is a company's own magazine primarily for internal circulation, with itself as the main theme. It has variants like bulletins and newsletters. It is circulated internally but also kept open for public reading. It is a reflection of the company's pride in itself. The house journal contains a good deal of pure entertainment also in which the employees and their family members participate as contributors and readers. The contents of a typical house journal are:

- New developments involving the company's top brass, their visits and meetings with leaders and dignitaries
- Inaugurations, new branches, major postings, reshuffles
- Employees' and their families' achievements in exams, public service, sports, fine arts, etc.
- Humour, especially related to the company's line of functioning. Scholarly writings on the company's field of activity
- Creative writing, viz. poems, stories, satires
- Photographs related to the above or of general interest

- Paintings, especially by employees or their relatives
- News on births, marriages, promotions
- Goodwill activities like donations, tree plantation, schemes for the handicapped
- Grant of scholarships by the company or award of scholarships to its employees or their relatives
- Letters by readers

Objectives of a house journal

1. To emphasise all that is positive about the company, its growth and its contribution to society's development
2. To create an awareness of its business breakthroughs such as bagging an export contract or an export council award
3. To give scope to creative talents of its employees and their family members
4. To keep harmonious relations with rank and file of the organisation. Employees in the lower posts may have talents in writing, photography, dramatics, singing etc. which get either projected or reported on in the house journal.
5. To entertain its readers in a unique way, that is in a way other than a general magazine
6. To acquaint the readers with the top brass through their photos, messages or write-ups
7. To reflect the corporate philosophy which is generally more than just making profits, viz. fostering self-reliance, raising the standard of living of the people, bringing innovations, global competition, etc.
8. To create the feeling of a shared culture and family bond among the employees

20.2.2 Nature and Functions of a Corporate Brochure

Brochures are printed handouts as small as a leaflet or as large as a booklet or folder, usually using glossy paper and colour pictures to enhance the effect. Brochures inform in brief and in polished language about a company or an aspect of it. The writing and designing of a brochure is a specialised job of copywriters, graphic artists and publicity personnel. Brochures may be distributed through a company's marketing personnel to reach the clients or prospects. They may be given to distributors and dealers for their information and to the public at POP (point of purchase), and to various connected organisations.

A well-produced brochure can give a major boost to a company's sales efforts. The quality of its production is taken as a symbol of the company's worth. A glitzy and colourful brochure tells half the story before it is opened and read. Hence a company pays much attention to its brochure in its promotional activity.

The following may be remembered about the nature of a brochure:

- It is an instrument of publicity that is compact and impressive.
- The writing of it is in polished prose, using minimal words.
- Pictures, diagrams, charts, tables etc. are used in a highly orderly manner.
- Close-up technical pictures help to explain finer processes and this sometimes earns the respect of a technically informed reader. For example, why is a particular kind of steel more weldable or how a particular toothbrush cleans the teeth better than others.
- Pictures of a company's plant, office, employees at work, its machinery, and testimonies of satisfied users, etc. to help convince the reader.
- Sometimes, a brochure incorporates a sample of the product itself, e.g. a perfume, a piece of fabric, etc.
- A brochure often uses a catchy headline or a matter-of-fact statement about the company or its product. E.g., a car brochure may be captioned, "What drives the stars in their orbits." An agricultural product may simply state (for its less sophisticated reader)

"Better yield, more disease resistance."

- Brochures are produced in the language best understood by the target audience. In India, however, there is a peculiar tendency to use English for producing a brochure even if the target audience understands the regional language better.
- Brochures are expensive to produce and need to be circulated accurately and without waste. Also, since information can become outdated in course of time, the quantity of brochures to be printed has to be properly estimated.

Functions of a brochure

1. It informs vividly and engagingly about a product, service or the company itself. Since it can be preserved, carried about, compared with other brochures, it acts as a powerful means of publicity.
2. The pictures sometimes tell the story better than long descriptions. In this age of audio-visual media, there is a right tendency to keep the pictures up front to arrest the eye without the need to read too much.
3. Technical processes and specifications are clarified.
4. Tables and charts help to show the comparative merits of a product over others, especially the conventional ones.
5. Unlike TV ads, they correlate pictures and words in a leisurely way. They help to redouble the impact of TV ads.
6. They can be stacked in a special stand at the sales outlet, for customers to pick up at their choice. A customer un- approached by a salesman feels more free to make a choice.
7. Brochures are extensively used in tourism.
8. Sometimes a brochure is disguised as a supplement to a general magazine and delivered along with it. Such a brochure offers attractive general information or advice, and marketing appears to be a secondary aim.
9. Some brochures try to enhance their preservation value by giving tips on maintenance, healthcare, financial advice, etc. They win the goodwill of the reader and make him feel grateful towards the company.

20.2.3 Information Booklet

A business house has to compile various types of information in a handy, readable form for ready reference by different categories of people it deals with. Thus the details of a scheme, the addresses and features of its branches, regulations, etc. may be published in an information booklet.

Good information booklets help the readers to understand the products, schemes, method of use (as in the case of cosmetics) and serve to reinforce marketing. A financial service provider may bring out a booklet on its investment schemes or, in public interest, on calculating income tax. This serves as indirect advertisement. Employees of an organisation may benefit from a compilation of essential service rules including facilities available.

An organisation needs to plan what information booklets it should have, how they can be made reader-friendly (simple language, illustrations, analogies etc.) and arrange for their distribution. An information booklet helps to reduce the mental distance between management and potential users of the information.

When an organisation is expanding rapidly – geographically or in terms of products and services (e.g. cellphones in the first decade of the twenty-first century) – timely issuance of information booklets and their updating can help the company's customers etc. to keep track of the developments.

An information booklet is simpler and more detailed than a brochure, which is a pithy publicity device.

A variant of information booklet is the instructions manual. In case of modern and complex gadgets, an instructions manual/user's manual is a must. Technology is expanding rapidly, there is little standardisation, and non-technical readers have to be attracted to new technology. They should benefit from it to the point of delight. While such manuals are being issued as rapidly as new technology is pushing its way into common use, they are at present generally unsatisfactory. Often one has to be a patient linguistics expert or a technocrat to make headway with them. Again, although American English is little used in India in school and college education, these manuals tend to use American usages wholesale. This is a sorry state of affairs and a good field of action for able communicators. The lack of good writing here is slowing down technology and business. Hence, when a business house launches new technological products, it would do very well to hold workshops, short training programmes etc. with live demos.

20.3 PRESS RELEASES AND PRESS CONFERENCES

To keep the public or a target section of it properly informed about a company's activities, especially those of news value, it has to issue timely press releases. In these, mass media reporters are given the company's version. These releases are mailed, handed personally in the media office (to newspapers, magazines, TV channels, radio etc.) or presented at a press conference. The conference, whether in a hotel or a press bureau, allows the reporters to ask questions and clarify things even better. Companies use various methods to induce the newspapers to print their version. This may be by giving simultaneous ads (the bigger the ad, the more the coverage to the press release!) or through samples, customary gifts, etc.

20.3.1 Nature of a Press Release

Since it is meant for creating a news item or influencing an editorial, a press release is primarily informative and persuasive.

1. It is generally given on the company's letterhead by a responsible officer (PRO, general manager etc.).
2. It incorporates accurate, official information with names, places, figures, endorsements, etc.
3. Skilled writers or ad agencies are employed for writing press releases.
4. Most newspapers have a business page where the press releases appear after conversion into news items. Some companies try to give a draft that may be straightaway used as a news item, editing the press release from the newspapers' point of view. However, most companies prefer to use their own formula.
5. If it is to promote a product, the AIDA formula (Attention, Interest, Desire, Action) is used. A press release is usually supported by an ad either the same day or thereabouts. The terse and appealing message of the ad and the detailed message of the news (based on the press release) supplement each other.
6. A press release can be supported by signed documents, statements, etc. which help to convince the newspaper about the truth of the release.
7. To get the press releases a good coverage, a company needs to maintain cordial relations with the media.
8. The PR department has to follow up after giving a press release to ensure that it is reported duly and accurately. Some omissions can be critical to the company's image and interests. For instance, if a report omits the fact that the product is technologically the best (to appease competing products and get their ads), the PR department has to get active.
9. A press release is part of a complex PR operation and requires much activity before, after and alongside to make the best impact.

20.3.2 Functions of a Press Release

A press release is as much an opportunity for a company as a duty. Its chief functions are:

- It is an instrument of timely mass information. It can inform the public about the formation of a business house, its expansion, reorganisation, merger, collaboration, relocation, new appointments, etc. Press release at the time of a new share issue (initial public offer) can influence the fate of the issue and the company together.
- It helps to remove misinformation. For instance, when bird flu had struck, press releases told how safe chickens were for eating. This controlled the panic reaction of the public and prevented the destruction of thousands of birds.
- Since a press release is presented through a reportorial third party (newspaper etc.), it may carry greater convincing power than an ad.
- While ad space is limited and expensive, a news item based on a press release allows the company to talk at length about itself.
- By devising something newsworthy every now and then, a company can remain in the news with regularity. It is an age of "publish or perish."
- Facts have the convincing power of cold logic. While these may look umimpressive in ads, they are the meat of a news report. Therefore, the facts in a press release are a necessity for winning public confidence.
- In times of strike, accident etc., if loud leaders carry the public opinion, a press release, supported by an intellectual medium, takes the wind out of them.
- Prompt and accurate press releases are a duty the company owes to its shareholders, investors, clients, franchisees, distributors, dealers, etc. Each has his own interest angle, as a user, dependant or financial partner, and he looks to the outcome of press releases. A press-mart company naturally surges ahead.

20.3.3 Composing and Delivering Press Releases

This is a job for persuasive writers. In organising a press release, the following points may be noted:

1. It should be prompt.
2. It should select the mass media to cover all concerned readers, viewers, etc.
3. The headline itself should sum up the story. Just as many readers browse only headlines, the news editor may also glance at a press release caption and decide about it.
4. A good headline should be followed up by a lead (opening line) that gets into the heart of the story. This will keep the editor interested enough to read it through.
5. Since the news editor is an intellectual, he may not be impressed by gimmicky headlines or leads. They should appeal to *him/her*.
6. It should not hurt any interest group or the news editor's sense of values.
7. It should be neatly typed and be free from errors.
8. How a press release is presented is also important. It should get as close as possible to the person who decides whether and how to publish it. In a newspaper office, it should reach the specialised desk and find the functionary in a favourable mood about it.
9. An ignored and delayed press release serves no function. Hence press cooperation has to be sought and there has to be a follow-up.
10. Some press releases are in two parts – a letter requesting the editor to publish it, and then the release itself.
11. The language of a release has to follow all the principles of effective writing discussed elsewhere (in chapters on letter writing and report writing) such as clarity, conciseness, completeness, use of simple language, and the sales formula of AIDA.

20.3.4 Specimen Press Releases

1. Press release informing about the Easy Exit Scheme of Ministry of Corporate Affairs

Covering Letter and Press Release

15th December 2010

The Editor
The Times of India
Nagpur

Dear Sir,

Kindly publish the below mentioned press release of the Ministry of Corporate Affairs in your esteemed newspaper and oblige.

Dr. V.K. Jain,
Chairman
Nagpur chapter, ICSI

Press Release

The Ministry of Corporate Affairs has decided to introduce a Scheme namely, "Easy Exit Scheme, 2011" under section 560 of the companies Act, 1956 to give an opportunity to the defunct companies, for getting their names struck off from the register of companies.

The scheme will be in operation from 1st January, 2011 to 31st January, 2011.

For details, refer to General Circular No. 6/2010 dated 03.12.2010 available at www.mca.gov.in

2. Press release to inform that now every Indian state has HERBO distributors

Press release
HERBO presence in all states

With the appointment of distributors in all the states of India now, HERBO Natural Medicines has more reasons to let people believe what it has always believed itself – that purity pays. The recent appointment of distributors in four north-eastern states of India gives us the rare record of being a herbal medicine company with distributors in all the states of the Union.

While the market is continually being flooded with cheap, fantasy-promising tonics, HERBO has stood its ground where many herbal companies compromised. HERBO has not changed its formula to accommodate allopathic medicines. On the contrary, it has reinforced its formulation with the help of constant feedback and research, but staying close to the ancient and time-honoured formulations for giving vigour and vitality to men and women. Thus we can safely claim to be purely ancient, nicely up-to-date.

20.3.5 Press Conference

A press conference is held to interact with the media rather than just pass on one-way information (as in sending press releases by messenger etc.). It creates a sense of occasion. It is helpful to:

- Launch a product, a new model, etc.
- Declare the opening of a new business establishment, regional entry
- Announce a merger, takeover, new appointment, etc.
- Give company's version in case of rumours or crises
- Give news of achievements, breakthroughs, etc.
- Announce schemes, discounts, etc.

20.3.6 Planning a Press Conference

In planning a press conference, the organiser has to think of a suitable place, time, spokesperson and message. The attendees need to be induced to be present. This is done by an alluring invitation and intellectual bait, and well-timed repeat contacts.

The spokesperson has to make a presentation with all the devices he can command – slides, film clips and so on.

The seven stages of a press conference are:

1. **Greeting:** It has been found by researchers that in an oral presentation 7% of a message is by words alone. Nearly 38% is through tone, accent, voice modulation and 55% through non-verbal factors like gestures, posture, dress, etc. Hence a cheerful, whole-hearted greeting is necessary.
2. **Outline:** This is to communicate in about 20 seconds the conference plan.
3. **Important information:** Now you can tell about the length of your talk, the handout or press release, the question-answer session and the refreshments (if any).
4. **Body message:** After this you can launch systematically with your detailed briefing. One male and one female speaker together hold the attention better. Graphic aids should be used for relieving monotony. It is a fine achievement if you can make the audience feel, "How

time has flown! Highlight the main points with a combination of emphasis and subtlety. How is subtlety used? "That will cost the company an additional rupees three crores, but let's skip that."

5. **Summary:** Make a summary of your talk before you close. If it is a product launch, e.g. a water filter, you can highlight the technology, the availability and the discount (early bird scheme).
6. **Question-answer session:** The organisers may need to go as a group to face media queries and also for mutual moral support. The media persons must be encouraged to speak and led into asking questions. Overcome the silences by raising questions yourself and answering them. Let the microphone go to the questioner and let the question be clear. Let the questioner be introduced. Among organisers, decide who will handle the query. A good question-answer session makes it a proper two-way communication and is a halfway victory.
7. **Conclusion:** Now conclude the sum of the question-answer session in just a few words, thank the attendees for their participation, make sure there are no more questions – or, if time is up against you, continue the questions over the refreshments. Invite the guests to refreshments.

20.4 COMPANY MEETINGS, AGENDA, NOTICES AND MINUTES

20.4.1 Requisites of a Valid Meeting

Meetings of a company must be convened and held in perfect compliance with the applicable provisions of the Companies Act, 1956 and rules framed thereunder. Every meeting, in order to be valid, must be properly convened, properly constituted and properly conducted.

I. Meeting to be "Properly convened" means that

(a) the meeting must have been convened by the *proper authority,* namely the Board of Directors, shareholders or Company Law Board and

(b) proper and *adequate notice* must have been given to all those entitled to attend.

The notice of a meeting to be valid should be of proper length (twenty-one clear days - in case of meetings of shareholders); must be sent to every member at his registered address in India, the legal representative of a deceased member, the official assignee or official receiver of an insolvent member, and the auditor of the company. The notice must mention the place, day and time of holding of the meeting and agenda of the meeting, Audited official statement of accounts, directors' and the auditors' reports, proxy form, explanatory statement, if necessary, should accompany the notice of the meeting.

II. Meeting to be legally constituted means that

(*a*) there must be a proper quorum and

(*b*) there must be a proper chairman

Quorum means the minimum number of members who must be present at a meeting as required by law/rules.

(i) In the absence of any provisions in the articles, the quorum, in respect of a general meeting, is **five** members in case of a public company and **two** members in case of private company.

(ii) Only members present in person and not proxies, can be counted for the purpose of quorum.

(iii) Quorum must be present throughout the meeting.

(iv) If the quorum is not complete, the chairman and members need to wait for half an hour after the scheduled time for the meeting. Then it is adjourned and postponed to the same day in the next week, at the same time and place. However, the board may fix any other day, time and place. At the adjourned meeting, business can be transacted without quorum.

(v) The quorum for a Board meeting is one-third of its total strength or two directors, whichever is higher. Interested directors are not counted for the purpose of quorum.

Chairman

The articles usually designate the Chairman of the Board of Directors to preside over the general meetings of the company in addition to presiding over Board meetings. A Chairman is required to maintain order and decorum at a meeting, to give rulings on points of order, to decide priority of speakers, to maintain relevancy and order in debate, to adjourn a meeting, to exercise a casting vote in case of a tie, and to ascertain the sense of a meeting and declare the result of voting.

III. Meeting to be properly conducted means

That proper rules for ascertaining the sense of the meeting, the rules for discussion and order in debate must be observed. Also, the proceedings should be recorded properly. The sense of the meeting may be ascertained by various methods including by acclamation, voice vote, division, show of hands, ballot or by poll.

In case of voting, voting rights are essentially conferred upon the equity shareholders. Preference shareholders have the right to vote only on resolutions which directly affect the rights attached to the preference shares held by them. Under the Companies Act, voting, in the first instance, is to be by show of hands unless a poll is ordered/validly demanded. In a poll, votes are counted on the basis of the shareholding of members and as such helps in ascertaining the true sense of the meeting. One share, one vote is the basis of counting in this method.

Sec. 179 governs the method of demanding poll. A poll is taken if the Chairman or a prescribed number of members are dissatisfied with the result of voting by show of hands. When a poll is demanded and ordered to be taken, the result by show of hands in negatived.

20.4.2 Types of Company Meetings

Meetings play a very important role in the management of a company. In fact all the important decisions of the company are taken in the meetings only. The shareholders express their will and exercise their rights in the general meetings of members. The directors exercise their powers and take decisions through board meetings. Company meetings may be classified as:

A. Shareholders meetings

(i) Statutory meeting
(ii) Annual general meeting
(iii) Extraordinary general meeting
(iv) Meetings of a class of members

B. Directors meetings

(i) Meetings of all the board of directors
(ii) Meetings of a committee of the board of directors

C. Creditors meetings

(i) Debenture-holders' meeting
(ii) Other creditors' meeting

20.4.3 Drafting of Notice

Notice is an intimation to the concerned persons of certain facts by which they are able to attend and participate in the proposed meeting. Notice generally includes the venue, date, time, and agenda of the meeting. The three main requirements of a notice are that:

1. It is given to every person entitled to receive it.
2. It is given at the proper time.
3. It contains the necessary information and fairly discloses the purpose of the meeting.

Contents of notice

Notice of a general meeting must –

(*a*) Be in writing

(*b*) Contain the company's full name and the address of its registered office in legible characters

(*c*) Specify the place and the day and hour of the meeting

(*d*) Contain a statement of the business to be transacted at the meetings

(*e*) Contain the statutory reminder as to proxies

(*f*) Be signed by a director, or the manager, or the secretary, or some other authorised officer of the company

(*g*) Have annexed to it an explanatory statement where any items of special business are to be transacted at the meeting.

Agenda

A notice usually contains agenda of the meeting. Agenda refers to the list of the items of business to be transacted in a meeting. Agenda is prepared for all kinds of meetings with a view to conduct the meeting conveniently and systematically. A good agenda will consist not merely of a list of items, but would amplify the heading with a brief note to give guidance as to what precisely the meeting is intended to discuss and form decision upon. The items listed in the agenda are normally taken up in the same order in the meeting.

In case of general meetings of company, the agenda items are divided into **ordinary business items** and **special business items**.

According to section 173(1) of the Companies Act, the following items are regarded as **ordinary business items.**

1. The consideration of the accounts, balance sheet and the reports of the board of directors and auditors
2. The declaration of dividend
3. The appointment of directors in the place of those retiring
4. The appointment of, and the fixing of remuneration of, the auditor

According to section 173(2) of the Companies Act, all the business other than ordinary business is deemed to be **special business**. Where any items of special business are to be transacted at any meeting of the company, there must be annexed to the notice of the meeting an explanatory statement setting out all material facts concerning each such item of business, including in particular the nature of the concern or interest, if any, of every director in such business.

How to draft a notice

1. Notice must be issued on the authority of those persons who are empowered to convene meetings. In case of a company this power is given to the board of directors.
2. The notice must comply with the statutory requirements and articles of association.
3. The notice must be signed, dated and, where appropriate, should indicate that it is issued "by order of" the convening authority.
4. The notice must state the date, time and place of the meeting.
5. Proper length of notice must be given as required by law or the articles.
6. The notice must contain a statement of the business to be transacted at the meeting.
7. If any special business is to be transacted, then explanatory statement as required u/s 173(2) must be given.
8. The notice must be sent to all members and other persons entitled to receive such notice.

Specimens

1. Annual General Meeting

NOTICE

Notice is hereby given that the Twenty-fifth Annual General Meeting of the members of Nagpur Industries Limited will be held on Monday, the 30th September, 2011, at 11 am at VIA hall, Civil Lines, Nagpur to transact the following business:

Ordinary Business

1. To consider and adopt the balance sheet as at 31st March, 2011, profit and loss account for the year ended on that date and the reports of the Board of Directors and Auditors thereon
2. To declare dividend on shares
3. To appoint a Director in place of Shri Atma Ambani, who retires by rotation and being eligible, offers himself for reappointment
4. To appoint M/s. Chaturvedi & Shah, Chartered Accountants who shall hold office from the conclusion of this Annual General Meeting until the conclusion of the next Annual General Meeting and to fix their remuneration.

By order of the Board of Directors

Place: Nagpur

1st September 2011

Rohit Patil

Company Secretary

Notes:

1. A member entitled to attend and vote is entitled to appoint a proxy to attend and vote instead of himself and the proxy need not be a member.
2. Members/ Proxies should bring the attendance slip duly filled in for attending the meeting.

2. Notice of a meeting of the Board of Directors

NAGPUR INDUSTRIES LIMITED

Regd. Office: 111, Ramdaspeth, Nagpur

NOTICE

20 August 2011

Shri A B Deshmukh
Director
28, Model Town
Nagpur

Dear Sir

A meeting of the Board of Directors of the Company will be held at the registered office of the Company on Monday, 1st September, 2011 at 3:00 p.m. Agenda for the meeting is enclosed.

You are requested to make it convenient to attend the meeting.

Yours faithfully
Company Secretary

20.4.4 Drafting of Minutes

Minutes may be defined for our purpose as the written record of the proceedings, business transacted, and decisions arrived at, by a meeting of the directors or shareholders of a company. In brief, the minutes are an authoritative record of the business of the meeting.

The essentials of good minutes-writing are:

1. **Accuracy:** As the minutes may subsequently be required as evidence in court of law, they must be accurate. Any inaccuracy in the minutes is fatal to their value and usefulness.
2. **Free from ambiguity:** Minutes should give the full terms of resolutions and avoid over – condensation, lack of clarity or inexactness. Dates, numbers, amounts, quantities, etc., must be clearly stated, and documents must be clearly identified. If the meeting gives any direction or instructions to be carried out, the officials receiving such directions or instructions must be named or otherwise described.
3. **Precision and conciseness:** Minutes must be brief but comprehensive. They must set out exactly what was done and no more, so that members who were absent may, by reading them, fully understand what was done at the meeting. They should not be overburdened with redundant statements or matters.
4. **Completeness:** Minutes should be complete so that it may be safely assumed that any matter not mentioned in the minutes was not dealt with.
5. **Index:** Minutes should be indexed for ready reference. A convenient arrangement is to give each minute a marginal title consisting of a few words (e.g. Finance, Borrowing, Appointment of Managing Director, etc.), and to number all minutes consecutively right throughout the book. This greatly facilitates cross-referencing.
6. **Use of past tense:** The past tense should be used to narrate things that happened at the meeting, viz. "It was reported that," and past perfect tense for things that happened prior to the meeting, "The chairman reported that the company had sent an application on…
   to the Controller of Capital Issues seeking his approval to the issue of bonus shares, etc."

Minutes should always be looked on as legal documents. They should contain no more and no less than what is really necessary. It is customary to record in the minutes votes of thanks to the chairman, directors, staff, etc. This is unobjectionable on special occasions, but it too often becomes a routine, and the minutes become loaded with courtesies, which serve no purpose except to obscure the more important items. For example, the minutes of an annual general meeting contained: "The chairman opened the proceedings by saying how pleased he was to see so many old friends present, as well as some newcomers, to whom he offered a special welcome." These minutes were not read at the next annual general meeting, and the recording of the chairman's amiable sentiments was a complete waste of time, ink and paper (quoted from Shackleton on *The Law and Practice of Meetings*, 6th Ed. at pp. 120-121).

Minutes consist mainly of resolutions and narrations. The former consists of decisions of the meeting, arrived at by voting upon a motion. A resolution should be minuted in the form. "It was resolved that …" If, as is often the case at Board meetings, a decision is arrived at by common consent without voting, it may be recorded in the form "It was agreed that…." Not all items of business require resolutions to record them, e.g. recording that the minutes of the previous meeting were read and signed by the chairman, or recording the vote of thanks to the chair. Narrations record items of business not calling for the framing of a formal resolution. These are known as minutes of narration. Some items of business do require formal resolutions and are known as minutes of resolution, e.g. where the Act or the articles require that some acts or transactions shall only be on the authority of resolutions passed at a general meeting or a Board meeting. Some minutes are recorded partly by narration and partly by resolution.

20.4.5 Specimen Minutes of Board Meeting

XYZ LIMITED

MINUTES OF THE 30TH MEETING OF THE BOARD OF DIRECTORS OF THE COMPANY HELD AT ITS REGISTERED OFFICE ON WEDNESDAY, 15TH APRIL, 2011 AT 3.00 P.M.

Present:
Shri A (Chairman)
Shri B
Shri C
Also present
Shri D Company Secretary
Shri E Vice-President (Finance)

1) **Minutes:** The Board approved the minutes of the last meeting held on March 10, 2011. Accordingly, the same were signed by the Chairman.
2) **Leave of Absence:** Leave of absence was granted to Shri F and Shri G for their inability to attend the meeting.
3) **Register of Contracts:** The Register of Contracts was signed by all the directors present.
4) **Operations Report:** The Board noted the Operations Report of the Company for the quarter ended 31st March. The Managing Director reviewed the problems faced and the market position. This was noted by the Board.
5) **Share Transfer:** The Share Transfer Register of the Company was placed before the meeting and the following resolution was passed.

   "RESOLVED that share transfer Nos. … to … (inclusive) consisting of … equity shares of the Company, be approved and the names of the transferees be entered in the Register of Members."
6) **Next Meeting:** It was decided to hold the next Board Meeting on Monday, 15th June 2011 at 3 pm at the Registered Office of the Company.
7) **Termination of the Meeting:** The Meeting ended with a vote of thanks to the chair.

……………………
CHAIRMAN

25th April, 2011
Nagpur

20.4.6 Specimen Minutes of Annual General Meeting

MINUTES OF THE PROCEEDINGS OF THE SECOND ANNUAL GENERAL MEETING OF XYZ LIMITED HELD ON TUESDAY, 24TH SEPTEMBER 2011, AT 3:30 P.M. AT 123, CENTRAL AVENUE, NAGPUR.

The following were present:
Mr. X (Chairman)
Mr. Y (Director)
Mr. Z (Director)
Mr. A (Director)
Mr. B (Director, Chairman of Audit Committee)
Mr. C (Company Secretary)
Members present in person 120
Members present by proxy 11
Mr. D, Partner of M/s AB & Co. Chartered Accountants, Auditors of the Company, was present.
Mr. E. Practising Company Secretary, was also present.

(1) Chairman: In accordance with Article 30 of the Articles of Association, Mr. X, Chairman of the Board of Directors, took the chair.

(2) Welcome: The Chairman welcomed the Members and introduced the Directors seated on the dais.

(3) Quorum: The Chairman declared that the requisite Quorum was present and called the Meeting to order.

(4) Register of Directors' shareholding: The Chairman informed the members that in accordance with section 307 of the Companies Act, Register of Directors' shareholding is available at the meeting for inspection.

(5) Notice of Meeting: With the consent of the Members present, the Notice convening the Annual General Meeting of the Company was taken as read.

(6) Auditors' report: The Chairman requested the Company Secretary to read the Auditors' Report. After the Auditors' Report had been read, the Chairman delivered his speech.

The business of the Meeting as per the Notice thereof was thereafter taken up itemwise.

(7) Adoption of Accounts

The Chairman requested Mr. B to read the Ordinary Resolution for the adoption of the Accounts for the year ended 31st March 2011 and Mr. B read out the Ordinary Resolution as follows:

"RESOLVED that the audited Balance Sheet of the Company as at 31st March 2011 and the Profit and Loss Account of the Company for the financial year ended on that date, together with the Schedules and Notes attached thereto, along with the Reports thereon of the Directors and the Auditors, as circulated to the Members and laid before the Meeting, be and are hereby approved and adopted."

After the above Resolution was proposed and seconded, but before it was put to the vote, the Chairman invited Members (other than those present by Proxy) to make observations and comments, if any, on the Report and Accounts, as well as on the other Resolutions set out in the Notice convening the Meeting.

Some Members made their observations and comments and raised queries on the Annual Report and Accounts and other items set out in the Notice and the Chairman answered their queries.

On a show of hands, the Chairman declared the aforesaid Ordinary Resolution carried by the requisite majority.

(8) Declaration of Dividend

Mr. A read the following Resolution as an Ordinary Resolution:

"RESOLVED that the dividend @ Rs. 2 on the equity shares of Rs. 10 each, fully paid-up, be and is hereby approved for payment, after deduction of tax at source, if any, to those Members whose names appear on the Company's Register of Members on Tuesday, 24th September 2011."

The Resolution was proposed by Mr. Y and seconded by Mr. Z, and was put to the vote as an Ordinary Resolution.

On a show of hands, the Chairman declared the aforesaid Ordinary Resolution carried unanimously.

(9) Appointment of Director

Proposed by : Mr. Y

Seconded by: Mr. Z

The following Resolution having been proposed and seconded by the aforementioned two Members, was put to the vote as an Ordinary Resolution:

"RESOLVED that, pursuant to Section 256 of the Companies Act, 1956, Mr. A, who retires by rotation and, being eligible for re-appointment, offers himself for re-appointment, be and is hereby re-appointed as a Director of the Company and that his period of office be liable to determination by retirement of Directors by rotation."

On a show of hands, the Chairman declared the aforesaid Ordinary Resolution carried unanimously.

(10) Appointment of Auditors

Proposed by : Mr. Y

Seconded by: Mr. Z

The following Resolution having been proposed and seconded by the aforementioned two Members, was put to the vote as an Ordinary Resolution:

"RESOLVED that M/s. AB & Co., Chartered Accountants, Nagpur, be and are hereby re-appointed as Auditors of the Company to hold office from the conclusion of this Meeting until the conclusion of the next Annual General Meeting of the Company on a remuneration of Rs.50,000, plus applicable service tax and other out of pocket expenses incurred for the purposes of the audit."

On a show of hands, the Chairman declared the aforesaid Ordinary Resolution carried unanimously.

(11) Termination of Meeting

The meeting ended with vote of thanks to the Chairman.

Chairman

24th September 2011

20.5 PUBLIC RELATIONS (PR)

20.5.1 Definition

We can define public relations as follows:

(*a*) This is a company's effort to understand the public (both within the company and outside) and make itself understood for the sake of its enlightened self-interest.

(*b*) It is an organised effort of a company to build a good image for itself among those who count, i.e. those on whom it depends for survival and growth.

(*c*) Public relations means the way a company relates with its publics, both within and without, to generate goodwill for it in pursuit of its business goals and other ideals.

(*d*) Public relations signify the smile which a company wears. Through PR, a company tries to present its human face, make itself approachable and likable. As such, public relations have to cover a range of activities – from singing praises of the company to giving outright donations for public causes. In between, there are mass awareness campaigns, publication of an internal circulation magazine (house journal), organising consumer/dealer get-togethers, sponsoring prizes and scholarships, conducting surveys, analyzing feedback, keeping track of news headlines about it, responding to news appropriately, meeting individual clients, etc. to solve their grievances. Public relations include both inward and outward communication. They cover not only a transmission of messages but also conduct of activities.

20.5.2 Objectives of Public Relations

Within the overall objective of understanding the public and making itself favourably understood, public relations have these objectives:

1. Creating an awareness about the company, its goals, products and services where this counts.
2. Sustaining the awareness as an ongoing process, keeping in mind what the competitors are doing, and knowing that public memory is short.
3. Striving to be accepted by the various publics. Special efforts are required to be accepted by employees. A foreign company has its own requirements for being accepted on this soil.
4. Creating a bond of trust. In times of rumours, misinformation, etc. , a company has to establish the truth. In normal times, too, a company has to promote its reliability. Just consider the frequent use of words like *believe, trust, reliable, safe, 100%, etc.* in building a company image.
5. Getting cooperation from various quarters. A company has many publics on whom it has to depend. Government organisations, providers of various services etc. have to be wooed in such a way that they willingly help the company.
6. Earning recognition. It is not enough to perform feats but it is necessary to get these noticed and talked about. Through winning awards, certifications etc. and getting these read and seen, a company gets recognition. Having so-and-so as a client or collaborator may itself be a recognition. This has to be publicised.

20.5.3 How Public Relations Differ from Propaganda and Advertising

Whereas propaganda suggests a blatant and crude kind of publicity, sometimes by bulldozing the audience, public relations are a gentlemanly effort to inform properly and create an understanding. Public relations try to win hearts.

As for advertisements, public relations exercises differ from the common run of marketing ads. Public relations may, of course, use press appearances as a medium for creating an understanding, but that is at a level different from marketing. While "ads" are normally understood to be out-and-out sales device, public relations create an atmosphere in which the ads may function effectively. Good public relations are, thus, a subtle and indirect mode of advertisement. Ads and PR are a doubles team to enhance a company's business and business image.

20.5.4 The "Publics" of an Organisation

Every organisation has to list out the bodies and segments of population on whom it depends for its smooth functioning and growth. Let us take a few examples.

Publics of a supermarket

1. Customers who visit it and buy from it
2. Its suppliers
3. Its staff
4. Its potential customers (and that may include the whole town, even visitors from nearby towns)
5. Licensing and taxation authorities
6. Providers of infrastructure facilities and services (e.g. electricity, security, etc.)
7. Its publicity agents, newspapers, etc.
8. Regulatory authorities such as Food and Drugs Administration

Publics of a holiday resort

1. People who have the spending power to visit it and have an access to it
2. Its staff
3. Travel agents who may do bookings for it
4. Transport operators
5. Government maintenance agencies like the municipal corporation
6. Law and order authorities
7. Professional entertainers
8. Emergency service providers like doctors, divers, adventure experts
9. Publicity machinery

The relative importance of each public for the company is determined from experience. Equitable attention is required to be paid to each public.

20.5.5 Internal Public Relations

It is curious that when we say "a company," sometimes we mean all its employees and sometimes only the top management or owners. For the top management, the rank and file are a public, to be entertained and befriended as a category.

Internal PR are maintained by means of:

1. **Counselling and dialogue:** Employees may have to be advised suitably to get adjusted to their jobs.
2. **Self-expression forums:** Employees should have access to higher management to convey their problems and useful ideas. The employees may express themselves through suggestion schemes. These contribute a fund of ideas based on actual working conditions. However, it is necessary not to promise that the suggestions would all be translated into schemes. At the same time, good ideas need to be rewarded. If a company conducts its own slogan contest, it may give a prize to the winning slogan and save on publicity expenditure.
3. **Publications:** As seen earlier in this section, house journals help to create a family feeling in an organisation. If a house journal is supplemented by get-togethers (of employees within a town) and camps (of employees from different towns), a bond of cordiality is created. The publication can serve as a base for such get-togethers and camps.
4. **Free films, entertainment shows, educative lectures:** Even in the days of overexposure to films through TV, rare and attractive films can be screened specially for employees. Similarly, magic shows, hypnotism shows, gymnastics shows, etc. can be arranged for them. Educative

lectures, yoga and meditation camps and celebration of special days (e.g. Hindi Day), poetry meets, etc. are some more means of solidifying employee bonds.

5. **Felicitations:** Employees and their family members can be felicitated for their achievements – merit ranks, scholarships, adventure feats, etc.
6. **Inviting family members by creating occasions:** A campaign like a tree plantation drive can be used to create a good image in the outside world and an occasion for employees' family members to meet in informal surroundings. Family members may also be invited for national days like the Independence Day and the Republic Day.

20.5.6 External PR

This is a wider area, with many interest groups.

1. **Customers:** They constitute the biggest public for a company. They can be wooed by having a grievance cell, enquiry booth, "disinterested" educational campaigns (e.g. "night brushing is vital" – message from a toothpaste company), display of posters and pamphlets explaining schemes, creating convenience for weaker age groups and weaker sections, etc. Courtesy and promptness are time-honoured PR devices that function through every representative of the company.
2. **Financiers:** The company's shareholders, bankers, depositors, etc. like to know about the financial status of the company. By issuing prompt, truthful, self-explanatory and reader-friendly financial publications and reaching them into the hands of the financial partners, a company can earn their goodwill.
3. **General public:** There is a vast group of people who are not actual consumers of the company but may be potential consumers. For an airline, there are many who have no plans to fly in the near future but who still view with interest the coming into existence of a new company in this line, its standard of service, etc. Their general discussions help to create a climate of opinion. Thus an overall good image needs to be projected at all times. A company can stay in the memory of the general public by doing society-useful jobs, e.g. cleanliness campaigns, ecofriendly activities, help in disaster management, etc.
4. **Institutions:** They include government departments, corporations and public bodies. They are power centres with much capacity to do or undo. To stay good in their eyes, a company needs to do that which appeals to an enlightened group. It needs to project an image as a law-friendly company. A clean administration and standards of probity in the product help to woo institutions.

20.5.7 Feedback in PR

To know what the public is thinking of the company in general and on specific points in particular is necessary for its image-building. This becomes especially necessary when sales decline despite heavy publicity campaigns. Publicity is a heady wine and likely to induce pride and self-complaceney. Excessive publicity sometimes produces a reverse reaction - sympathy for the underdog. People sometimes don't want to go where everybody goes. And yet monolithic reputations (one company outshining all others) are possible. They are achieved by staying close to the ground. A company can stay in touch with the public at large by getting constant feedback from its publics. This is done through surveys and questionnaires, as also through "casual" talk and by listening to casual remarks. Some film-makers arrange for a pre-release show and watch the facial expressions of the spectators as they leave the theatre. Good face-readers and listeners are an asset to a feedback compaign.

Just as a company uses celebrity endorsements (support of famous persons) as a tool of advertisements, it does well to listen to disinterested intellectuals who may not be celebrities. Because of their superior intellect and dispassion, they can mouth an opinion that may be of lasting value. At the same time, an ignored warning from this precious minority can be a sign of decline of a company. Publishers get their books read by such disinterested intellectuals for a frank and balanced opinion.

20.5.8 PR and Media

Media planning is truly a specialist job today. From hoardings at busy suburban railway stations like CST or Churchgate, daily seen by lakhs of commuters, to internet – deep inside the computer tube, there are too many media today. But audio-visual media maintain their primacy.

The tools of public relations are:

1. **TV:** Here your skill in PR is seen in the programmes your sponsor and in the decorum of your presentations. The TV announcer's voice is often more effective to drive home your slogan than the paid artist or the celebrity!
2. **Print media – newspapers and magazines:** While ads do their work, good PR lies in contributing useful scholarly articles to appropriate magazines and newspapers. An article on motivation or on economy by a company's chairman would do much to enhance its image. Then there are interviews, panel discussions, etc. in which top executives can take part.
3. **Films:** Films about a company's working and its unusual activity (e.g. oil exploration, disease control) can be used for fostering public relations. These films can be shown at customers' meets, exhibitions, press meets, in-house get-togethers, etc.
4. **Literature:** Brochures, information booklets, leaflets etc. are specially devised literature for image-building. They can be coupled with calendars, lists of holidays, useful telephone numbers, etc.
5. **Direct mail:** Some banks send birthday greetings to their customers. Similarly, season's greetings, sympathy cards, invitations etc. can be used as a bridge to reach a company's established as well as new clients.
6. **Internet:** Internet is an ever-expanding medium with unexplored possibilities. It is also a very effective tool for reaching special interest groups who would be visiting certain sites or using certain features of internet (like email).
7. **Radio:** The Radio, an audio device, has certain advantages over the TV. It can play in the background without involving the eye. Its importance needs to be properly rated, since it is a highly under rated medium in today's India. Executives have an extra opportunity of reaching rural audiences by giving radio talks in regional languauges. Agricultural products can be popularised by effective use of the radio.
8. **Oral communication and stage manners:** This is not the least device of public relations. Customers see employees' dresses and manners with some attention. Consider a savings account clerk in a bank. Customers have to stand and wait in front of him/her. They get ample time to watch the functionaries. All personnel who have to deal with the public need to be trained, groomed and counselled from the PR angle.

In conferences, press meets and public appearances, executives are judged by their courtesy, stage manners and gift of the gab. A systematic development of personality is needed. Also, sometimes a subject expert may not be a good speaker or a presentable person. What a mistake it is in such cases to project him as the company's spokesperson! It is better to impart the expertise to a proficient communicator and use him for presentations.

20.6 BASICS OF ADVERTISEMENT

20.6.1 Defining an Advertisement

To advertise a product, service or an idea is to draw attention to it favourably using a mass medium.

Supreme Court definition: If by any communication, communicator tries to influence people to buy his product or service or attract towards his product or service, the communication amounts to an advertisement. *(The Supreme Court in ICICI Bank v. Municipal Corporation of Greater Mumbai [2006] 4 STT 20 (SC))*

An ad performs several functions:

(*a*) To introduce a new product in the market

(*b*) To tell of its comparative merits in a competitive market

(*c*) To increase the use of a product and the frequency of its use

(*d*) To bring new areas and new population groups into the fold of buyers (e.g. a chocolate promoted for all age groups and not just children)

(*e*) To bring together a group of related products (e.g. cosmetics with a variety of applications)

(*f*) To make the brand name noticed and popular. There are, for instance, ads which say nothing except the name of shoe brand around a cricket ground.

(*g*) To educate the public about a useful product which they had been missing

(*h*) To remove misunderstandings about a product

(*i*) To influence opinion leaders

An ad addresses an existing need or creates a need which was unfelt. Its appeal is to the mind (desires), intellect (judgement) and the senses. For attracting clients, it offers money-saving, better quality, durability, pleasure, prestige, profit, healthy living, convenience and such other benefits as motivate people to act. When the appeal is to the senses, the message is remembered better. With an average city dweller's exposure to thousands of ads at home and outside, the competition for attention is high and the imagination is stretched to the limit to find out new ways of attracting attention and being remembered.

20.6.2 Writing an Advertisement Copy

Drafting and designing an ad is a specialist job, often requiring the services of a professional ad agency. Many companies, however, have their own ad wing as part of its publicity operations.

The message of an ad copy is multiplied by a good visual. A copy may contribute 50% of the appeal and the visual the remaining 50%. The percentage may vary, of course. So the copywriter has to work in a team with the graphic visualiser and graphic artist. These days visuals are generally taken from the huge banks of pictures and photos which some computer programmes have, reducing the need for sketching or taking photographs.

An ad copy must reveal the consumer benefit and the reason why.

It consists of a headline and then a body copy. On a newspaper page, for instance, there are ads and ads, and the headline has to be catchy to hook the reader's attention. Generally, about 90% of the work of attracting reader attention is done by the headline.

The five steps in converting a potential buyer into an actual buyer are:

1. Getting attention
2. Creating interest
3. Arousing desire
4. Convincing of merits
5. Inspiring action.

We shall see how this works through a specimen written for study and some real-life ads used by advertisers in the media.

Specimen ad for a business school

Headline	**Capitalise on our business course, invest in yourself**
Body copy	Investment in yourself is the best investment. Two years of study for MBA in Central India's foremost business school will enrich you variously: • Professional managers of high repute to teach • Up-to-the-minute computer lab • 100 % job placement • Interaction with industry's leading lights • Quiet, congenial campus • Homelike hostel and mess • Makes you a global manager **Entrepreneurs Business School** Village Devri, Katol Road Nagpur Tel : xxx xxxx Fax : xxx xxxx Email : ebschool@priority.com

The headline uses financial terms like "capital" and "invest" which are related to business. The body copy is given in bullet points for easy, quick reading.

Nowadays, small ads that are classified into subjectwise categories are quite popular and constitute the largest number of ads in a newspaper. A further development in this type of ads is classified display ads that use visuals and various layout techniques while being placed on the classified ads page. The classification ranges from situations vacant, matrimonials, accommodation… to sale or purchase of goods or services.

The language of ads is usually concise and imaginative. Various literary devices are used in the headline and body copy.

To sample a few of them:

1. Slogans
   - Binny – a great name in textiles
   - Be wise buy the best – Britannia biscuits
2. Puns
   - The <u>Kinetic</u> energy of youth at Limbanna Scooters (showroom)
   - I'm a Khaitan <u>fan</u>
3. Coining new words
   - Utterly butterly delicious
   - Skintoxication
4. Sensuous appeal
   - Finger-licking good
   - Sound you can see (TV ad)
5. Alliteration
   - The zing thing (soft drink)
   - Think bigger. Think better. (Corporate ad for an industrial group)

6. Parallelism
- Neighbour's envy, owner's pride (TV ad)
- Light as mist, soft as spring

7. Questions
- Someone special is coming your way, did you Cherry Blossom your shoes?
- Do you make these mistakes in English?

Specimen ads from print media

1.

BIG BAZAAR

THE GREAT EXCHANGE OFFER

Exchange Everything Old For Anything New

Exchange your old garments, newspapers, stationery, plastics, luggage, footwear, household items, crockery, cutlery, leather goods, electronic items (in working or non-working condition), mattresses, etc.

We will weigh them and value them at the rates given below and issue exchange coupons for their total value.

Now you just shop with us for (a minimum of) four times the value of these coupons. E.g,. if you have brought goods worth Rs.200, you shop for Rs.800, of which you pay only Rs.600.

You can choose from a wide range of garments, utensils, home linen, luggage, footwear, toys, furniture, plastics, etc.

Our buying price:

1. Garments @ Rs.200/kg.
2. Newspapers @ Rs.25/kg.
3. Plastics, utensils, glass, leather goods, furniture @ Rs.75/kg.
4. Footwear and luggage @ Rs.100/kg.
5. Pet/beer bottles @ Rs.15/kg.
6. Other goods @ Rs.20/kg.

Terms of the offer:

- The exchange coupon is valid for 7 days from the date of issue.
- Management reserves the right to change the exchange offer on any product category from time to time.
- The coupon is valid for a single transaction.
- The coupon is not transferable to any other location.
- The coupon is not valid at Food Bazaar, Gold Bazaar, Mobile Bazaar, Dollar Shoppe and some other points in the Store. (Details at venue.)

BIG BAZAAR
Is-se sasta aur achchha kahin nahin!

Adapted

Good morning goodness
Here's to 365 days of happy mornings. Mornings where bath tantrums surrender to a splash of strawberry fun. Mornings that are awash with love. And drenched with goodness: the goodness of olive oil. New Pears Junior gently moisturises and nourishes even the most delicate skin. So you can be sure that when it comes to skin care, your junior gets nothing but the best.
OLIVE OIL GOODNESS
Pears
Pears JUNIOR

Reproduced

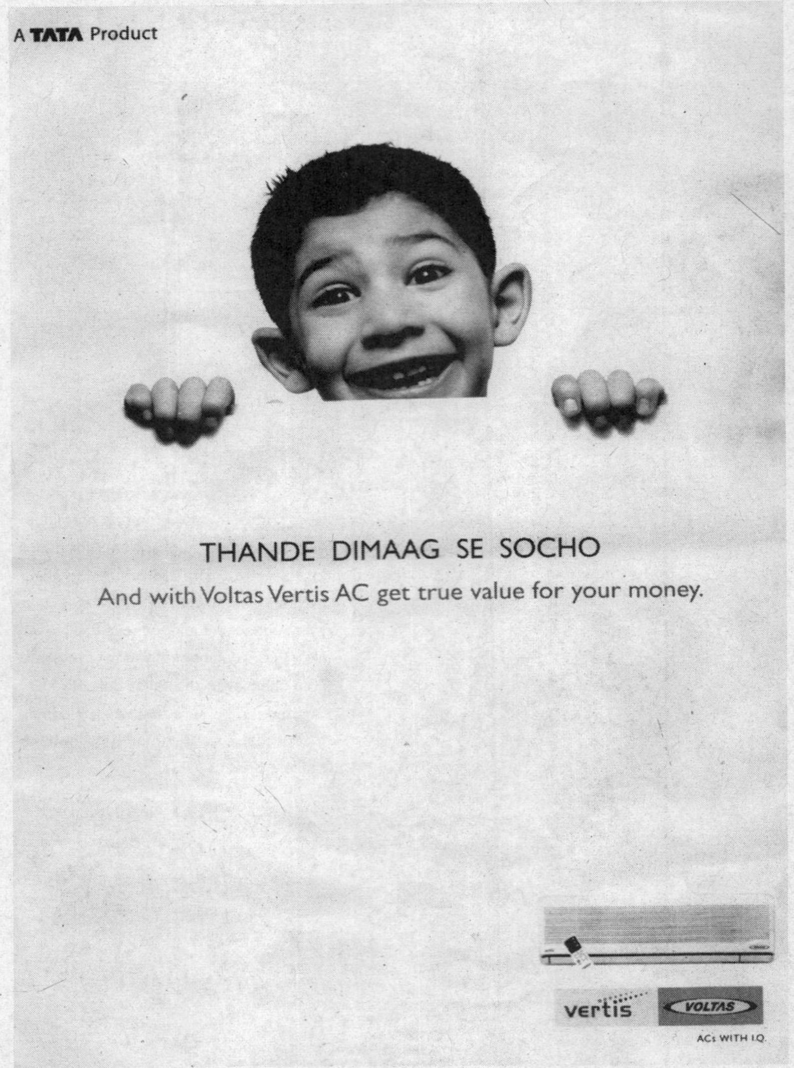

Reproduced

WANTED FRESHERS / experienced Web Designers, Programmers, VB, ASP, Net, SQL, Oracle, Business Development Executives with software knowledge, lady Telephone Co-ordinator with English fluency. Contact: BIIT Pvt. Ltd. Ph. 2630211. hr@bilt.in.info@bilt.com.

Facsimile

Facsimile

20.6.3 Media for Advertisement

Broadly we can classify the media as indoor and outdoor.

Indoor media

1. **Television:** Being an audio-visual medium, it is the most powerful in affecting the senses, mind and intellect. Advertisers use professional models, cartoons or celebrities to drive home their message. With colours and music in play, and special effects to add, these ads can be quite entertaining. And yet the excess of them that we see these days, stretches to the limit the ability of the viewer to respond to them or to remember the product names and their benefits. Since these ads follow in a chain, consumers tend to get up from the TV-front seat or mute the TV when the ads rush in.
2. **Radio:** This medium has been in use for nearly a century now. Radio can be heard without the need to fix one's eyes to a spot, and can be played while working, cooking, studying, etc. Its reach is farther than that of TV though the ability to engage attention is much less. Music and jingles make radio ads more memorable.
3. **Newspapers and magazines:** Almost every educated home gets a newspaper and some magazines. Ads account for about half the newspaper space though the percentage varies for magazines. Now most newspapers use colours to add charm. Newspapers ads can be made more effective by putting them on the appropriate page and timing them well. A financial product can be advertised on the page for financial news, youth-related ads (educational institutions) on the sports page, and festivals can be used for announcing discount schemes.
4. **Direct mail :** An advertiser procures addresses of potential buyers from various sources (e.g. by giving a free gift to an existing contact). There is a socio-economic research study behind effective mail-selling. The *Reader's Digest* is one of the more prominent users of this type of advertising.

Outdoor media

1. **Hoardings/billboards:** Huge boards are set up by the roadside or at squares and a brief, easily graspable message painted on it. These serve very well to supplement TV ads. At night one may see a new TV ad and the next day see the same product advertised, in a different way, on a hoarding. While the TV advertiser appears someone remote in a metro city, the hoarding ad brings him closer. The local contact can be given in a hoarding ad. Hoardings are especially used for promoting stores in the neighbourhood and major sales outlets anywhere in town.
2. **Posters:** Posters are often displayed at POP (point of purchase) where the consumer takes the decision to pay for a product. Posters can be seen anywhere and everywhere: on buses, autorickshaws, in stores. Sometimes they are as small as the thickness of the shelf in a medicine shop. That is miniaturisation for you. City walls and empty spaces anywhere - electric poles included – are used for displaying posters.
3. **Electric or neon signs:** They are similar to hoardings except in the technology. Neon signs and electric displays are visible at night. They are made more effective by an on-and-off mechanism or a movie message where the words rotate, and curiosity pushes the reader to wait and read the whole.
4. **Balloons:** At fetes and exhibitions one sees large balloons held high in the sky, displaying an ad.

The ground for advertising is – any place you can think of. Large business houses are heard saying, "Half the money we spend on advertising is a waste. But the question is, which half?" It is necessary to measure the pulling power of an ad and use the feedback for the next ad. Trading houses measure the responses simply by counting the phone calls they receive on a day in response to an ad.

20.7 INTERNATIONAL COMMUNICATION

20.7.1 Scope

With new technology connecting countries, connecting people, connecting hearts and minds, we can communicate at the speed of thought. We are in a global village. Hence the need to think globally and act locally. International communication is the specialised study of how to deal with cultural differences when dealing with widely different international audiences.

A classic example of cultural difference is the British journalist who does not understand what *biodata* is (in *The Tiger's Eye*, a radio play) and only understands the term *CV* (which is short form of the Latin phrase *curriculum vitae*!). It is an ongoing question - how to communicate across cultures?

Today, international job–hunters are numerous, and occasions for cross-cultural business talk even more. This situation requires us to adapt as well as standardise.

Aspects of culture we need to note

Culture is the customs and habits peculiar to a group of people and includes the civilisation, arts, ways of greeting and parting, the ways of paying respect etc. We talk of Stephen's College culture, Brahmin culture, South Indian culture, Chinese culture, IBM culture, hippie culture, pop culture and so on. The different headings under which we achieve our cultural identity should make us think and take heed.

An international businessman needs to develop an awareness of:

1. **Etiquette and social customs:** They differ between countries. In the late 1970s, Indian Prime Minister Morarji Desai, during his visit to America, suggested that when toast was proposed in his honour, no alcoholic drink should be served but only water. American President Jim Carter responded positively. Generally, the two parties arrive at a mean of two cultures. However, for this you have to know the other group's social customs.
2. **Dress habits:** Dress habits show a wide range across the international cultural spectrum. A typist may go in a short skirt in a Hollywood firm. But when she goes to work in an Arab country, where most women wear a burka, she has to cover her head, her legs, and dress least provocatively. Indian leaders have repeatedly shown their independence from the western dress of a business suit. But, for everyday business, it may be wiser to conform to the dress code expected in a business meet.
3. **Respect for time:** It is often believed that European countries insist on to-the-minute punctuality. But as one goes from Germany to Spain, the expectations of timely arrival and start of business differ a good deal. Indians are known to be rather lax about maintaining time. One has to know the standards of punctuality in an international situation and act accordingly.
4. **Roles of men and women:** Where women's liberation has taken major strides, the roles of women have evolved a good deal. A woman may go alone to meet a male dignitary at the airport. But such a practice is known to have created misunderstandings in a very traditional society.
5. **Religious notions:** Man's behaviour ultimately rests on his concept of his place in the universe, which is what religion is about. In certain cultures, hard work and profit through it is preached from religious platforms. In India, among Hindus, we have a system of pooja and celebration of Diwali as a part of business rites. One may exclaim in the name of *God* or *goodness*. Utmost consideration is required to appreciate the other group's religious values.
6. **Decision-making process:** We in India have more hierarchical business organisations, with more and more decisions centred at the higher levels. In Western countries there is greater decentralisation, delegation of powers and individual authority. Japanese, who are Orientals but businesswise second only to Americans, take a long time deciding. In China and Japan,

decisions are generally taken collectively and not by individual managers. In USA, elaborate planning and foresight precede a business meet. The executive is prepared with two or three responses and can decide quickly and convey the decision on the spot. Russians, by contrast, are thoroughgoing and even somewhat suspicious and take longer to decide, with several rounds of talks.

7. **Different uses of English:** Bernard Shaw remarked that England and America were divided by the English language (and not united by it). How much greater must be the division, then, with so many countries developing English language skills in their own ways, under the influence of their native languages. Prepositional phrases are quite common in USA, but these may fox (or "take in") others.

   Hold on = wait
   Put up = stay, take residence
   Meet up with = meet
   In back of = behind

A phrase which is not understood or, worse, wrongly understood can be a source of trouble. The airlines crew are trained to use clear expressions (e.g. "I didn't get you" for "Beg your pardon"). It is good to study phrase books of the country with which you are doing business, especially if it is an English-speaking country like USA, Britain, Australia, New Zealand, Canada, South Africa, etc.

It is also necessary to understand the accent and express oneself with clear pronunciations.

20.7.2 Tips for Effective International Communication

From the foregoing, one can crystallise a few tips for dealing with global communication:

1. Study the cultural habits, business customs, manners etc. of the country with which you have to deal. Video clips are especially helpful.
2. Take the responsibility of making sense and getting your meaning across. An oral meet may use signs and symbols, pictures and diagrams to convey what you cannot explain in words. Use repetition. Ensure that the meaning is clear.
3. Start with a feeling of respect and let it find suitable expression in verbal and non-verbal communication. A gesture like drawing a chair for an old person or offering to carry a lady's suitcase tells more than what words do.
4. Treat the other party as an individual without putting him into a cultural stereotype. Keep your mind free from prejudice.
5. Celebrate all that is common, the two countries' mutual contributions in the past, the symbols of unity between the two cultures.
6. Modify your accent (when you can) to match the other speaker's. This is especially necessary when the other person's mother tongue is being used.
7. Be kind to the other party's communicative deficiency. He may be making up for it by his business smartness.
8. Try to meet halfway about food habits, manners, etc. The other party may also be doing the same. That's what friends do anyway.

20.7.3 How to Achieve Better International Written Communication

You may be running a business house in another country or dealing with foreigners in your country or writing for import or export. The written communication may take the form of letters, reports, memos, trade documents or sales literature. Here is what you may do:

1. In the case of letters and memos, you may write them in a language with which you are comfortable (perhaps English) and may get your writing translated into the other party's language through an expert professional translator. Use the block or modified block format.

Keep the language simple and clear, avoiding informal expressions. It is better to be specific than general.

Note the specialities of different national groups (without, of course, jumping to universal conclusions about the group).

Americans are straightforward and to the point, the Japanese a little ceremonial (with enquiries of health etc.), the businesspersons from the Arab block countries elaborate with deep courtesies.

2. If you are drafting a sales message, note the different approaches of different cultures: Americans – direct; Japanese – action-oriented, Arab block people – deeply polite and emphasising the relationships. Show careful respect to the other party's cultural value and use appeals with which it is comfortable.

   Sometimes the other party may be using a calendar other than the Christian one (i.e. a lunar calendar). Use the appropriate calendar.

3. Documents which accompany an import or export transaction need to be in an acceptable usage. Some countries use multilingual printed forms (e.g. for the covering letter to documents). In translation, there are radical changes in construction and wording. This can be easily judged from the fact that the equivalent of "nameste" can be "good morning." Be sure of where you stand in a multilingual document. This may depend on the jurisdiction of the deal. Make sure that the technical and routine terms put you on the safe side of the law.

A. Questions based on critical understanding. Comment in about 30 words.

1. **Communication is an important functional area like production, marketing, finance, etc. of a modern commercial organisation.**

Ans. We are living in an age of information and people are conscious of the overall image of the company with which they deal as buyers, sellers, etc. Hence good image-building is necessary for an organisation. This is best done by improving its quality of communication within and without and using communication as an instrument to form better relationships.

2. **House journals can bring to an organisation the feeling of belonging to one family.**

Ans. A house journal is not like a general magazine but rather a magazine to celebrate an organisation. It highlights news about the top officials and common employees of the company and gives scope to their creativity. Thus it brings the employees a feeling of belonging.

3. **A press release has to please two publics – the press editor and the readers of the periodical.**

Ans. Through a press release, a company reaches out to the readers of newspapers etc. through their editors. Naturally, it has to please the editor first and satisfy his standards. At the same time the company has to make sure that its version reaches the public undistorted.

4. **Public relations are the same as advertisements.**

Ans. False. Whereas product/service advertisements are aimed primarily at enhancing the sales, public relations aim at image building. They create an atmosphere of goodwill and trust for a company in which advertisement may function effectively. Public relations comprise many kinds of activities including social and charitable work.

5. **One can praise one's product to any extent in an advertisement.**

Ans. An ad is legally bound to make only those claims which it can substantiate. Moreover, in public judgment, an ad is believable only when the company has a reputation of being truthful. False and exaggerated claims erode a company's credibility, making its ads nearly useless. You cannot fool all the people all the time.

6. A common business culture prevails in all the countries of the world.

Ans. On the contrary, the cultural practices of businessmen of different countries differ. To succeed in business across cultures, one has to familiarise with the other party's culture, respect it and modify one's behaviour approximately.

7. Public relations are the smile which a company wears.

Ans. It is not enough any more to produce goods and sell them. People wish to know about the company with which they deal as buyers, sellers, shareholders etc., and the PR wing reveals the company's personality, non-commercial objectives etc. An outgoing, winsome (cheerful) public image helps a company to make a place in public hearts – as a smile does. (An airlines once made a TV ad based plastic smiles and rosy smile.)

8. International communication is about knowing the rules of import and export.

Ans. Understanding and relating to foreign cultures with which a company deals – that's what international communication is all about. The international charter of impex formalities is only part of the story. In writing and speaking to one's overseas business counterparts, one has to learn to respect their culture, whatever it may be.

B. Questions for revision

1. What is a press release? How is it different from a press report?
2. What do you understand by corporate communication? Outline the activities governed ly it.
3. Write short notes (about 150words each) on: a) House journal b) Corporate brochure
4. What are the contents of a house journal and what purpose do they serve?
5. Explain how a press conference should be conducted.
6. What are the occasions for issuing a press release? What are the conditions for its success?
7. What are the objectives of public relations?
8. Name the media available for public relations and their merits and limitations.
9. Define an advertisement and enumerate its functions.
10. "Ads are all-pervasive." Comment with reference to the media used for advertisements.
11. What is the importance of learning cross-cultural communication? Explain with examples.
12. What can a business house do for effective international communication?
13. How can corporate image be built through public relations?
14. Distinguish between corporate image and public relations. What are the various factors that will establish the corporate image of your company? Explain.

C. Drafting exercises

1. Draft a press release scotching the rumours of management excesses which have allegedly led to a strike in your company. Write a suitable covering letter for it.
2. Write a press release at the introduction of a scooter that gives the mileage of a motorcycle.
3. Draft a press release announcing the setting up of a joint venture in a related field in collaboration with a multinational company.
4. Write a press release on the performance of your company last year.
5. Write a press release announcing a seminar-cum-workshop organised by your company, inviting participation in it.
6. Draft a press release on getting the award for the highest exports.
7. Draft an appointment ad for salesmen and salesgirls for an automobile showroom.
8. Write an advertisement for a school that lays much stress on sports and cultural development of its students.
9. Write a classified ad seeking an accommodation of about 4000 sq.ft. in a business area for opening a branch of a bank.
10. Yahoo Bank, having head office at Manipal, Karnataka has fully compurterised its branch at 1643, Thane Road, Najafgarh, New Delhi which is to be inaugurated on 23rd June, 2006 at 9.45 a.m. by Vijay Kumar, Chairman and Managing Director of the bank. The bank is soliciting gracious presence of one and all. Draft an invitation for putting it as an advertisement in Delhi newspapers. (CS exams)

■■■

CHAPTER

21

Presentation Skills and Public Speaking

What should you know?

21.1 WHAT IS A PRESENTATION?

A presentation is a form of public speaking and sometimes the two terms are interchanged. However, in business practice, **presentation** usually means presenting your point of view on a subject orally, formally and with preparation. A presentation may be to inform, argue out your case, persuade.

Your method of making a presentation may be –

1. By preparing a talk, making notes, memorising only the ideas and illustrations, and speaking extempore (that is without reference to any written material)
2. By memorising an entire speech and delivering it
3. By reading out a speech (for example a company report) so that every word is spoken exactly as you planned it

The reading method, to be interesting, requires that the person presenting the speech be a very good reader. He should vary the tone to prevent monotony.

These days it is getting increasingly popular to use illustrations, charts, slides or film clips along with an oral presentation. These devices help to involve the visual sense in receiving the communication and present the information summarily and graphically.

21.2 ELEMENTS OF A PRESENTATION

In an oral presentation, the audience sees the speaker and hears him. Hence the standing personality must corroborate the spoken words. A speech on simplicity must be accompanied by the same quality in the speaker. A speech on confidence should show this quality shining in the speaker's gestures and posture, voice and delivery. Hence the dictum "Dress before address" is only appropriate. The essential elements of a presentation are:

1. Confidence
2. Sincerity
3. Mastery of the subject
4. A friendly feeling for the audience

1. **Confidence:** In a way, standing before a group of people to speak for a length of time, and speaking with force and conviction, is a difficult undertaking. You need to prepare yourself psychologically for the occasion and be ready to stand your ground. This is what confidence amounts to. If you are sure of yourself and sure about your message, you find it easier to carry your audience with you. On the eve of discovering America, Columbus faced a revolt from his seamen who did not believe that a continent existed in the direction they were going. But Columbus was sure. Hence he could manage to make his team work along with him. Confidence comes out of your own intellectual and emotional satisfaction with your message and cause. To be thoroughly sure of your grounds, it requires a good deal of research into your subject, preparation, and anticipating the audience you are going to face.
2. **Sincerity:** When does a preacher succeed in preaching? When he means what he says and has the interests of the listeners in his heart. A good presentation begins in the heart and reaches the listeners' hearts. However, *having* sincerity and *being able to communicate it to the audience* are not the same. Your inner state, your attitude needs to be translated into the delivery. The ability to convey your sincerity is the ability of an actor. As a sincere speaker, you are playing before the audience a role – that of a bringer of a useful message. Now, as an actor becomes one with his role, you have to be one with your message.
3. **Mastery of the subject:** Every effective speaker vouches for this, that he went deep and wide into his subject. A good speaker gathers more information than may be required for the speech. That is how he has a back-up, a reservoir of facts and opinions on which his speech stands. When you say, "The farmer in Vidarbha is pushed to the wall," let's say you have at the back of your mind the figures of farmer suicides and the circumstances and factors related to them. A mastery of the subject requires that you see the subject from many points of view including that of your opponents. Then you can be effective.

   If, for example, you are speaking in favour of economic liberalisation in India, you need to see the issue from the standpoint of the *svadeshi* supporters, the trade unionists, the communists, etc. also.
4. **A friendly feeling for the audience:** When you stand before a group of people, many of whom are strangers to you and with their own opinions, you can be effective by radiating a friendly feeling. A motivation speaker started her speech before a large crowd of restless youths with the resounding words, "I love this audience." This was said in a radiant tone and eye-to-eye contact with the listeners. Instantly, a friendly bond was established. You need to have the listeners' welfare in mind as the purpose of your talk. You need to take care that through your actions or words, you don't militate against any of their pet likes.

21.3 DESIGNING YOUR PRESENTATION

Structurally, a good presentation has an introduction, a body and a conclusion. The speaker may organise his thoughts upon any of these formulas:

1. (a) State your facts
   (b) Argue your facts
   (c) Appeal for action
2. (a) Show that something is wrong
   (b) Show it can be remedied
   (c) Seek the listeners' cooperation.

Now we discuss the parts of a presentation.

1. **Introduction:** This is to prepare the listeners to receive your message and to arouse their interest. As Dale Carnegie, the renowned author on public speaking says, the beginning and ending of a speech are its most important parts. The beginning hooks the listener to your message, the ending leaves a lasting impression on his mind.
   (a) Speakers use a story, a humorous piece or joke, a shocking fact, a noble quotation, a question, etc. to kickstart their speech. Swami Vivekanand did even better in the all-religions' meet in Chicago in 1893 by starting his immortal speech with the words "Brothers and sisters"(when the others were addressing them "ladies and gentlemen").
   (b) You can present your idea by quoting some surprising statistics. Talking on pollution, you may start: "The safety level of X chemical is 25 ppm (parts per million) but in some areas of Mumbai it is 4000 ppm." If your statistics concern the health and security of your audience, its money status or honour, the audience may awaken to your message at once. "In X country, 90% husbands help their wives with kitchen work, while in Y country (audience's country) only 10% husbands do so." Women are quite likely to awaken to the speech.
   (c) Quotations are pearls of wisdom, often in felicitous wording: "Eternal vigilance is the price of democracy." A quotation gives authority to your speech.
   (d) You may ask a question like, "Are you sure that the air you breathe has 20% oxygen and not just 15%?"
   (e) A speaker may produce an exhibit out of his pocket and start. "This object the size of a pocket calculator can put you in touch with 120 TV channels of the world."
2. **Body:** The body of your speech is the main course of the meal, wherein you should arrange the facts in a logical order. Let us say you are talking on the low standards of English in our set-up (to sell audio and video cassettes for self-learning). You may tell systematically about what happens during the teachers' training, and then the inadequate teaching of the language from the primary stage onwards. You may talk of what happens when a regional language is the medium of instruction. You may analyse the facts, driving to the conclusion that the English communicative ability of most of our students is below par in the global scenario. When "Shining India" is the buzzword, it requires global competitiveness in English.

   If you go into the minor and finer aspects of your subject and if you have a solid back-up of examples, the body of your talk is strong. During this part of your talk, it is necessary to keep the audience on its toes (and out of its daydreaming) with periodic use of humour, change of tone and pace, exhibits and other devices that keep the interest and receptivity high.
3. **Conclusion:** Your conclusion aims that the audience should act in the way you want. You may want them to buy your product or service, or to speak well of your company or acquire a new habit (e.g. punctuality, better proofreading, greater courtesy, etc.). The conclusion has to emerge logically out of the talk like the proof of a mathematical theorem. And yet, the speech should be anchored more in an emotional appeal than an intellectual one. You have to make a good idea likable.

In the concluding part of your speech, you may restate your main arguments, give a summary of the talk or produce a resounding conclusion line. In good rhetoric (art of speaking) the last line remains in the listeners' minds. George Orwell's novel *The Animal Farm* is a satire on the double standards of rulers who profess equality but corner the best for themselves. Towards the end, one character raises the question, "How is this done when all animals are equal?" The leaders says, "Yes, all animals are equal, but some animals are more equal than others." This impossible twist of language echoes in the reader's mind for a long time.

In general it is a good idea not to cover too many themes in one presentation. Keep the number of points few and argue these with force. One has to allow for the listeners' limited attention span while listening.

21.4 A Brief about Sales Presentations

In business life, one has to make a presentation for selling a product or a service before various types of audiences – distributors, the press, a family (in a house-to-house sales campaign) or customers gathered in a showroom. The sales presentation may be accompanied by a live demo, a test ride or a film clip. We recall here the sales formula of AIDA – attention, interest, desire, action. It is not always that you have an audience ready and waiting for you to deliver your talk. You may have to, like the roadside seller, gather an audience using your magnetism. Hence a sales presentation requires the best of persuasive skill.

For making a good sales presentation, the following maybe remembered:

1. **Study the product technically:** If you are merchandising a surgical instrument, you may have to learn a good deal about surgery even if it is not your specialisation.
2. **Competitors:** You have to study the competitors' products.
3. **Consumer benefit:** You have to point out what gap in the consumer's life the product can fill. Cold drinks, chocolates, etc. tend to *create* a need. A life that was getting along well without these foods suddenly looks incomplete after the product is presented interestingly. You have to point out how the product can enrich a life that was seemingly content with itself. People were used to paper currency, but then cheques came in, then plastic money, and now internet transfers.
4. **Reliability:** The product should be presented as reliable. It is often the most wanted quality in a product. Hence the frequent use of the word *money-back guarantee*, ISI (now BIS - Bureau of Indian Standards) or ISO 9001: 2000 certification, hallmark etc.
5. **Easy to use:** The product should be presented as easy to use. A live demo or the instructions manual should convince the consumer of this.
6. **Easy to buy and maintain:** It should be presented as easy to acquire and easy to maintain. You find phrases like, "We have 3000 outlets, and surely there is one close to you," or, "We have a servicing network of 20 garages in your town," or, "In case of any difficulty, ring us toll free on xxx."
7. **Protect consumer ego:** A good sales talk avoids hurting the audience's opinions and biases. It avoids showing the consumer as a fool. We have often heard the saying, "You may win an argument but lose a friend." Instead, "The customer is always right" approach pays better.
8. **Simple language:** The language of a sales presentation needs to be simple and as far as possible non-technical. If it is technical, it is educatively so. "This is a carburettor, which does the function of lungs."
9. **Avoid humour:** Jokes are not necessary in a sales talk and in general they are rarely used. But a figurative twist to the language can be used to make the consumer smile. On driving safety, "Better be late, Mr. Motorist than be Late Mr. Motorist."
10. **Eye contact:** When using visual aids for a sales pitch, you should as far as possible look at the audience and not the exhibit or screen. You should not stand in the way of the visual aid. The light and visibility should be good enough for all viewers to see the visual aid clearly.
11. **Offer a trial:** It is often effective to ask one of the members of the audience to try your product.
12. **Collect orders on the spot:** You should be ready for making spot sales or getting commitments after the presentation. If it has been a good presentation, you should not allow the effect to wear off with time and distance, competitors or distractions.

21.5 TIPS FOR AN EFFECTIVE PRESENTATION

From the moment a presentation is proposed, these are the steps to make it effective:

1. Know your audience and the place and occasion of your talk.
2. Get ready your text and visual aids, models etc.
3. Keep your dress and appearance appropriate.
4. Practise your talk.

We now discuss these tips at length.

1. Knowing the audience and the occasion:

(a) A good speaker's first question after being asked to speak on a topic is, who am I going to talk to. And what is the occasion?

(b) The speaker finds out about the organisation which is organising the talk and the background of the audience. This decides the tone and register (level of language) to be used. The speaker finds out what arrangements are there for speaking and using demos. Some speakers carry a battery and microphone on their person if they anticipate a large gathering and absence of a mike. He has some say in the seating arrangement, lighting and ventilation of the place. The speaker may have to instruct that no food and drinks should be served during the talk.

(c) The speaker should know the occasion and the background of the organisation – what happenings have taken place lately, and what is the organisation's motto.

(d) He should check out the time allotted to him and plans his message for the given number of minutes. Overshooting the time limit is in bad taste and he loses the audience support.

(e) He should find out who the other speakers are and what aspects of the topic are they likely to cover.

(f) He should visualise his relationship to the audience. He should take care to be properly introduced to the audience. He may ask that some background material be circulated among the listeners or he may ask them to do some background reading.

(g) He should find out whether he will be presented as an expert to the audience or as a colleague. The term **teacher** and the term **resource person** have different suggestions of meaning.

2. Getting ready the text and the visual aids, models etc.:

(a) While organising the material for his presentation, the speaker should make his notes, arrange them and if possible write out the entire talk. Writing out the speech is advisable for beginners and when the occasion is so important that every word counts.

(b) The style of a presentation should be formal, with occasional use of short forms like *couldn't*, *isn't* etc. But usages like *for free*, *guy*, *fellow*, etc. are inopportune. The speech should sound easy on the ears – you need to avoid tongue-twisters.

(c) A speech can be spiced up with humour. But one has to take care that the jokes are not worn out. They should be decent, too. Difficult moments are made bearable by humour. "Individually we think that one cannot do anything about this problem. But in a conference we can collectively decide that nothing *can be* done about it."

(d) As for addressing the dignitaries and the audience, one may simply address the chairperson (or the host if one is oneself the chairperson), the audience and begin. Or one may take the care to address all the dignitaries on the dais.

(*i*) Mr. Chairman Sir, ladies and gentlemen,

(*ii*) Honourable Principal, members of the teaching staff, and my dear student friends, (*iii*) Chairman of today's function Mr. Ramesh Gandhi, guests of honour Mr. Khanna and Mr. Pardesi, representative of the sponsors Mr. Deole, ladies and gentlemen,

(e) The text of your speech, as discussed before, has to have three parts: introduction, body, and conclusion.
During the introductory part, the speaker may make a topical remark about the day's news or what has happened in the hall or during the previous speaker's talk. If the speaker has to repeat something said by earlier speakers, for supporting it or showing difference of opinion, he may quote that part carefully.

(f) The speaker gains audience support by saying how happy or privileged he feels to be there. He may express his gratitude or react to the introduction given to him. This ought to sound straight from the heart.

(g) The main body of the talk has to use facts and figures to suit your purpose. If it is to inform, the information must be well classified and made memorable by converting figures into visuals. "This factory, small as it is, produces one matchbox for every citizen of Mumbai." If the purpose is to persuade, the logic of the facts should drive to the conclusion. "We see that the number of asthma cases is directly proportional to he number of automobiles in the city. In short, the vehicles need to stop spoiling our breathing systems."

(h) Devices like visuals, cinema clips etc. give relief to the speaker and whet the curiosity of the audience. Moreover , the variation in the mode of presentation makes it interesting. Besides, the visuals leave a deeper impress on the viewer's mind. There has to be, though, a judicious mix of script and visuals. One good picture is worth a thousand words, but it takes eight words to state this truth. In other wrods, we have to come back towards.

3. Suit your dress and appearance to the occasion:

(a) Once during a famous speaker's talk, video filming was going on, and close-ups of his face were shown on screens in different parts of the hall. And people remarked that some parts of the speaker's chin were not properly shaved. A formal speech is an occasion for looking smart and well-tailored. Sometimes there is no speaker's desk or table where half of the speaker's body may be hidden. Hence the speaker needs to take care of himself from top to toes.

(b) Moreover, the body language is read by the spectators even before the speaker begins his talk. So your way of getting up from the chair, making your way to the speaker's post, the way you carry your hands about your body, etc. need to be rehearsed and managed. Impressive body language requires:

(i) **A comfortable posture:** You should stand at ease, your weight equally balanced on your feet. You should not tie your hands behind your body but rather keep them by the side or at the belt level.

(ii) **Eye contact:** You should look the audience in the eye. You should try to locate a friendly face and use it to your advantage. You should run your eyes over all sections of the audience.

(iii) **Graceful movements:** If you walk about during the course of your talk, you should do so as unnoticeably as possible. You may have to move to get close to a chart and then come back to the front part of the stage. Do this smartly.

(iv) **A pleasant expression:** You need to smile, and even if you do not, the effect should be pleasant and cheerful. Serious news can be delivered with a sober, calm expression.

(v) **Mastery over the voice:** A good voice for presentations is cultivated like a singing voice. Indeed, the two have much in common: increased breathing capacity, breath control, cheerful overtones, clear pronunciation, absence of harshness, and variation of the pace of delivery.

(vi) **Pauses also speak:** From time to time, the speaker has to pause even while keeping control over the audience's attention. How much to pause and when, is an art. But even seasoned speakers are found to overdo it, which only shows how much care one needs to exercise here.

(vii) **Energetic appearance:** The speaker should radiate energy. He had better speak on an empty stomach or with only a light snack. Then the stomach muscles throw the air out forcefully and the blood circulation is more in the brain and not in the digestive system.

(viii) **React to the audience mood:** The audience may get dull or highly responsive during the speaker's talk. If it gets dull, the voice has to become vigorous or a joke or story has to be used. If the audience gets very responsive, a remark may be added about its enthusiasm.

4. Practising your talk

There may be four stages in practising a presentation:

(a) Reading your text either word for word or from the points written down. This is in the mind.
(b) Talking to a wall, a mirror or alone in your room in a slightly audible voice
(c) Rehearsing your speech before a trial audience, friends or relatives
(d) Speaking on the occasion

A speaker who goes through these four stages finds himself at ease on an occasion which tends to make the best of us a little bit nervous.

Practice makes one perfect. Indeed, practice also enables you to adjust the length of your talk and find out if any tongue-twisters have crept into your speech. Preparation and practice are the all-important tools for generating confidence, which is the foundation of a presentation.

21.6 PUBLIC SPEAKING

Every business leader or manager has to learn the art of public speaking. In modern business set-up, one generally spends more of one's communicative time speaking than writing.

Skill in public speaking is distinct from skill in private conversation. Indeed, sometimes one may be a good public speaker but not an expert conversationalist.

While **public speaking** is the conventional term for talking to a group of people formally, the modern usage has brought in the word **presentation**. This shows a shift in values. In public speaking you talk to a group of people which is your public. In a presentation, the focus is on the message which you are presenting. As such, in business, the term presentation is preferred. The term *public speaking* also includes political speeches in election campaigns, mass education or mass awareness talks for public causes. The word presentation conveys the sense that something has been made presentable just as a product is dressed up for sale or a candidate for a job.

Another useful distinction between a presentation and a public speech is that a light talk on an anniversary or an inauguration would rather be called a public speech than a presentation. A speech is to encourage, applaud, felicitate or entertain. The audience for a speech is generally large.

A presentation is a studied talk and relatively heavy. It is made before a relatively small and well-informed group of people. It is made at a conference, seminar or business meeting.

Distinction between a speech and presentation:

Speech	Presentation
1. Audience is generally large.	1. Audience is compact.
2. The occasion is light.	2. The occasion is serious and purposeful.
3. It is made at anniversary, inauguration etc.	3. It is made at a conference, seminar or business meeting.
4. The purpose is to congratulate, entertain etc.	4. The purpose is to inform, explain, persuade, present one's side.
5. There are no question–answers.	5. It is followed by questions.

A. Questions based on critical understanding. Comment in about 30 words.

1. Some are born with the gift of the gab and don't have to prepare at all to speak on the stage.

Ans. Stage speaking is an art, and no one is born a perfect artist. The potential, the talent may be there, but to attempt speaking unprepared an all occasions is to perform far below one's best. Preparation is the backbone of a speech. A well-prepared speech is nine-tenths delivered.

2 In modern parlance, presentation and public speaking are the same.

Ans. Modern usage, on the contrary, distinguishes between the two. A presentation is the more formal, more purposive speech. A public speech is for lighter occasions such as felicitation, celebration, etc.

3. The first ten seconds of a speaker on the stage win the audience one way or the other.

Ans. This is a truth derived from observation and studies. Well begun is half done. The first impression is, for some if not all listeners, the last impression. The ground lost in the first ten seconds is hard to recover.

4. Good oratory is all about good acting.

Ans. Acting is role-playing and it is temporary and dramatic. In oratory, on the other hand, the speaker's personality and actual feelings are involved. Without sincerity of the heart, the acting skill carries limited conviction. Acting is only admired, but sincerity wins hearts.

5. Dress before address.

Ans. Before a speaker opens his mouth, he is seen from head to foot, the way he walks, uses his eyes, and so on. The speaker's dress (and appearance) should show his concern for looking pleasant to the audience. Neatness and appropriateness are more important than gaudiness.

B. Questions for revision

1. What are the essential elements of a presentation?
2. "Speaking is an art." Elaborate it and explain the pre-requisites needed for effective speaking.
3. What are the principles that are to be followed to become an effective speaker?
4. "Speaking and listening go hand in hand." Do you agree? Discuss in brief the features of good speaking. Also, explain the role of eyes in listening. (Refer to Chapter 3.)

5. How should a business executive design his presentation? Discuss, taking a hypothetical situation to illustrate your views.
6. What strategy would you adopt to make a sales presentation?
7. What is the role of planning, preparation and practice in a presentation or public speech?
8. Write a note on the use of visual aids in a presentation.
9. What roles do body language and voice qualities play in your presentation?

■■■